Policies of Economic and Social Development in Europe

SOFIA CONFERENCES ON SOCIAL AND ECONOMIC DEVELOPMENT IN EUROPE

Edited by
Prof. Dr. George Chobanov,
PD Dr. Jürgen Plöhn,
Prof. Dr. Horst Schellhaass

Volume 2

PETER LANG
Frankfurt am Main · Berlin · Bern · Bruxelles · New York · Oxford · Wien

George Chobanov
Jürgen Plöhn
Horst Schellhaass
(eds.)

Policies of Economic and Social Development in Europe

11th Annual Conference of the Faculty of Economics and Business Administration
Dedicated to the 120th Anniversary of St. Kliment Ohridski University of Sofia
Sofia, October 10 to 11, 2008

PETER LANG
Internationaler Verlag der Wissenschaften

Bibliographic Information published by the Deutsche Nationalbibliothek
The Deutsche Nationalbibliothek lists this publication in the Deutsche Nationalbibliografie; detailed bibliographic data is available in the internet at http://dnb.d-nb.de.

Cover illustrations:
Printed with kind permissions of the universities of Cologne and Sofia.

ISSN 1867-562X
ISBN 978-3-631-60412-0

www.peterlang.de

Contents

Chapter Four
Studies on the European Union and Germany

Attachments

INTRODUCTION

JÜRGEN PLÖHN
(MARTIN-LUTHER-UNIVERSITY HALLE-WITTENBERG, GERMANY)

1. The 11th Annual Conference of the Faculty of Economics and Business Administration at Sofia University

As a contribution to the 120th anniversary of the foundation of St. Kliment Ohridski University Sofia, the eleventh international conference of the Faculty of Economics and Business Administration enjoyed the special support of Bulgaria's oldest university. Once again held in the impressive Boyana Residence on the outskirts of Sofia, the conference induced scholars teaching in 12 different countries to hand in their suggestions for oral presentations. Thus the annual conference provided a useful platform for the exchange of ideas between East an West.

The title of the first volume in this series ("*Towards a Knowledge-Based Society in Europe*") named a *goal*, indicating a challenge for the European development and demonstrating its actual variety at the same time. The volume on hand, instead, bears a title which can easily serve as a headline for all the contributions presented in the following chapters. Like the 2007 conference, the publication of these proceedings has been supported by a grant of the University of Cologne, due to the long-established partnership with Sofia University. Moreover, several scholars of the University of Cologne actively participated in the discussions.

16 papers out of 34 presentations have been handed in for publication in the proceedings of the conference. According to the results of the peer review, eleven contributions have been selected. The editors are grateful to the German and American experts for their well-reasoned opinions. Finally, the volume collects articles of 19 scientists out of six countries.

2. The contributions collected in this volume

The papers have been grouped in four chapters:

I. Generalized Approaches,
II. Studies on East Europe,
III. Studies on Southeast Europe and
IV. Studies on the European Union and Germany.

In the first part, *Jean-Pierre Gern* discusses the term "sustainable development". Following a French tradition, he presents his critical attitude towards the existing socio-economic system and some of its adherents in a thoughtful essay, not in an annotated scientific article.

Contrasting to *Gern* in style and contents, *George Chobanov* continues his studies on the Walras equilibrium which he had already approached in the preceeding conference. Now *Chobanov* develops equations for a Walras equilibrium in an open economic system.

The second section starts with an article on Russia: *Tatiana Dolgopyatova* presents an empirical analysis on Russian joint-stock companies. She clearly pleads for professional managers.

The following text by *Cornel Oros* and *Camelia Romocea-Turcu* encompasses six Central and East European countries that have joined the EU. Studying interest rates and exchange rates, the authors identify signs of a gradual rapprochement of the new EU Member States to the Euro zone.

In section three *Nicolae Dardac* and *Iustina Alina Boitan* analyze the Romanian banking system. According to their data, the productivity within that branch still has to be improved.

Contrasting to that short-term analysis of a competitively organized private banking sector, *Kalina Dimitrova* describes the development of the monetary and fiscal policies in Bulgaria in a long-term perspective. In her research *Dimitrova* combines theoretical approaches and portrayals of different phases in history with econometric analyses.

Henrik Egbert, Maria Ivanova and *George Chobanov* try to assess the size and the development of the Bulgarian transaction sector during recent years. The authors recognize a substantial increase of that sector within the first decade after the consolidation of the Bulgarian currency.

Ivan Ivanov and *Julia Dobreva* study public goods. On the background of Bulgaria's accession to the EU they argue in favour of a strengthening of municipal budgets in order to finance a localization of public goods.

From a German perspective, *Thomas Lenk, Oliver Rottmann* and *Tatsiana Makarevich* deal with a similar topic: the delivery of services by municipalities. The authors discuss whether public-private partnerships should be recommended as instruments in order to improve the services.

Jürgen Plöhn and *Alexander Peniuk* present a study on labour market policies in Germany. The paper deals with the respective programmes of the two major political parties in Germany as well as with empirical results of approaches to turn unemployed persons into entrepreneurs.

Finally, *Frank Schulz-Nieswandt* and *Michael Sauer* turn the readers' attention to the interference of European law with national welfare systems. The authors discuss developments towards a "guarantor state".

Chapter one:

GENERALIZED APROACHES

Sustainable Development: A Challenge for the Decisional Process

Jean-Pierre Gern
(Neuchâtel, Switzerland)

1. The problem of sustainable development

The future of the economy of the world and of the world's economic systems is a dominant preoccupation. It involves many issues. Sustainable development is only one of them. Attaining a better level of sustainability does not bring a solution to the others. It may help to solve them, but it could also be hindered by them.

1.1. The historical origin

For over two centuries industrialization has been progressing around the world. Previously economic activities and innovations only raised occasional problems for the sustainability of development. But now all the evolution of economic activities through the world is unsustainable in the long term.

In primitive societies the sustainability of economic activities belonged to the social order; the relationship to the environment was part of it. With the emergence of what is called "civilisation", social inequality arose and most members of those societies lived well below what could have been achieved with existing resources and technologies. Consequently, the main factors for the lack of sustainability of development were to be found in dysfunctions of the socio-economic system, which were the source of tensions, or in tensions between socio-economic systems.

With the emergence of industrialization, a new challenge gained in importance: the relationship between human activities and the natural environment. For the first time the challenge is global. In new terms it raises the question of the human, social, organizational and cultural resources necessary to face the issue.

1.2. The present challenge

By sustainable development we understand an evolution of techno-economic and social structures, which tends towards an equilibrium between human activities (economic and others) and natural environment, as well as towards a social equilibrium, in order to avoid increasing tensions on either front. It excludes the possibility – often advocated for – of innovations which have no long term validity but which are expected to be replaced in time by others, which in turn will often have to be replaced (and so on) with a deeper and deeper impact on nature.

The development is sustainable, if risks of crises and decline are minimized. There are three levels of risk:

- ups and downs of the economic activity;
- structural crises, as in the late 19th Century or in the seventies;
- destruction of a social system (economic, social, political), as at the end of the Roman empire.

Sustainable development does not exclude ups and downs.

As for structural crises, the very necessity of reorientating development towards sustainability involves a structural transition, just as a structural crisis would. But a higher level of sustainability can be expected to smooth future structural crises.

As for the decline of the industrial civilization, while a more sustainable development cannot be expected to avoid it, it may postpone it or make it less dramatic. There may be various reasons for such a decline, for instance:

- the decline in population;
- the complexity and fragility of the socioeconomic system;
- increasing imbalances;
- destruction of the environment.

The critical issues of today are just apparent effects of a deeper problem. More and more critical issues will emerge in coming years. Facing them one after the other and remedying the scarcity of energy, the lack of raw materials in turn, the congestion of megapoles, the overweight of transportation, population imbalances, distortions in social relations and so on, is not only an endless job, it is also too demanding to be fulfilled: crisis after crisis, remedies to one raising another ... It is, of course, easier to mobilize social action against a single problem (such as pollution) than for the complete revaluation of the overall technological, economic, social, institutional and cultural system of an industrial society. But to avoid the endless race just mentioned nothing less than this is required.

To minimize the impact of today's productive and other human activities on the environment and to avoid building up social tensions, requires new objectives for production and a new approach to "needs". The determinant factors of the constant increase in the production of goods and services have to be analyzed, as well as their dynamics. That trend has to be reconsidered in depth, which means a serious restructuring of the productive sector and a cultural change in all social actors. It requires a new relationship between economic actors, between them and the political power as well as between them and the particular society.

1.3 The scope of our reflection

We shall consider only one aspect of the problem. For that purpose we make two important assumptions:

First: Necessary technologies are potentially available and can be found and applied in a reasonable future.

Second: A social organization, able to survive without excessive tensions and able to manage its relations to the natural environment, can be found.

On the basis of such assumptions, we shall concentrate our attention on one issue: How far are today's societies able to take efficiently the decisions needed to achieve a sustainable development?

The problem is global at the world level - but can the answer be global? We will be brought to consider two levels of action and decision making:

- firstly, within a relatively homogeneous social system (institutional, techno-economic, social). Such relative homogeneity can be found, or developed, in areas like Europe, which we shall call "regions";
- secondly, we shall consider the relations between such "regions".

2. The inefficiency of the present approach

2.1. Similarity with the issue of development

Achieving sustainable development has much in common with the issue of development in the Third World, which has been the object of so much analysis in the last decades. Lessons from theory and practice and even more from errors may be of great value.

When the theory and policy of development were introduced after the Second World War, the attention was on *one* factor ("lack of capital" or "technical progress" and the like). Development efforts were scattered in the various fields: education, infrastructure, industry. Missing elements in comparison with industrialized countries were individually identified and acted upon. This approach has been a failure.

After decades of experiences, errors and catastrophes, the development theories that have been taught and used in practice, are now derelict; the issue has often been shifted to social scientists rather than to economists; or the proposition has been made to leave the populations concerned take care of themselves. Finally attention and action were just on remedying the disasters induced by erroneous development policies (poverty, mass migrations etc.). Similar mistakes should be avoided in the efforts to achieve sustainable development.

Today the concept of sustainable development is broad and all-inclusive, but concrete understanding and action are far from it. When it comes to policies, specific issues drain attention by their urgency and specific actions are launched, which will have a positive effect on some dysfunctions of the present system (abuse of some natural resource, excessive pollution and so on). But such actions will rapidly come to their limits:

- the chosen solution may solve more or less a specific problem, but may raise new ones, which have not been taken into account,
- many significant changes are ignored if they are not in themselves a direct source of concern, though they are crucial for the path to sustainable development,
- a better result may only be obtained with a more systemic approach involving correlative changes in different fields.

2.2 Techno-economic constraints on economic units (enterprises, individuals, communities, state etc.)

Figure 1: Techno-economic constraints on a productive unit

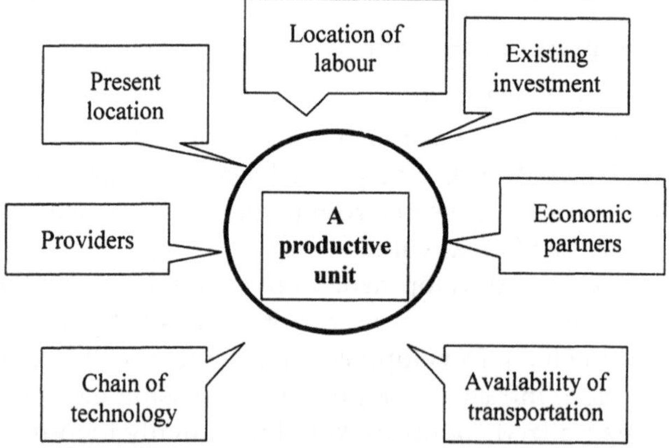

In the modern industrial system, the flows and networks of trade in goods and services are so dense and complex that a productive unit cannot change its technical process without correlative changes in its forward and backward linkages, in consumer practices, in government action and other relations. The same is true for individuals, for communities and for the state itself.

2.3. *Institutional or systemic constraints on social entities (enterprises, individuals, communities, state etc.)*

We shall use the above to describe all hindrances to action coming from the operational rules, which govern the socio-economic and political system.

2.3.1. THE CONSTRAINTS ON ENTERPRISES

In a market-based economy enterprises are fighting for their survival. The overall system operates in a way that imposes on them

- to stay small and marginal,
- to be absorbed or
- to aim at imposing themselves on others and, if possible, dominating the market.

To maintain and enlarge their scope of operation they use all possible tools:

- valorisation of the product through complexity, gadgeting, packing etc. at a higher price,
- lower production costs, which implies delocalisation, cheap quality or non-durable products, lower wages and salaries,
- abusive use of patents to avoid competition,
- financial strength, which leads to the accumulation of profits to the detriment of the distribution of income,
- deceiving publicity and high marketing costs.

2.3.2. THE CONSTRAINTS ON INDIVIDUALS

The operational constraints on individuals are stronger than generally perceived: Their choices are under pressure from publicity and marketing; they are not well informed about the characteristics and qualities of a good product.

Their choice is limited by the lines of technological development in the productive sector and trade. They can choose from what is offered. Years ago the shift to non reusable bottles was not their choice; it came from a glass factory. The orientation of research in the pharmaceutical industries is governed by the possibility of profits, not by the necessities of suffering people. For instance, fighting tropical diseases is suddenly rising as a result of higher income in the South.

2.3.3. For the Government

The present institutional system in industrialized countries is less and less favourable to efficient government strategies under the pressure of liberal and market ideals supported by economic powers dominating the markets and short sighted university teachers.

Besides, democracy – as desirable as it is – tends to enclose government activities into the application of norms established through a long and slow procedure, where categorical interests are stronger than farsighted views of the national wellbeing.

The burden on government shoulders is day by day heavier, as private activities require more and more specific action or intervention from the state to maintain the operation of the whole system. On the other side, governments are pressed to alleviate their financial weight on the economy, leaving aside activities of more strategic importance.

2.3.4. For all social actors

Each society largely derives its identity from its cultural model: ways of life, social relations, ways of consuming, system of values, relation to material and spiritual life etc. The cultural models are both very traditional and very volatile. They safeguard the identity of a society and shape its dynamism. Consumerism has imposed its impact on cultural models. After the wave of consumerism, will there be a revalorization of discredited values, or the creation of more ecological and sustainable ideals?

3. Necessary changes from the present socio-economic system

To reach sustainable development, *first* it is necessary to break the present socio-economic system. Its very coherence is an obstacle to sustainability as it makes change more difficult to achieve. It is not possible to save a particular natural resource, to avoid some pollution, to secure a minimum of social justice and coherence, without changes in all fields of social action. Each element of the system is contingent upon the others; each obstacle to sustainability is linked to a network of interdependences.

Of course, in the existing system each element is rational only relative to its context; it does not mean that the whole system is rational in itself and answers optimally the declared objectives of the economic agents. For instance, the present communication networks of industrial societies are a crying example. Their failure to meet social needs is a source of dynamism (it calls for reform) but sustainable development requires a more radical reconsideration of the system.

Secondly, it is necessary to conceive and work for the emergence of a new organization of the socio-economic system: new economic structures within a new social and institutional framework, with a different value system.

But if the coherence of the "nation state", which had achieved the "welfare state", is being broken by globalization, the presently emerging system, based on straightforward competition in all fields of life, may rather destroy the very basis for coherent social dynamics now.

4. The need for coordinated action and the implication for the decisional process

The previous paragraphs have shown both:

- the importance of the interdependences between all sectors, all fields of action and all social actors for the attainment of a sustainable development,
- and at the same time the fact that the drive to sustainable development is a worldwide affair.

The dream of a world government which would manage a worldwide project is still recurrent, as illusionary as it may be. How can this dilemma be overcome? There is no satisfactory solution. We shall consequently propose a compromise which seems a priori the most promising.

The transformation in depth of the social system, which allows the necessary changes for sustainable development can only be realised (if at all) within a region, which is relatively homogeneous institutionally, technologically, economically, socially and so on. This coherence is determined by the historical make-up of society, by its culture, by its institutions and by its political system. We may consider that Europe is working on building such a region, of course, with regional diversities. But we suggest that such diversities can be properly taken into account and managed within Europe (as long as it does not enlarge itself too far).

Between such regions, the necessary coordination for sustainable development is not the same. Its objective is limited to worldwide issues, but also to the pressure exercised by a particular regional socioeconomic system on another one through economic and other channels. The differences between regions in techno-economic structures, social organization, institutions etc. cannot be erased. But they are a serious hindrance to sustainable development in other regions, if any step in that direction in one region is challenged by economic competition from outside. To avoid this, a level of economic distance between regions is required. Maybe, it does not need to be advocated as it shall emerge anyway.

4.1. *Coordinated action and its implication for the decisional process within a region (relatively homogenous area)*

We shall consider four modalities of decision making in a region:

1. Starting from an utopia, from a coherent vision of an alternative to the present socio-economic system,
2. setting up an institutional elaboration of strategies of change, based on long term perspectives and on the "concertation"(an important concept of French planning) of all social actors,
3. setting up an industrial and agricultural policy, as a basis for the institutional power to rule and direct the development of economic activities,
4. depending on the interplay of social actors, as it is today.

4.1.1 FIRST MODALITY: STARTING FROM THE ELABORATION OF A COHERENT ALTERNATIVE SYSTEM

When there has been a problem in the working of a socio-economic system and tensions have been created, it often happened that the dream of an alternative came to life. The most typical example is to be found in the industrial society of the 19th century. The social groups, which were the victims of the power given to the industrial capital and traders, imagined alternative models of social organization. Today, socialists face the reproach of proposing no significant alternative and limiting themselves to palliatives.

To make development more sustainable from the social and environmental points of view, there is a need for innovative perspectives, in order not to fall into a mass of measures of all kinds, which may carry more contradictions than coherence.

Who can work it out? Who can decide? It cannot be a macro decision, be it international. It cannot be the decision of a philosopher (as Plato proposed) or of a social movement, as in the 19th century. The best approach would aim at a global, coherent solution, but it is the least likely, the least feasible.

4.1.2 Second modality: an institutional process to elaborate a strategy of change

This approach has more credible historical references. French planning, which was launched after the Second World War, constituted a wide system of consultation and coordination for the attainment of national objectives, which could only be reached through the convergence of the strategies of all social actors. Long term perspectives were elaborated in order to gear the strategies towards long term goals. In the seventies, the weakening of the constraints due to the post-war scarcities and the increase in international competition pushed aside the development process based on the coordination of decision making by all social actors. That approach enjoyed the context of the "nation state". The organizational link between productive systems, institutions and social organizations opened the way to successful coordinated strategies.

Is it presently possible to find a sufficient ground for such strategies, now that convergence is loosing ground even in individual countries?

4.1.3. Third modality: an industrial and agricultural policy

If the second modality was more modest than the first, the third is even more so. But it has also historical references; they are many and have proved quite efficient for the industrialization of a country. Such policies still exist in emergent economies; they even happen to give them an advantage over industrialized countries. The present emergence of Asian countries shows more than one example. Their rising competitive power may even bring some industrialized countries to reconsider this option. It is obvious that such strategies have been serving the need for competitiveness in some key sectors more than the building-up of a well integrated socioeconomic system.

Nevertheless, the fact that institutional authorities develop strategies for a coordinated development of a key sector rather than counting on everyone's desire for profit, may be an efficient instrument for change, even if it is limited in its scope.

4.1.4. Fourth modality: relying on the market economy itself

This modality corresponds largely to the present situation. Enterprises have enterprises' strategies, which differ from region to region and according to branches. States fix laws and rules, establish treaties; consumers follow their preferences; numerous intermediaries find occasions to intervene in all fields; the financial actors are active in speculation; marketing tries (often with success) to convince consumers to spend more than their income … - and the whole game covers itself with a slight layer of ecology. Occasionally, real preoccupations bring some significant research and innovations in the fields of environmental technology or behaviour. Can that game end up in sustainable development? With the presently declared purposes of the main groups of actors, certainly not. Relying on the so-called "law of the market" for the regulation of all activities - which means competition by all means (prices, marketing, financial power, domination of markets) - turns the "ecological consciousness" more towards new economic opportunities than to fulfilling the conditions for sustainable development.

Innovation has to play a crucial role on the road to sustainable development. It has to open the way to new modes of production, of organization, of satisfaction of needs, ways which would safeguard the relation to the natural environment and maintain the social equilibrium. Therefore it is useful to scrutinize the reasons for innovation of various social actors. In the relations between enterprises, it is the main instrument for winning or at least keeping market shares. Great changes are needed in the present dynamic of innovation, if it is to serve sustainable development.

The evolution of the real economy is more and more dominated by finance. If the purpose of finance is to facilitate real flows of goods and services, how are its recent overexpansion and its orientation to be understood? The disturbances brought by the financial sector to the real economy show that the former develops its own life and that the productive sector is more and more dependent on it. This evolution questions the rationality of the decisional system in the structuring of the productive sector.

Even if consumers add an ecological element to their preferences, they are under the increasing pressure of marketing. It is an illusion to pretend that the "signal" given to the market by consumers may be sufficiently significant.

Concretely all actors have attitudes and behaviours, which are strongly conditioned by the whole socioeconomic system and the cultural models which it has produced. A systemic change needs more than new preoccupations and purposes by everyone. The very coherence of the system sets a narrow limit on actions taken in that framework.

Besides, it is amazing to discover how inside each institution itself decisions are taken problem by problem. At the higher level legal procedures even enforce it.

For cultural as well as economic reasons (pressure of competition) the short term is the prevailing perspective. Maybe that ecology reintroduces longer term approaches, but they are under the pressure of short term survival in a world of generalized competition.

Finally, and probably as a result of the dominant economic theory, based on simultaneous adjustment between variables, structural changes and even more the management of such changes do not get the attention they deserve.

4.2. *Coordinated action between regions and its implication for the decisional process*

In a relatively homogeneous area, sustainable development depends on the coherence of the socioeconomic system. Between regions, it is not possible to pretend to reach such coherence. World cultures and social systems are too diverse to aim at such an objective. Diversity has to be accepted.

Consequently, there are two issues at stake:

- impacts on the environment, which have a worldwide dimension,
- actions which have a strong influence on the socioeconomic system of other regions and may compromise their way towards sustainability.

Other issues, like the relation between government regulation and management practices of enterprises or consumers' behaviour and urbanization, can only be considered within a given region, where the systemic coherence is meaningful and necessary for the sustainability of development. The present tendency to equalize conditions worldwide in order to reach a worldwide economy without limits is a dangerous utopia for us, which may be destructive to all socioeconomic systems, and may let the attainment of sustainable development get out of reach.

4.2.1. First issue at stake: pollution and resources

If some pollution incidents are purely local, most are worldwide dangers; they have to be the subject of worldwide negotiations. The way to restrict them is not the same everywhere. At present fixing worldwide rules shows its difficulties and limits. But negotiations can take place between regions. Each one participating with its specific possibilities and constraints and acting on the problem accordingly, a substantial discussion can take place and reciprocal or compensatory concessions can be made.

Pollution (charging the environment with damaging refuse) is half the problem; the other half is draining resources of all kinds from the environment, which are becoming scarce. Developing countries ask for their share of natural resources, and industrial countries defend their present economy. A good negotiation needs a greater understanding and collaboration, very far from present attempts. In the seventies with the report of the Club of Rome, conscience was raised that industrialization in its historical way would mean a world drama when new countries industrialize. It might have been the proper time for the industrial countries to innovate, saving both resources and refuse, in order to make it possible for newcomers to start on that line. Nothing has been really done, and the expected drama is at the door. Petrol is just the first, others are pressing already. The fight between national interests will not open the way; what is needed is another culture of negotiation.

4.2.2. Second issue at stake: not compromising sustainable development in other regions

Presently, world markets, as positive as they may be, are destructive of socioeconomic structures in all regions which try to adjust but pay the price of a loss of internal coherence. It is an obstacle to building structures compatible with sustainable development. Consequently, when necessary, a degree of specific external protection should be accepted.

The recent WTO negotiations are a good representation of the present problem: a conflict between those who dream of a worldwide economy, where every producer would be in competition with all others (a dream based on the generalization of the Walras equilibrium in the complete neglect of its limits and constraints), and those who fight to safeguard the consistency of the economic systems in place with no regard for its necessary dynamics – two ideologies, which block the way to a well understood future.

The present international relations (and especially the so-called division of labour) are based on temporary factors, which are misleading for long term global development. Inequality in labour costs, differences in technological development, concentration of financial power, pressure of dominating enterprises at the world level, inequality of income within countries and among them orientate any negotiations and agreements in the wrong direction from the point of view of sustainable development.

Nevertheless negotiations are based on present, temporary conditions. No government could consider negotiating on the basis of long term perspectives rather than present conditions. If negotiations had to be on a sound ground, they could only consist of conferences towards a common goal. Developing ecological structures and infrastructures on present temporary conditions is an obstacle for the future. But building up together adequate structures for the future requires that representatives of all regions, having a proper understanding of the way to sustainable development in their area, work at finding adjustments between them.

5. Summary and conclusions: which decisional process?

Sustainable development is one of the factors of survival of the industrial society, but not the only one. The industrial societies are facing many risks of crises, superficial or deep; sustainable development is concerned with those which concern the relationship of human activities with their environment and with increasing imbalances in social relations.

Facing the problems one by one, as is the case nowadays, is no valid solution and may raise deeper crises.

It is not possible to reach a really sustainable development (be it only for the size of the human population on the earth), but an appropriate level of sustainability requires a complete reconsideration of the socio-economic systems and of their institutional and cultural context.

We considered only one aspect of sustainable development; we assumed that the techno-economic aspects could be solved, the question we raised was: with such an assumption, can the necessary decisions be taken?

Though the issues are worldwide, we found that they have to be managed at two levels:

(1) At a regional level, in an area which has a relatively homogeneous social system (such as Europe, USA, China):

As solving problems one by one will prove impossible and inefficient, a *systemic approach* is needed and is feasible only within a socioeconomic system, which is sufficiently coherent and homogeneous.

In that framework we considered four ways of decision making only to find that none of them appeared to be adequate. Either they were well orientated but not feasible, or they were feasible (for instance, letting things go as they do), but not orientated in the right direction. Could they be combined? They will probably have to be so.

That means a new definition of the role of the political power: rather than being confined to regulatory and palliative activities, it should manage wide consultations and the co-ordination of action with all economic and social actors. The role of competition should be redefined and the relations between enterprises should be more largely built on co-operation towards a common goal. The productive system should be restructured to answer more efficiently and more exclusively socially useful needs. Social norms and values are presently changing more rapidly than expected, but they have to be orientated in a meaningful direction; they should be adjusted to a new pattern of production, consumption and recycling, to new urban structures, social structures and so on.

(2) At the world level:

Between such regions negotiations mean *coordination*. Negotiation between regions should be based on a proper understanding of the common interest, and consequently should be more orientated to co-operation than to confrontation of each party's interest, and aim at coordinating the long term aims and objectives of the various regions.

Issues for negotiation would mainly be:

- the impacts on the environment, which have a worldwide dimension and
- actions which have a strong influence on the socioeconomic system of other regions and may compromise their way towards sustainability.

WALRAS' LAW AND FLOW OF FUNDS ANALYSIS IN AN OPEN ECONOMIC SYSTEM[1]

GEORGE CHOBANOV
(SOFIA UNIVERSITY "ST. KLIMENT OHRIDSKI", BULGARIA)

1. Towards a micro-macro economics bridge

In the history of economic thought, micro and macro economic theory developed separately with only few connections with each other. The separation between micro and macro economic theories was started by the classic theory and is going on now in the neoclassic theory. A typical trait of the neoclassic theory is the separation of the economy in two sectors: the real and the monetary one, thus dividing the concept into the theory of value and the theory of money.

The theory of value is indeed the Walras theory of general equilibrium, which is the micro economic theory, because it tries to determine a set of equilibrium prices, based on real relations of the economic exchange and the behavioral norms of economic subjects, their preferences and available goods and production factors. Money is involved in this theory only as the unit of account - there is neither a money market nor a quantity of money.

The neoclassical theory of money is considering money from a macro economic point of view and is trying to determine the price level based on the quantity of money by using the so-called Cambridge equation, keeping the theory of value at the periphery of consideration.

In economics, on the micro level, *behaviour* is considered, i.e. activities of economic subjects on economic objects, on macro level, *relationships in the economic system as a whole* are investigated. Macroeconomic relationships are resulting from aggregated activities or relationships of economic subjects on the micro level. Aggregation means synchronized summation of quantities on the micro level, implying qualitative changes in the economic system as a whole on its macro level. Aggregation is a complicated process bringing the synchronized activities of a dominating part of randomly behaving components of the economic system to deterministic relationships on its macro level. In the world we live in, this is due to effects of the law of large numbers.

[1] Best thanks to the referee of this paper for his useful suggestions!

We need to know the mechanisms of aggregation processes, because signals of economic policy are given at the macro level in order to reach the individual economic subjects and influence a dominant part of them to cause changes on the macro economic level.

The separation of micro and macro economic theory implies misleading signals for economic policy and could have dramatic consequences for the economic theory and practice.

The discrepancies in the theory and practice of economic policy were among the reasons causing the Great Depression in the 1930s. The disability of economic policy makers to manage the crisis resulted in doubts in the regulatory power of market mechanisms and in criticism directed at basic statements of the neoclassic economic theory. The most serious alternative to the classical economic theory was developed by John Maynard Keynes in his seminal work "The General Theory of Employment, Interest and Money". Initially, the extreme version of Keynesian theory denying almost all the basic classics, lead to further separation of the micro and macro theory. Later on, as usual in contradictory theories, economic scientists tried to make them consistent with one another by selecting the most realistic of their principles. The researchers' efforts resulted in the theory of neoclassical synthesis, which develops the Keynesian theory on the base of neoclassics. The achievements of currently best known representatives of the neoclassical syntheses like Alvin H. Hansen, John R. Hicks, Lawrence Klein, Don Patinkin, Paul A. Samuelson, James Tobin and Franco Modigliani bring micro and macro economic theories closer to each other. First attempts for convincing or synchronizing both, micro and macro theories, have been made by Don Patinkin (1965) and Oskar Lange (1942). Later on, due to efforts of Don Patinkin, Robert Clower, A. Drazen, J.-P.Benassy, Robert Barro and others, Walras' law was proven for a closed economic system without public goods, but aggregated macroeconomic markets and involving money as a macroeconomic phenomenon (see Bernhard Felderer/Stefan Homburg 1999).

Economists recognize, that Walras' model is not only a bridge between micro and macro theory but it plays a central role, like a "Charta magna" for economic theory (Schumpeter), because the general equilibrium approach became a general framework for monetary analysis (see James Tobin 1969). Currently, the macroeconomic monetary analysis of an economic system is based on the flow-of-funds analysis in the national accounts system (see A. D. Bain 1973). So, we come closer to the idea of using the inflows and outflows in the sectors of the national accounts system in an open economy to prove formally Walras' law for that kind of system.

Walras' law is indeed a law of conservation of economic flows, saying that all positively signed inflows and all negatively signed outflows, flowing in and out through all markets of a closed economic system have to sum to zero, which means indeed, that in a closed economic system nothing can appear from nothing and nothing can disappear into nothing, flows can only transform into each other.

2. Walras' law in an open economic system

Here, we consider an open economic system of markets, which are aggregated to the macro level. The aggregation process starts on the level of single economic units and, passing through different aggregation levels, reaches the macro level of an open economy consisting of five sectors, namely: the households H, the enterprises E, the state (government) G, the capitalization sector K and the rest of the world ROW.

The economic flows of an open economy are passing through the transaction mechanisms of six markets: domestic goods, domestic money, domestic public goods, domestic labor, domestic capital and the foreign exchange[2]. These six markets build a closed set of non-overlapping markets covering all inflows and outflows in an open economic system. So, for this economic system, Walras' law has to be true.

Open economy system's Walras law:

The excess demands of the markets of domestic goods, domestic money, domestic labor, domestic capital, public goods and the foreign exchange in an open economy sum to zero:

$$\begin{aligned} &E^{(d)}(DomGoods) + E^{(d)}(DomMoney) + E^{(d)}(DomLabor) + \\ &E^{(d)}(DomCap) + E^{(d)}(PubGoods) + E^{(d)}(ForegnExchange) = 0 \end{aligned} \tag{1}$$

with $E^{(d)} = Excess\ Demand = Demand - Supply$

[2] Notice: Here, we refer to "public goods" as all produced in the public (government) sector, like external and internal security, knowledge, information transfer, etc. Furthermore, we assume, that there are no cross border externalities of public goods.

In order to state this theorem more formally, we need the following notations:

$E^{(d)}(DomGoods) = PY^{(d)} - PY^{(s)}$ (2)

$E^{(d)}(DomMoney) = M^{(d)} - M^{(s)}$ (3)

$E^{(d)}(DomLabor) = WN^{(d)} - WN^{(s)}$ (4)

$E^{(d)}(DomCapital) = K^{(d)} - K^{(s)})$ (5)

$E^{(d)}(PubGoods) = G^{(d)} - G^{(s)}$ (6)

$E^{(d)}(ForeignExchange) = F^{(d)} - F^{(s)} = -BP = EP^* N\,\mathrm{Im} + NTr_{ROW}^{LR} =$
$= E^{(d)}(ForeignGoods) + E^{(d)}(ForeignMoney)$ (7)

$E^{(d)}(ForeignGoods) = F_g^{(d)} - F_g^{(s)} = -EP^* NEx = -EP^* Ex - EP^* \mathrm{Im}$ (8)

$E^{(d)}(ForeignMoney) = F_m^{(d)} - F_m^{(s)} = -NTr_{LR}^{ROW}$ (9)

P - domestic prices
P^* - foreign prices
E - exchange rate
W - wage level
i - interest rate
$PY^{(s)}$ - supply of domestic goods
$PY^{(d)}$ - demand for domestic goods
PC - private consumption (households)
PC_G - public consumption (government)
$WN_E^{(s)}$ - income of households for labor $N_E^{(s)}$ supplied to enterprises
$WN_G^{(s)}$ - income of households for labor $N_G^{(s)}$ supplied to government
$WN_E^{(d)}$ - demand for labor by enterprises
$WN_G^{(d)}$ - demand for labor by the government
$WN^{(s)} = WN_E^{(s)} + WN_G^{(s)}$ - income of households for the labor supplied
$K^{(s)}$ - supply of capital
$K^{(d)}$ - demand for capital
OW_H^G - one way transactions from state to households (social help)
OW_E^G - one way transactions from state to enterprises (subsidiaries)
S - savings of households
I - investments
G_S - budget surplus (savings) of government
T_E – taxes paid by enterprises
T_H – taxes paid by households

T - taxes
G government spending
$EP * Ex_E$ - income from export of enterprises
$EP * \text{Im}_E$ - spending for import of enterprises
$EP * Ex_G$ - income from export of the state
$EP * \text{Im}_G$ - spending for import of the state
$EP * Ex$ - export
$EP * \text{Im}$ - import
$EP * NEx$ - net export
NTr_E^{ROW} - net transfers from ROW for enterprises
NTr_G^{ROW} - net transfers from ROW for the state
NTr_H^{ROW} - net transfers from ROW for households
NTr_{LR}^{ROW} - net transfers from rest of the world (ROW) to local residents (LR)
$NTr_{ROW}^{LR} = -NTr_{LR}^{ROW}$ net transfers from (LR) to (ROW)
π - profit of enterprises, received by household, being their owners.

With the notations above, Walras' law becomes:

$$\begin{aligned}&(PY^{(d)} - PY^{(s)}) + (M^d - M^{(s)}) + (WN^{(d)} - WN^{(s)}) + \\ &(iK^{(d)} - iK^{(s)}) + (G^{(d)} - G^{(s)}) + (F^{(d)} - F^{(s)}) = 0\end{aligned} \tag{10}$$

Proof of the Walras law

The processes in an open economy system and their ruling mechanisms could be better investigated in the knot points of the system – the aggregated markets, where the exchange between economic sectors happens. A flow diagram of these processes is presented at Figure 1. The five sectors of an open economy, namely: the households *H*, the enterprises *E*, the state *G*, the capitalization sector *K* and the rest of the world *ROW* are presented by rectangles. Only the monetary inflows and outflows between sectors are shown by arrows.

Figure 1: Flow diagram of an open economy

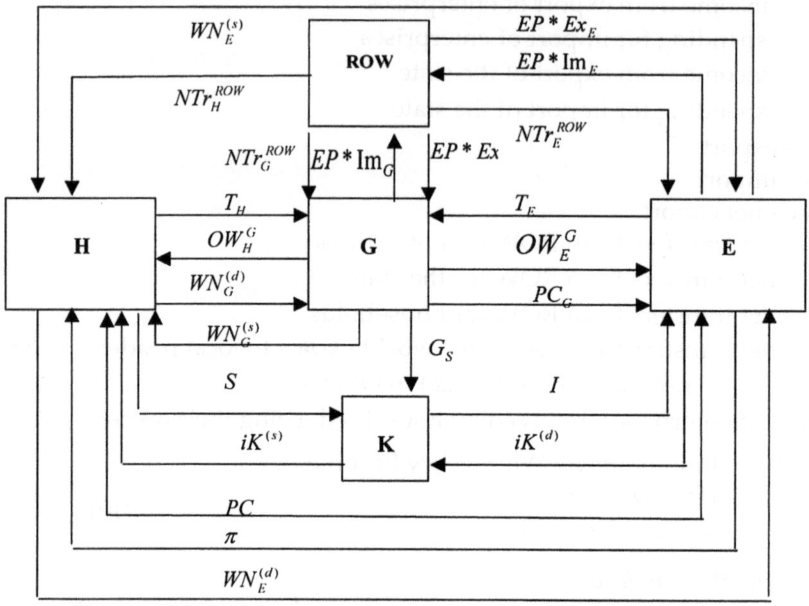

At Table 2a all the inflows, outflows and their outstanding (difference) for the corresponding sectors are given.

Table 2a: Sector inflows, outflows and their outstanding

	Inflows	Outflows	Outstand.
H	$WN_E^{(s)} + WN_G^{(s)} + iK^{(s)} + OW_H^G + NTr_H^{ROW}$	$PC + S + T_H$	$-\pi$
E	$PC + PC_G + EP * Ex_E + NTr_E^{ROW} + OW_E^G$	$WN_E^{(d)} + iK^{(d)} + EP * \mathrm{Im}_E + T_E$	π
G	$T_E + T_H + EP * Ex_G + NTr_G^{ROW}$	$PC_G + WN_G^{(d)} + OW_H^G + OW_E^G + EP * \mathrm{Im}_G$	G_S
K	$iK^{(d)} + S + G_S$	$iK^{(s)} + I$	$(1+i) E^{(d)}(K)$
ROW	$EP * \mathrm{Im}_E + EP * \mathrm{Im}_G$	$EP * Ex_E + EP * Ex_G + NTr_E^{ROW} + NTr_G^{ROW} + NTr_H^{ROW}$	$-BP$

Table 2b: Aggregated sector inflows and outflows

	Inflows	Outflows	Outstanding
H	$WN^{(s)} + iK^{(s)} + OW_H^G + NTr_H^{ROW}$	$PY^{(d)} + T_H$	$-\pi$
E	$PY^{(s)} + PC_G + EP * Ex_E + NTr_E^{ROW} + OW_E^G$	$WN_E^{(d)} + iK^{(d)} + EP * \mathrm{Im}_E + T_E$	π
G	$T + EP * Ex_G + NTr_G^{ROW}$	$G + EP * \mathrm{Im}_G$	G_S
K	$(1+i)K^{(d)}$	$(1+i)K^{(s)}$	$(1+i)E^{(d)}(K)$
ROW	$EP * \mathrm{Im}$	$EP * Ex + NTr_{LR}^{ROW}$	$-BP$

In table 2a, we bring together some of the inflows or outflows and get table 2b by using the following obvious equations:

$PY^{(s)} = PC$

$PY^{(d)} = PC + S$

$K^{(d)} = S + G_S$

$K^{(s)} = I$

$T = T_E + T_H$

$G = PC_G + WN_G^{(d)} + OW_H^G + OW_E^G$

$EP * Ex = EP * Ex_E + EP * Ex_G$ - export

$EP * \text{Im} = EP * \text{Im}_E + EP * \text{Im}_G$ - import

$EP * NEx = EP * Ex - EP * \text{Im}$ - net export

$NTr_{I.R}^{ROW} = NTr_E^{ROW} + NTr_G^{ROW} + NTr_H^{ROW}$

Based on the principle that the sum of all inflows is equal to the sum of all outflows plus its outstanding, and using table 2b, we get the ***fundamental equations of sector balances in an open economy***:

$$H : WN^{(s)} + iK^{(s)} + OW_H^G + NTr_H^{ROW} + \pi = PY^{(d)} + T_H \quad (11)$$

$$E : \pi = PY^{(s)} + EP * Ex_E + NTr_E^{ROW} + OW_E^G - WN_E^{(d)} - iK^{(d)} - EP * \text{Im}_E - T_E \quad (12)$$

$$G : G_S = T + EP * Ex_G + NTr_G^{ROW} - G - EP * \text{Im}_G \quad (13)$$

$$K : (1+i)E^{(d)}(K) = (1+i)(K^{(d)} - K^{(s)}) = (1+i)(S + G_S - I) \quad (14)$$

$$ROW : -BP = -(EP * Ex - EP * \text{Im} + NTr_{I.R}^{ROW}) \quad (15)$$

The equations (11)-(15) express basic economic activities of economic subjects.

According to equation (12) an ***enterprise*** plans to get a nominal profit π - for a period of time, maximizing the difference between the income $PY^{(s)}$ of goods supplied in the country, $EP * Ex_E$ of goods supplied abroad, NTr_E^{ROW} of net transfers from ROW for enterprises, OW_E^G of one way transactions from the state for enterprises (subsidiaries) and the costs for demanded labor $WN_E^{(d)}$, for demanded capital $iK^{(d)}$, importing $EP * \text{Im}_E$ and for paying taxes T_E.

According to equation (11) a ***household*** is demanding to get a nominal income $PY^{(d)}$ by a given price level P, maximizing the relationship:

$$PY^{(d)} = WN^{(s)} + iK^{(s)} + OW_H^G + NTr_H^{ROW} + \pi - T_H \quad (16)$$

by supplying labor $N^{(s)}$ at wage level W, getting income from capital $K^{(s)}$ supplied at interest i, receiving OW_H^G - one way transactions from the state (social help), NTr_H^{ROW} - net transfers from ROW, the profit π of enterprises, because households are the owners of enterprises, but paying taxes T_H. The household decides to distribute the demanded income $Y^{(d)}$ for consumption PC, for savings S after paying taxes T_H:

$$Y^{(d)} = PC + S \quad (17)$$

By inserting (17) in (16), we get the balance of income of households according to its distribution:

$$PC + S = WN^{(s)} + iK^{(s)} + OW_H^G + NTr_H^{ROW} + \pi - T_H \quad (18)$$

Bringing together (16) and (12), we get the basic equation of the economic circle: production - distribution - consumption or saving and, again, production. The savings S of households and the government surplus G_S are expected to be invested to increase the initial capital stock by the capital supplied: $K^{(s)} = I$.

Inserting π from (12) into (11) we get consequently:

$$WN^{(s)} + iK^{(s)} + OW_H^G + NTr_H^{ROW} + PY^{(s)} + PC_G + EP * Ex_E + NTr_E^{ROW} +$$
$$OW_E^G - WN_E^{(d)} - iK^{(d)} - EP * \mathrm{Im}_E - T_E = PY^{(d)} + T_H$$
$$(PY^{(d)} - PY^{(s)}) + (WN_E^{(d)} + WN_G^{(d)} - WN^{(s)}) + (iK^{(d)} - iK^{(s)}) + T_E + T_H + NTr_G^{ROW} + EP * Ex_G$$
$$- EP * \mathrm{Im}_G - WN_G^{(d)} - PC_G - OW_H^G - OW_E^G - EP * Ex_G + EP * \mathrm{Im}_G - EP * NEx_E$$
$$- NTr_G^{ROW} - NTr_H^{ROW} - NTr_E^{ROW'} = 0$$
$$(PY^{(d)} - PY^{(s)}) + (WN^{(d)} - WN^{(s)}) + (iK^{(d)} - iK^{(s)}) + (T + NEx_G + NTr_G^{ROW} - G) +$$
$$(EP * \mathrm{Im} - EP * Ex) + NTr_{ROW}^{LR} = 0$$
$$(PY^{(d)} - PY^{(s)}) + (WN^{(d)} - WN^{(s)}) + (iK^{(d)} - iK^{(s)}) + (G^{(d)} - G^{(s)}) + (F^{(d)} - F^{(s)}) = 0 \qquad (19)$$

In order to derive (10), we need to consider money as a value measuring good (numeraire) and to add it to the ordinary goods Y to get an enlarged set of goods denoted by Y_e, $Y_e = Y \cup Money$. We denote by $Y_e^{(d)}$ - demand and by $Y_e^{(s)}$ - supply at the enlarged market of goods. For the "new" system of markets, equation (19) holds:

$$(PY_e^{(d)} - PY_e^{(s)}) + (WN^{(d)} - WN^{(s)}) + (iK^{(d)} - iK^{(s)}) + (G^{(d)} - G^{(s)}) + (F^{(d)} - F^{(s)}) = 0 \qquad (20)$$

Now we can split the enlarged market of goods into *two* markets: the market of "ordinary" goods and the market the "measuring" (numeraire) good, called "money". This can be expressed by:

$$(PY_e^{(d)} - PY_e^{(s)}) = (PY^{(d)} - PY^{(s)}) + (M^{(d)} - M^{(s)}) \qquad (21)$$

By inserting of (21) into (20) we get (10), which was to be proved.

3. Flow-of-funds analysis and financial programming in an open economic system

The Walras law is a proper frame for a flow of funds analysis and designing corresponding financial programs. Here, I would like only to draw attention to using the Walras law as a theoretical fundament for a flow of funds analysis and the development of economic policy mechanisms for restoring or keeping the balance of payments equilibrium in an open economic system.

An open economic system has an internal and an external part. It is often a problem to balance the internal part of the open economy with the rest of the world economy. Considering an open economic system with respect to its markets of domestic goods, domestic money, domestic labor, domestic capital, public goods, foreign exchange, we would have the internal part of the system consisting of all the markets in consideration, without the foreign exchange market (the closed system indeed). Due to the Walras law (equation (1)), the internal economic system is in balance with the rest of the world economy, if - and only if - the foreign exchange market is in equilibrium. For bringing the internal economic system into balance with the rest of the world economy, economic policy tools like financial programs can be used.

Generally speaking, any financial program is a set of coordinated policy measures intending to achieve certain economic targets. Some publications devoted to this subject are: Chorng-huey Wong, Oystein Pettersen 1979, Boerje Kragh et al. 1970, Stanley Fischer 1997, Polak, J.J. and Victor Argy 1971, J.J. Polak 1997 A. Schaechter 2001, S. Sriram 2001.

Financial programs are often designed for an IMF member country in order to restore its *balance of payments viability*, and more generally to restore its *macroeconomic stability* - seen as necessary condition for economic growth. Using the terminology we introduced, an IMF financial program could be designed to restore the balance of the country's economic system, which means the restoring of its foreign exchange market equilibrium.

The foreign exchange market is in equilibrium, if:

$$E^{(d)}(ForeignExchange) = F^{(d)} - F^{(s)} = -BP = EP * N\,\mathrm{Im} + NTr_{ROW}^{LR} = 0 \qquad (22)$$

with

$$E^{(d)}(ForeignExchange) = E^{(d)}(ForeignGoods) + E^{(d)}(ForeignMoney) \qquad (23)$$

$$E^{(d)}(ForeignGoods) = -EP * NEx - (EP * Ex(Y, \frac{EP}{P*}) - EP * \mathrm{Im}(Y*, \frac{EP}{P*})) \qquad (24)$$

$$E^{(d)}(ForeignMoney) = -NTr_{LR}^{ROW}(r, r*) = -(Tr_{LR}^{ROW}(r, r*) - Tr_{ROW}^{LR}(r, r*)) \qquad (25)$$

But how can foreign exchange markets come into an equilibrium?

The approach that can be chosen for restoring the foreign exchange market equilibrium essentially depends on structural issues of the economic system in consideration, particularly determined by its exogenous and endogenous variables. In case of a floating exchange rate regime, the exchange rate variable E is considered to be endogenous, in case of a fixed or pegged exchange rate regime, E is considered as an exogenous variable.

If the economic system has a floating exchange rate regime, then a market-equilibrium approach can be used for balancing the foreign exchange.

Another source for compensating a negative net export $EP*NEx$ could be a positive flow of net transfers from the rest of the world to local residents NTr_{LR}^{ROW}. Two main components of NTr_{LR}^{ROW} play usually the most important role in compensation of the negative current account $CA = EP*NEx$: ***the foreign direct investments and transfers of local residents of the country who are working abroad.***

If the economic system has a regime of a fixed or pegged exchange rate, a good source for compensating for a current account deficit is the public goods market. Among the markets in consideration, the market of public goods is the most specific one. It is a highly regulated monopolistic market because the state is the only provider of public goods. Just because the market of public goods is a highly regulated monopolistic market, it is often used as an economic policy mechanism if some of the other markets are negatively misbalanced in order to compensate them by a ***positive excess demand of the public goods market, which is indeed the government's budget surplus***. More formally, using (7) and (10), the Walras law can be written in the form:

$$BP = (PY^{(d)} - PY^{(s)}) + (M^{d} - M^{(s)}) + (WN^{(d)} - WN^{(s)}) + (iK^{(d)} - iK^{(s)}) + (G^{(d)} - G^{(s)})$$

This last equation shows, that a negative balance of payments $BP < 0$ can be at least partially compensated for by a positive excess demand flow of public goods $G^{(d)} - G^{(s)} > 0$, which means that the government has to keep a budget surplus flow.

The development of a financial program for restoring the foreign exchange equilibrium is usually based on flow-of-funds analysis (see, for example A. D. Bain 1973, Ray C. Fair and Dwight M. Jaffe 1972, Janos Kornai 1971, Donald P. Tucker 1971; Carl F. Christ 1969).

Basic tools for a flow-of-funds analysis are flow-of-funds accounts and social accounting matrices. The ***flow-of-funds account*** is a well known component of the national accounts system, showing the financial transactions between sectors of the economy and providing a framework which gives a systematic, comprehensive and consistent description and analysis of the facts. It brings the various financial activities of an economy into explicit statistical relationship with one another and with data on the non-financial activities that generate income and production[3].

References

Bain, A. D. 1973: Flow of Funds Analysis: A Survey. The Economics Journal, vol. 83, pp. 1055-1093, London

Christ, Carl F. 1969: A model of Monetary and Fiscal Policy Effects on the Money Stock, Price Level and Real Output. Journal of Money, Credit and Banking, vol. 1, Columbus, Ohio, pp. 683-705

Copeland, M. A. 1962: Some Illustrative Analytical Uses of Flow of Funds Data, in: National Bureau of Economic Research, Studies of Income and Wealth, vol. 26, The Flow of Funds Approach to Social Accounting, Princeton University Press

Fair, Ray C./Dwight M. Jaffe 1972: Methods of Estimation for Market Disequilibrium. Econometrica, vol. 40, New Haven, Conn., pp. 497-514

Felderer, Bernhard/Stefan Homburg 1999: Makroökonomik und neue Makroökonomik. Springer Verlag, Berlin

Fischer, Stanley 1997: Applied Economics in Action: IMF Programs. The American Economic Review, vol. 87, no. 2 (May), Papers and Proceedings of the Hundred and Fourth Annual Meeting of the American Economic Association, pp. 23-27

Kragh, Boerje et al. 1970: Financial Programming. OECD Publications No. 27, 143, Paris

Kornai, Janos 1971: Anti-Equilibrium. In: On Economic Systems Theory and the Task of Research, Amsterdam/London

Lange, Oskar 1942: Say's Law: Restatement and Criticism, in: O. Lange et al (eds.): Studies in Mathematical Economics, Chicago, Chicago University Press

Patinkin, Don 1965: Money, Interest and Prices. Harper and Row, New York

Polak, J.J./Victor Argy 1971: Credit Policy and Balance of Payments. IMF Staff Papers vol. 18, Washington DC, pp. 1-24

Polak, J.J. 1997: The IMF Monetary Model at Forty. IMF Working Paper, April

Schaechter, A. 2001: Implementation of Monetary Policy and Central Bank's Balance Sheet. IMF Working Paper, October

Sriram, S. 2001: A Survey of Recent Empirical Money Demand Studies. IMF Staff paper, vol. 47, no. 3

---

3 The flow of funds analysis has been developed nearly parallel to the national accounts system by seminal contributions of authors like M. A. Copeland 1962, R. Stone 1965, and J. Tinbergen 1965.
Social accounting matrices were used first by R. Stone 1966. They are the tools for designing procedures for achieving economic policy goals. In this paper, I am not intending to go in more details of implementation of social accounting matrices to the matter concerned here.

Stone, R. 1965: Social Accounting Matrix Models - Framework for Economic Decisions, in: C. M. Berners-Lee (ed.): Models for Decisions, London

Stone, R. 1966: The Social Accounts from a Consumer's Point of View, Review of Income and Wealth, Series 12, March

Tinbergen, J. 1965: A Model for Flow of Funds Analysis of an Open Country, Rivista Internationali di Scienze Economiche e Commerciali, vol. 12, March

Tobin, James 1969: A general equilibrium approach to monetary theory. Journal of Money, Credit and Banking, vol. 1, no. 1, Feb., pp. 15-29

Tucker, Donald P. 1971: Macroeconomic Models and the Demand for Money under Market Disequilibrium. Journal of Money, Credit and Banking, vol. 3, Columbus, Ohio, pp. 57-83

Wong, Chorng-huey/Oystein Pettersen 1979: Financial Programming in the Framework of Optimal Control. Weltwirtschaftliches Archiv, vol. 115, issue 1, pp. 20-37

Chapter two:

STUDIES ON EAST EUROPE

Corporate Control and the Role of Business Integration in Russian Companies[1]

Tatiana G. Dolgopyatova
(State University Higher School of Economics, Moscow, Russia)

1. Introduction

Researchers of the Russian economy have unanimously identified the most important features of stock ownership and control (NCCG 2008: 12-16): *First,* the concentration of capital in the corporate sector resulting from its aggressive redistribution for more than 15 years tends to be high. *Secondly,* the high concentration of ownership affected the development of corporate control and evolution of the mechanisms of corporate governance. This high concentration provides the basis for control by the majority shareholder or a consolidated group of such shareholders exercised by various formal and informal means. Majority shareholders are constrained only by the need to comply with the formal legal provisions and often imitate the activities of intra-corporate tools (Yakovlev 2003: 42-43).

Thirdly, the prevailing model of corporate control is that in which majority shareholders participate directly in management as top managers of companies (Dolgopyatova, 2007: 270). A combination of ownership and control has become a formal institution of Russian corporate practices, which restrict the demand for "outside" managers who do not own company shares. This institution has become widespread not only as a result of privatization ("red directors" becoming owners of enterprises) but also as a tool intentionally chosen by owners who established their businesses from scratch. In a situation of underdeveloped markets for managerial staff and institutions for protection of property rights, this arrangement was preferred as compared to high costs of preventing opportunistic behaviour of hired managers.[2] This resulted in the elimination of the agency problem of corporate governance.

Conjecturing about the evolution of the Russian system of corporate governance continues; however, it would be interesting to answer the question which model of governance dominant shareholders choose and

---

[1] The research is carried out within the framework of the Fundamental Research Program of SU HSE in 2008. I would like to thank Ichiro Iwasaki, Heiko Pleines, and Yurii Simachyev for their useful comments, and Ol'ga Uvarova for her assistance in data processing.

[2] At the time of economic transition, this behaviour would take the extreme form of asset stripping and business raiding (Black-Kraakman-Tarassova 2000: 1750-1752; Fox-Heller, 1999: 18-22; Gaddy-Ickes, 1998: 4-8).

whether or not they consent to the separation of executive management from company ownership. Reliance on hired management prompts owners to seek other methods of control over a business entity, and they sometimes resort to the use of internal corporate mechanisms.

Our main objective in this paper is to identify, on the basis of a representative sample, a set of factors underlying the preference of dominating shareholders for top managers who do not hold shares of a given company. We identify two types of companies, one, independent businesses, which are stand-alone entities and parent companies of holdings, and the second, business divisions, which are the rank-and-file entities of a company group. We will empirically test two core assumptions regarding the role of corporate integration in the choice of the form of control.

The *first hypothesis* is that integration is a tool that replaces direct control by the shareholder and suggests a preference for a form of control with the separation of management and ownership.

The *second hypothesis* is that two types of companies will respond differently to demands of property rights protection and enhancing the quality of management. For divisions of larger businesses, factors of preference for hired managers are linked to the state of corporate management, which includes that at the level of business groups. For stand-alone companies, the main determinants for the departure of shareholders from management are linked to the protection of property rights.

The paper uses the results of a survey of top managers of 822 large and medium-sized joint stock companies (JSCs) in industry and communications carried out in 2005 at 64 regions of Russia by the "Analytical Centre of Yurii Levada" within a joint project that is being carried out by the Institute for Industrial and Market Studies of the SU HSE and the Institute of Economic Research (Hitotsubashi University) on corporate governance and integration processes in the Russian economy (for details: Dolgopyatova/Iwasaki 2006: 5-12).

Based on the findings of the survey, the second section of this paper gives a description of stock ownership and corporate control forms, with management and ownership functions either separated or combined. The third section contains the driving factors of choice of the form of control with separate functions and measurement indicators, while the fourth section presents a comprehensive analysis of their possible impact on the choice using a binary logistic regression. The final section is a summary of the outcome of the analysis.

2. Corporate control under concentrated ownership

2.1 Quantification of ownership concentration

In an atmosphere of imperfect legal institutions the Russian corporate sector took the predictable way of creating a type of large shareholder, an owner of stakes that could give him or her the right to control executives (Stiglitz 1999: 6). Privatized enterprises evolved in this direction, while newly established companies, as a rule, belonged to large shareholders from the outset. A high level of ownership concentration is natural to transitional economies in spite of differences in initial ways of privatization and in the quality of institutions (Berglöf/von Thadden 2000: 152-153).

Russian companies have a characteristically high level of stock ownership concentration that increases annually. The aggressive ownership redistribution in the wake of privatization resulted in the rapid emergence of large shareholders. According to various surveys, in the beginning of the 2000s, the largest shareholder would own, on average, 40 to 50 percent of the assets; JSCs including a blockholder accounted for 40 to 65 percent of the total sample, while those with a controlling stakeholder accounted for up to 45 percent of the sample. Qualitative surveys (e.g., interviews and case studies) generally suggested a higher level of concentration of real control, as opposed to formal ownership, in one person and practically the universal presence of a controlling shareholder (Dolgopyatova 2008: 96-97).

Our survey has confirmed a very high degree of ownership concentration (more than 50 percent of the shares were owned by one shareholder) in the sample, which was observed in almost 70 percent of the surveyed companies. Companies with the average level of concentration (25 to 50 percent of shares owned by the largest shareholder) were approximately 18 percent of the total, while those with a low level of ownership concentration (in Russian terms) with the blockholder (owner of more than 25 percent of the total stock) not yet to emerge accounted for only 13 percent of the sample.

High-concentration companies included two subgroups depending on whether there was a second large shareholder with at least a blocking minority ownership (counterbalance) or not. Almost half of the companies had a dominant shareholder not contained by the stake of the second shareholder (Figure 1). The pattern of distribution of businesses by the degree of ownership concentration was approximately the same in manufacturing and communications and was not dependent on company size, type of incorporation, corporate background, and lack of international or domestic tradability of stock. A high concentration of ownership became an intrinsic feature of Russian companies.

Figure 1: Classification of surveyed joint-stock companies by level of ownership concentration

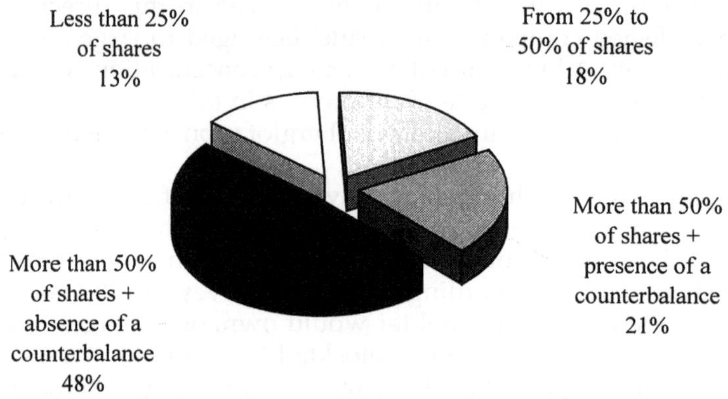

Source: Author's illustration based on survey data.

A very high level of concentration was also characteristic of large public companies. According to a survey by Standard & Poor's (S&P) of 80 Russian companies with the most liquid shares, about 71 percent of them had shareholders with more than 50 percent of the stock in 2007, and only 8 percent of the companies did not have a blockholder (S&P 2007a: 20). Among the 75 public companies accounting for 90 percent of the capitalization of the Russian stock market, the largest shareholder would own, on average, 58 percent of the shares (S&P 2007b: 6).

2.2 Control tools of large shareholders

The existence of controlling shareholders brings the solution of the key problem of corporate governance, i.e. coping with opportunistic behaviour of the management, to another level (Stiglitz 1999: 5-7): On the one hand, the free-rider problem gives principal shareholders the incentives to develop and provide control of the business. On the other hand, there are various opportunities, including formal and informal tools, to achieve corporate control. The Russian practice includes the entire range of control procedures.

Control through direct participation of the principal shareholder in corporate management in the capacity of top manager (CEO and/or other top managers) has been widely practiced, thereby resolving the agency problem. Our survey analyzed the inseparability or separation of ownership and management by using two variables. The first variable is the question of whether or not large shareholders work as company managers; the second, that of whether or not a company CEO holds company shares. A joint consideration of these questions makes it possible to divide the surveyed JSCs into four groups (Figure 2). We can define JSCs in which large shareholders are managers as a cluster with a combination of ownership and management. This cluster includes two unequal groups. One group has large shareholders who are managers, and, at the same time, the CEO is a shareholder - as a rule, of a large proportion of shares. This group is identified as having "complete inseparability." In the smallest group, large shareholders are company managers, but the CEO is not a shareholder. Such situations occur infrequently; they are usually temporary or related to the geographical isolation of an enterprise from its major owners.

Figure 2: Classification of surveyed companies by participation of shareholders in their management

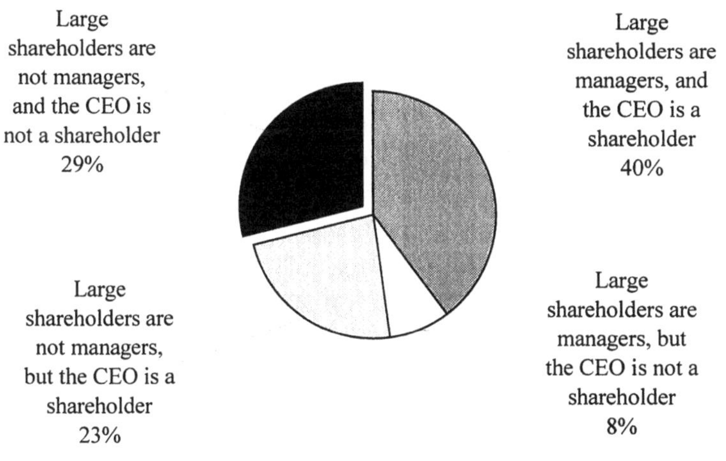

Source: Author's illustration based on survey data.

There is a substantial group in which only the CEO is a small or medium size shareholder. Even a modest stake in the hands of a top manager gives him or her additional control. In JSCs in which respondents gave negative answers to both questions, the ownership was formally separated from the management in accordance with our working definition.

Along with the institution of inseparable functions, large shareholders have other ways of gaining control over companies. One of them is to capture the corporate boards. Principal shareholders can legally adopt basic decisions at the meeting of shareholders by domination, including the formation of the board of directors and management boards while ignoring the interests of minority shareholders. Although such a method allows a JSC to be virtually controlled as a private company, it remains legal and even helps shareholders to become accustomed to the use of intra-corporate tools.

A tool in order to exert a tight control is the possibility of dismissal of the management staff - or the threat of dismissal - which comes easy in the case of stock domination. Personalities may cause problems in these cases. In addition, opportunistic behaviour on the part of the new managers may also contribute to the situation.

Another possibility for gaining control is related to having additional links to the company's executive management by establishing head companies or by including special supervisory managers into the procedure for the coordination of decision making. In many cases these are not staff members of a given company, or they may have a title (like "commissioners") that does not reflect their real functions. Such links are normally governed by in-house business management regulations and operated beyond the scope of intra-corporate procedures.

Finally, another possibility is the use of informal schemes of control directly through the owners on a regular basis or case by case. In fact, such a possibility means a permanent, direct intervention of principal owners into the management procedures - which can be done without any agreement or taking into account other shareholders' or stakeholders' interests.

2.3 Separation of ownership from management

In academic studies (for instance, Yakovlev et al. 2006: 271), it had been predicted that owners would tend to depart from business management, and this practice has received the attention of industry experts and the business community (NCCG 2007: 60-63). The separation of ownership from management and the delegation of authority to hired managers are the products of two opposing trends. The institutionally underdeveloped economy promotes the combination of both functions to protect the rights of large shareholders. At the same time, specific skills and competences still remain in demand under the current conditions as well as in the long-term perspectives for the development of Russian companies in the framework of a market embedded in the global economy; therefore, the requirements for management quality are likely to become exclusive.

The issue of the gradual separation of executive management from ownership was discussed on the basis of records of 20 in-depth interviews with senior managers of JSCs (Dolgopyatova 2008: 104-107). It was demonstrated that as Russian business underwent an intense integration, the ways and means of corporate control also saw extensive change.[3] The separation of the ownership and management functions (in terms of the working definition presented above) was primarily characteristic of subsidiaries companies within company groups. Formal separation resulted in real changes in the distribution of competences, gradual delegation of some managerial issues to hired managers, and, in particular, production and operational issues and some strategic issues related to logistics and marketing. The separation contributed to a more active use of boards of directors by dominating owners to exercise control over hired managers.

Figure 3: Links between ownership and management in integrated and independent companies

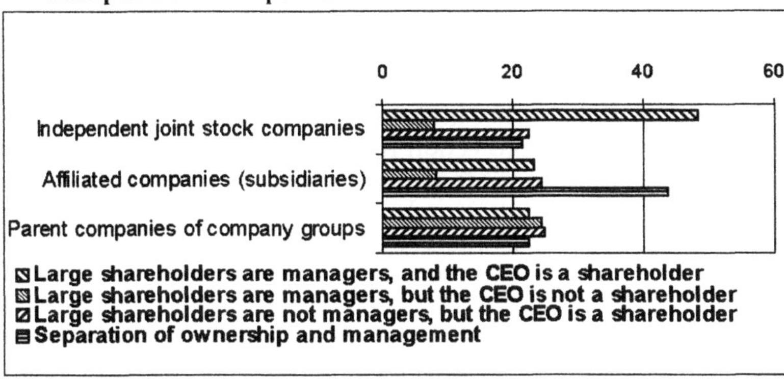

Source: Author's illustration based on survey data.

The patterns of a combination of ownership and control are different in JSCs that represent a business or a part of a business (Figure 3). The separation of ownership from management is typical (twice as often) of the enterprises that are rank-and-file members of holding company groups, but independent firms and parent companies are mostly operated on the basis of the inseparability of these functions. The stakes owned by a CEO are practically the same in all types of surveyed companies, but the few cases in which large shareholders participate in management when they are not CEOs are typical of parent companies.

Patterns of control in rank-and-file members of company groups were correlated with their features. The separation of management is typical of large-scale business groups with complicated management structures:

---

[3] The reader can find a wider picture of the development of business integration in Russia in Avdasheva 2007.

massive groups with large numbers of entities, or holding company groups that are widely dispersed geographically and diversified by industry. Exceeding the boundaries of a single region gives the companies with separate ownership and management an advantage of nearly 11 percentage points. A separation of functions is evident in 55 percent of conglomerates, in 42 percent of vertically integrated groups and in 35 percent of the horizontally integrated company groups.

3. Determinants for the hired management choice

Various methods of corporate control provide the dominating owner with choice options. He or she must decide whether the type of operational environment of the particular company is in favour of the selection of a hired management and the separation of ownership and management. In our empirical analysis, we included four sets of factors influencing the owner's choice and define the specific hypotheses for testing.

3.1 Corporate governance and ownership

Direct participation of the owner in management under a formal contract is a tool of property rights protection from the opportunistic behaviour of managers when institutions are weak. There are other tools of control that substitute or complement a combination of management and ownership. The basic tool is the integration of enterprises into company groups, thus providing the top-management with other instruments of control and making it possible to enlist hired managers among the rank-and-file members of business groups. In this case, parent companies and stand-alone enterprises will be less likely to separate ownership from management.

Another tool is a very high concentration of capital, which makes it legally possible to take control of company boards. It can also be used as a substitute for a combination of ownership and management. With a lower concentration, a combination provides for a strengthening of controlling positions of shareholders, thereby complementing the ownership.

Another mechanism of protection (substitute) is property nontransparency or ultimate owner (beneficiary) concealment behind a multi-level chain (5-8 levels) of affiliated firms or individuals, and multistage company management systems (Dolgopyatova 2007: 266). The Standard & Poor's study of transparency cited above revealed that less than a quarter of the large public companies reported shareholders who owned 10 and more percent of stock (S&P 2007a: 16). Recent in-depth research demonstrated that public companies masked holdings of insiders through nominee and foreign offshore arrangements (Chernykh 2008:

170). This nontransparency can be reflected by stake holdings of different legal entities or foreign investors[4].

The existence of special owners, such as the government and real foreign investors, multiplies the chances of selection in favour of the division of the functions.[5] The degree of a company's publicity should follow the same direction. Open JSCs and, particularly, companies whose securities are traded in stock markets must be more inclined to engage hired managers because it may be a positive signal for retail investors.

3.2 Path-dependency

Voucher privatization provided employees at enterprises with shares and created preconditions for the redistribution of ownership. The managerial corps had strong informational and organizational advantages over other potential owners in terms of the purchase of shares of the company, in which case the former used their own assets, which they had previously accumulated in the shadow turnover. The scheme with a shareholder being in the capacity of a manager is more likely to be used at JSCs established during privatization than at new (start-up) businesses or reorganized companies. At the same time, the effect of privatization might have lessened after such a long period of intensive redistribution of ownership upon its completion.

3.3 Corporate management and markets

A complex operational environment often requires professional managerial skills and expertise. The size and industrial classification of a company are indirect indicators of managerial complexity. The bigger the number of employees, the bigger the number of special competences required for its management. With regard to production particularities, the only existing aggregated industrial classification fails to allow such industries to be clearly identified.

Management complexity can be characterized by the particularities of the organizational structure and management techniques, in particular, the methods of strategic planning required due to the extension of the decision-making horizon in the 2000s (Yakovlev 2003: 39-40). The strategic planning indicator of a company is the duration of the company's decision-making horizon beyond 3 years, during which its chances of engaging hired managers should multiply.

---

[4] Although such ownership indicates, to some degree, an enterprise's participation in the holding company group, it may have an individual value as a signal of nontransparency.

[5] The existence of a foreign or quasi-foreign investor does not have any effect on the formulation of a quantitative hypothesis.

Restructuring plays a special role in the area of corporate management. There is much truth in the literature on management (Shekshnya-Ketz de Vries 2007: 36) in that restructuring is much easier to perform with a single center for decision making when a single person is acting in the capacity of owner and top manager.[6] To measure the level of restructuring, we selected the introduction of new technologies and R&D activities in the period between 2001 and 2004. In the weak innovative economic environment marked by the production decline of the 1990s, R&D may suggest the intensification of production and technology restructuring and, thus, negatively affect the choice of hired managers.

Management complexity and peculiarities are also associated with market conditions, namely competition including global markets.[7] In many empirical studies it is competition with manufacturers of developed market countries, rather than competition with Russian manufacturers or CIS enterprises which are mostly based on the prevailing stereotypes of operation and interaction in the market (mainly price competition and administrative leverage) that becomes the indicator of a truly competitive environment with an impact on enterprise behaviour and forcing Russian manufacturers to resort to modern methods of competition (Kuznetsov 2005: 84). Estimates of competition with Russian companies are often reflecting a low demand, poor competitiveness and, thus, an incomplete restructuring. Therefore, we used the existence of both, severe and moderate, competition with companies from developed foreign countries as the key indicator of competition, assuming that it should multiply the chances of appointment of a hired top management.

3.4 Managerial labour market

Operational conditions govern the demand for hired managers; in addition, their engagement is also encouraged by the management labour market's development and the growth in the supply of qualified managers. Unfortunately, it is very difficult to provide an adequate assessment of it as part of a survey on the micro-level. Taking into account the Russian labour market's well-known regional dimension and low labour force mobility, its development can be estimated by using the assessment of the average wages in the regions, derived from the data of a sample

---

6 Restructuring was required for the overwhelming majority of Russian companies, both privatized ones whose assets were collected under the state-planned economy and new ones, because they emerged in the real sector from what was left from old Soviet enterprises by accumulating their assets.

7 Although the point is the company's external factor of competition in the market of its products, in fact we have only a subjective assessment of the level of competition by the respondents that can be developed through a set of conditions.

survey on wages of CEOs conducted by the Federal Service of State Statistics as a proxy for the labour market supply (Rosstat 2006: 112-114). The higher the wages are, the faster the division of functions may be chosen. The wage level does not only show the market development, but also managers-shareholders' behaviour. They may use other channels of remuneration: They may prefer informal methods of shadow income extraction or dividend payout.

4. Empirical analysis: results and discussion

The holding of an enterprise's shares by its CEO (general director) could give the director solid advantages in decision making, particularly because a JSC with a limited interest of the director is distinguished by a lower concentration of ownership and a higher share of the state in equity. This suggests that a comprehensive analysis of factors could be made by using the binary logistic regression and excluding from the sample a group of enterprises in which the CEO has shares. The dependant variable *CONTRL* was therefore expressed by the chances of choosing a form of control with separation of ownership from management, which adopts a value of "1" in the case of separation and one of "0" in the case of inseparability (that principal shareholders are top managers of the companies).

Table 1 shows a comparison of JSCs according to the value of basic indicators (descriptive statistics), which we assume have an effect on the choice of the control configuration. The names of variables used in the regression analysis are presented in parentheses. Nine industries were used for industry classification (*INDDUM*), with the communication sector being the basic category. JSCs with a high level of concentration were considered as the basic category for ownership concentration. The logarithm was taken from the quantitative variable of the number of employees in a company.

The model of choice "A" was assessed for all JSCs (sample I) and for JSCs with the exclusion of enterprises of the communication and of the fuel and energy sectors due to their features (sample II). Large holding company groups organized and controlled by the federal state operate in these two sectors. They are distinguished by a high public interest and by a developed market regulation.

Table 1: Comparison of JSCs with separation or combination of ownership and management

	Combi-nation	Separa-tion
Average number of employees in a JSC, persons *(COMSIZ)*	1096	2154
JSCs in communications, %	4.7	9.2**
Open JSCs, % *(OPECOM)*	60.2	68.3**
Privatized enterprises, % *(PRICOM)*	70.0	61.7**
JSCs with securities traded on stock markets, % *(STOCKM)*	7.9	13.3**
Independent JSC or parent company in a group of companies, % *(BUSINES)*	77.4	49.1***
Parent company of a group of companies, % *(HOLCOM)*	5.8	4.1
Average percent of shares owned by foreign investors, % *(OWNFOR)*	2.4	7.6***
Average percent of shares owned by authorities, % *(OWNSTA)*	3.7	7.0
Average percent of shares owned by all legal entities, % *(OWNENT)*	11.0	26.3***
The largest shareholder owns less than 25% of shares *(CONLOW)*	9.0	11.4
The largest shareholder owns less than 50% but more than 25% of shares *(CONMED)*	20.6	11.0***
The largest shareholder owns more than 50% of shares	70.3	77.6*
JSCs invested in R&D, % *(R&DEXP)*	61.0	49.5***
JSCs introduced new technologies, % *(NEWTEC)*	58.2	49.5**
JSCs faced intense competition with Russian enterprises, % *(COMPRU)*	67.5	55.3***
JSCs faced competition with enterprises of developed countries, % *(COMPFO)*	26.6	30.7
JSCs with horizon of strategic planning of 3 years and more, % *(STRPLA)*	22.8	33.5***
Average wages of enterprises top managers by regional statistics data, thousand Russian rubles *(SALCEO)*	16.041	16.627

Note: Comparison of frequencies by χ^2 test; comparison between means by Kruskal Wallis test. – ***: Significant at the 1% level. – **: Significant at the 5% level. – *: Significant at the 10% level.

Table 2 shows the results of the calculations. Close estimates of selection options of the form of control were obtained with two samples. A significant effect is typical of ownership characteristics: the chances of selection in favour of separation multiplied at open JSCs, with an increase in the interest held by legal entities, foreign investors, and government bodies at all levels; on the other hand, the chances were reduced with a medium level of equity concentration in comparison with a high level (only for industries outside of the fuel and energy and the communication sectors). Furthermore, a positive effect was demonstrated by the existing competition with companies of developed market economies. Fewer chances for using hired management were observed in companies under restructuring or severe competition with Russian companies as well as in those related to privatized enterprises.

Integration had a stable and strong influence: the chances of engaging hired managers were considerably reduced for enterprises classified as independent businesses. Model A was tested separately at companies representing independent businesses (subsample 1) or a division of them (subsample 2). Similar specifications for these subsamples (including an indicator identifying the enterprise as the parent company) allowed us to see an appreciable difference in the effect of the tested independent variables.

The history of a company ceased to have an effect. While the choice of a form of control for businesses remained heavily influenced by factors of ownership, enterprises which were integrated into company groups remained under a positive effect of the interest held by legal entities (exclusive of the energy and communication sectors), state, and foreign investors. The interests of legal entities as well as, to some extent, those of foreigners were previously interpreted as a means to reduce ownership transparency used by ultimate owners as a tool to protect their property rights.

Restructuring had an effect on independent businesses and rank-and-file members of the holding company groups. With regard to the latter, both indicators manifested themselves with an added effect from the use of strategic planning. Competition with foreign manufacturers always had a positive effect on independent businesses as well as on rank-and-file members of company groups in industry (exclusive of the fuel and energy sector). Competition with Russian manufacturers always was significant for independent businesses and, in some cases, divisions of the holding company groups. It is only the rank-and-file members of the company group that experienced a positive effect from the labour market, mostly due to the existence of enterprises of the energy and communication sectors. Naturally, all-Russian holding companies of these sectors have to take into account the situation in the regional labour market when hiring new managers.

Table 2: Logistic regressions for shareholders' choice of separated ownership and management

Sample	I	II	I-1	I-2	I-2	I-2	II-1	II-2	II-2	II-2
Model	A	A	A	A	B	C	A	A	B	C
Constant	0.719* (0.396)	1.106** (0.468)	-0.658** (0.311)	-1.315 (0.805)	-1.044 (0.826)	-2.007** (1.001)	1.043 (1.163)	-1.132 (0.884)	1.031 (0.733)	-2.939** (1.376)
BUSINES	-1.187*** (0.250)	-1.410*** (0.291)	X	X	X	X	X	X	X	X
HOLCOM	X	X	X	X	X	X	X	X	X	X
COMSIZ	X	X	X	X	X	X	-0.893* (0.449)	X	X	X
OPECOM	0.670** (0.264)	0.739** (0.299)	X	X	X	X	0.723** (0.356)	X	X	X
PRICOM	-0.594** (0.255)	-0.660** (0.288)	X	X	X	X	X	X	X	X
STOCKM	X	X	X	X	X	X	X	X	X	X
CONLOW	X	0.719 (0.444)	0.710* (0.427)	X	X	X	0.865* (0.457)	X	X	X
CONMED	X	-0.719* (0.375)	-0.566 (0.424)	X	X	X	-0.580 (0.457)	X	X	X
OWNSTA	0.015** (0.007)	0.020** (0.009)	0.036*** (0.010)	X	X	X	0.030*** (0.010)	X	X	X
OWNFOR	0.020*** (0.007)	0.029*** (0.009)	0.032*** (0.012)	X	X	X	0.039*** (0.014)	0.023** (0.010)	0.020* (0.012)	0.032** (0.015)
OWNENT	0.015*** (0.004)	0.013*** (0.005)	0.016*** (0.006)	0.018*** (0.006)	0.018*** (0.006)	0.016** (0.006)	0.014** (0.007)	0.017** (0.007)	0.021*** (0.008)	0.021** (0.009)
COMPRU	-0.599** (0.236)	-0.776*** (0.268)	-0.680** (0.292)	X	X	X	-0.741** (0.317)	X	-0.975* (0.589)	-2.088*** (0.809)
COMPFO	0.700*** (0.260)	0.859*** (0.279)	0.700** (0.320)	X	X	X	0.770** (0.339)	1.030** (0.487)	1.173** (0.569)	1.144* (0.687)

STRPLA	0.490* (0.264)	X	X	1.273*** (0.445)	1.485*** (0.470)	1.360*** (0.496)	X	X	1.343** (0.627)	X
R&DEXP	-1.117*** (0.250)	-1.263*** (0.284)	-1.232*** (0.308)	-1.047** (0.429)	-1.199*** (0.449)	-1.170*** (0.462)	-1.258*** (0.340)	X	-1.689*** (0.645)	-1.430** (0.687)
NEWTEC	-0.528** (0.234)	-0.626** (0.261)	X	-1.332*** (0.443)	-1.453*** (0.468)	-1.356*** (0.496)	X	-1.503*** (0.496)	-1.778*** (0.589)	-1.463** (0.674)
SALCEO	X	X	X	0.125*** (0.047)	0.110** (0.049)	0.090* (0.051)	X	0.083* (0.051)	X	X
INDDUM	X	X	X	X	X	X	X	X	X	X
SIZHOL						1.382*** (0.531)				5.699*** (1.473)
INTVER					-0.126 (0.450)	-0.286 (0.466)			0.008 (0.579)	0.413 (0.681)
INTCON					1.940*** (0.663)	1.864*** (0.698)			2.374*** (0.775)	1.924** (0.881)
N	456	394	313	143	143	139	291	103	103	100
-2Log likelihood	476.68	385.21	307.77	159.49	150.29	138.48	270.92	116.40	97.64	73.14
R^2 Nagel-kerke	0.326	0.357	0.247	0.288	0.354	0.401	0.263	0.281	0.458	0.628
Test of the model χ^2	124.56***	123.70***	58.32***	34.36***	43.56***	48.94***	56.91***	24.20***	42.96***	62.92***

Notes: Standard errors are reported in parentheses. ***: Significant at the 1% level. – **: Significant at the 5% level. – *: Significant at the 10% level. – Forward Stepwise method was used: X: variables dropped from the final regression equations.

In addition, two other models were estimated for rank-and-file members of business groups, which took into account the scale and structure of the entire group of companies. The management complexity in the group was assessed by including an industry diversification indicator into model B (affiliation to a vertically integrated holding company *INTVER* or conglomerate *INTCON*, while affiliation to a horizontal type of association became the basic category), and the C specification was added with a variable for the size of the group of companies (*SIZHOL*, the logarithm of the number of legal entities integrated into the holding company). The use of these indicators in the model has a positive effect on the choice and increases its explanatory function with retained stability of basic dependences.

5. Conclusions

Business integration encourages a gradual separation of ownership from management, and shareholding relations among the members of a company group allow abandoning a combination of functions. Summing up the results of our empirical study, two basic hypotheses and most of the special assumptions with regard to the effect of suggested factors were confirmed. Indeed, factors of ownership and corporate governance, which are "responsible" for property rights protection, made a considerable contribution to multiplying the chances of an engagement of hired managers at Russian JSCs.

Another and more important result is that integration became a significant feature that predetermined differences in the role of other factors of choice for different types of companies. Direct participation of shareholders in management is preferred by stand-alone enterprises and parent companies, while engagement of hired managers is encouraged by both, competition with companies of the developed countries and the peculiarities of capital structure. Factors of management and restructuring play an important role at rank-and-file members of company groups, in which case the management complexity of the entire group is important as well. Holding company groups retain their nontransparency as an additional element of protection for principal shareholders.

At the same time, no evidence was obtained on a possible effect of company openness. While an identification as an open JSC showed the previously positive effect for all enterprises, free floating of company securities in stock markets had no significant effect on the selection of the form of control. The role of stock markets was not evident.

In general, a number of characteristics regarding the peculiarities of corporate management were relevant and significant. Irrespective of the JSC involvement in integration, we observed an adverse effect of restructuring on the chances of selection in favour of hired managers. Competition with foreign manufacturers encouraged the engagement of hired managers. The adverse effect of severe competition with Russian manufacturers remains a mystery. The existence of such competition may reflect restructuring in progress at enterprises, but it also demonstrates operation in relatively competitive markets requiring no special competences. As for the management labour market, its limited role may be defined by the quality of a selected proxy variable.

No steady effect of the size of the enterprise on the set-up of corporate control was revealed.[8]

The question of how Russian companies will advance is worthy of consideration. Whether owners will remain as managers or rely on the labour market for hiring top managers will be of interest. It is safe to predict that restructuring of the legacy of the state-planning economy will be up for completion and competition in globalizing markets will improve against the smoothing of the effect of privatization and the inevitable resignation of the "red directors" generation, thereby enhancing the intention to hire a professional management. It remains to be seen whether the costs from "self-administration" will outweigh company benefits from minimizing the risks of managers' opportunistic behaviour. From all appearances, the existence of an alternative mechanism of control through integration has already made these values comparable. The risks of the violation of shareholders' rights and of a poor corporate governance are as important for independent businesses as they were before. It is far more difficult to forecast the situation with property rights protection. However, a certain improvement in corporate governance in the 2000s was evident (NCCG 2008: 16-17).

References

Avdasheva, S. 2007: Russian Holding Groups: New Empirical Evidence, in: Problems of Economic Transition, vol. 50, no. 5, pp. 24-43

Berglöf, E./E.L. von Thadden 2000: The Changing Corporate Governance Paradigm: Implications for Transitional and Developing Countries, in: B. Pleskovich/J. Stiglitz (eds.): Annual World Bank Conference on Development Economics 1999, The World Bank, Washington, D.C., pp. 135-162

Black, B./R. Kraakman/A. Tarassova 2000: Russian Privatization and Corporate Governance: What Went Wrong?, in: Stanford Law Review, vol. 52, pp. 1731-1808

[8] The number of employees is closely correlated with the company's form of incorporation, and the last indicator includes the effect of size.

Chernykh, L. 2008: Ultimate Ownership and Control in Russia, in: Journal of Financial Economics, vol. 88, pp. 169-192

Dolgopyatova, T. 2007: Corporate Ownership and Control in Russian Companies: Trends and Patterns, in: B. Dallago/I. Iwasaki (eds.): Corporate Restructuring and Governance in Transitional Economies, Palgrave MacMillan, Basingstoke, pp. 250-274

Dolgopyatova, T. 2008: Corporate Control Models in Russian Companies and Business Integration, in: J. Pickles (ed.): State and Society in Post-Socialist Economies, Palgrave MacMillan, Basingstoke, pp. 92-110

Dolgopyatova, T./I. Iwasaki 2006: Exploring Russian Corporations: Interim Report on the Japan-Russia Joint Research Project on Corporate Governance and Integration Processes in the Russian Economy, Discussion Paper Series B, no. 35, Hitotsubashi University, Institute of Economic Research, Tokyo (available at: http://www.ier.hit-u.ac.jp/English/publication/ier.html)

Fox, M.B./M.A. Heller 1999: Lessons from Fiascos in Russian Corporate Governance, in: University of Michigan Law School Working Paper No. 99-012

Gaddy, C./B. Ickes 1998: To Restructure or Not to Restructure: Informal Activities and Enterprise Behaviour in Transition, in: William Davidson Institute Working Paper Series, WP No. 134

Kuznetsov, B. 2005: Vliyanie konkurentsii na protsessy modernizatsii i reformirovaniya rossiiskikh promyshlennykh predpriyatii (opyt empiricheskogo analiza), in: S. Avdasheva/ V. Tambovtsev (eds.): Vliyanie Konkurentsii i Antimonopol'nogo Regulirovaniya na Protsessy Ekonomicheskoi Modernizatsii, TEIS, Moscow, pp. 44-85 (in Russian)

National Council on Corporate Governance (NCCG) 2007: Korporativnoe Upravleniye v Rossii: Opyt i Perspektivy, Natsional'nyi sovet po korporativnomu upravleniyu, Moscow (in Russian)

NCCG 2008: National Corporate Governance Report (Issue 1) 2008, National Council on Corporate Governance, Moscow

Rosstat 2006: Zarabotnaya plata rabotnikov v Rossiiskoi Federatsii, in: Statisticheskii Bulleten', no. 9 (130), pp. 5-117 (in Russian)

Shekshnya, S./M. Kets de Vries 2007: Mnimyi ukhod, in: Ekspert, no. 5, pp. 34-41 (in Russian)

S&P 2007a: Issledovaniye informatsionnoi prozrachnosti rossiiskikh kompanii v 2007 gody: znachitel'nye izmeneniya v desyatke liderov, Standard & Poor's, Moscow (in Russian)

S&P 2007b: Portret soveta direktorov rossiiskoi kompanii kak otrazheniye kontsentrirovannoi struktury sobstvennosti kompanii i prepyatstvii na pyti razvitiya korporativnogo upravleniya, Standard & Poor's, Moscow (in Russian)

Stiglitz, J. 1999: Quis custodiet ipsos custodes? Corporate Governance Failures in the Transition, paper presented at the World Bank's Annual Conference on Development Economics (ABCDE) in Europe, in: Challenge, vol. 42, no. 6 (available at:

http://www.findarticles.com.com/p/articles/mi_m1093/is_6_42)

Yakovlev, A. 2003: Spros na pravo v sfere korporativnogo upravleniya: evolutsiya strategii ekonomicheskikh agentov, in: Voprosy Ekonomiki, No. 4, pp. 37-50 (in Russian)

Yakovlev, A., et al. 2006: Corporate Governance in Transition: New Trends and Challenges, in: A. Sell/A. Krylov (eds.): Corporate Governance, Peter Lang, Frankfurt am Main, pp. 269-280

Monetary Shocks in Central and Eastern Europe: Evidence from a VAR Analysis*

Cornel Oros / Camelia Romocea-Turcu
(Universite de Poitiers, Poitiers Cedex, France)

Introduction

The Central and Eastern European Countries (CEECs) joined the EU several years ago and they are also expected to follow the Slovenian example and become members of the Euro area in the near future. Within the framework of a widened European Monetary Union (EMU), the economic and social cohesion becomes an essential issue as the asymmetrical effects of the single monetary policy are likely to be considerably reinforced. Consequently, a thorough identification of the CEECs' channels of monetary policy transmission could represent an important step in the global evaluation of the huge institutional change represented by these countries joining the EMU[1].

In this context, the objective of this paper is to analyze the CEECs' monetary policy transmission mechanisms, over the recent period corresponding to stable monetary regimes. The exchange regimes' stability is the successful result of the long transition period these countries have experienced and is representative of a structural political and economical maturity in order to develop viable econometric analysis on these countries and to produce robust results.

In the vein of the literature, our analysis deals with three transmission channels of monetary policy, namely the interest rate, the exchange rate and the credit. Thus, from a theoretical point of view, if prices are rigid, a rise of the nominal interest rate points to an increase of the real interest rate which triggers a decrease in the total demand and in the price level. In a flexible exchange rate regime, these effects are amplified by the exchange rate channel as the increase in interest rates causes an appreciation of the real exchange rate which can be harmful to the external competitiveness. Finally, the credit channel transmits the initial monetary impulse towards the real sphere by means of a reduction of the credit mass offered by banks and by a degradation of borrowers' financial position.

---

* An extended version of this paper is published in Applied Econometrics and International Development.

1 See Oros and Romocea-Turcu (2009) for a review of the empirical literature related to the monetary policy transmission mechanisms in the CEECs.

At the methodological level, the distinction between the three transmission channels will be carried out via a VAR model based on a structural decomposition technique (SVAR) which will enable us to provide the basis for a comparative analysis of the relative effectiveness of these transmission channels within the CEECs. Formally, in order to facilitate this analysis, we chose to analyze only those CEECs whose monetary systems allow a relative flexibility of their national currencies and for which the existence of the exchange rate channel is thus effective. Consequently, our analysis will be concerned with six CEECs: Hungary, Poland, the Czech Republic, Romania, Slovakia and Slovenia. We did not include into the analysis the Baltic States (Estonia, Latvia and Lithuania) and Bulgaria as they are characterized by fixed exchange rate regimes or currency board arrangements for which the investigation of the exchange rate as a transmission channel of the monetary policy would be completely useless.

The paper is structured as follows: The first section describes the methodological framework used in this paper. We will analyze the technique of identification of the shocks and will present the data used in our study. The second section discusses the results of the estimations and points out the eventual national specificities concerning the reactions of the macroeconomic variables to the different types of monetary shocks.

1. Methodology

The empirical analysis of the channels of monetary policy transmission in the CEECs will be based on a VAR model that represents the most frequently used technique in the literature on the transmission mechanisms of the monetary impulses.

The VAR model is written as follows:

(1) $Y_t = A(L)Y_{t-1} + B(L)X_t + \varepsilon_t$

where Y_t represents the vector of the endogenous variables, X_t that of the exogenous variables and ε_t the vector of the errors which are normally distributed. The vector of the endogenous variables (Y_t) is composed, for each CEEC, of: the industrial production index (y_t) and the consumer price index (p_t), the monetary market nominal interest rate (i_t), the nominal exchange rate (e_t)[2] and the domestic credit (cd_t):

(2) $Y_t = [y_t \; p_t \; i_t \; e_t \; cd_t]$

[2] It is determined by a direct quotation of the national currencies with respect to euro.

The vector of the exogenous variables (X_t) contains the industrial production index (y_t^{UE}) and the consumer price index (p_t^{UE}) for the EU 25 and the monetary market nominal interest rate for the Euro area (i_t^{euro}).

As for the identification method of structural shocks, two possibilities need to be investigated: a Cholesky decomposition technique, on the one hand and a structural procedure, better grounded in theoretical terms, on the other hand. There is no unanimity at the academic level on the opportunity of one or the other of the two methods. The relative advantage of the structural technique, that is usually used to analyze the small open countries (Kim and Roubini (2000), Elbourne and De Haan (2006)) might not be adapted to the CEECs case because of their macroeconomic instability (Ganev *et al.* (2002), Héricourt and Matei (2007)). However, this problem can be avoided if we choose to analyze very recent periods that correspond to stable monetary regimes and are not characterized by the structural changes of the beginning or middle 1990s. Thus, we chose to apply a structural technique which enabled us to have more flexibility in defining the short term interactions between the endogenous variables[3].

The structural method (SVAR)[4] consists in the definition of a sufficient number of restrictions allowing to orthogonalize the residuals of the equation 1 and to determine their structural components. Thus, by distinguishing between the real variables (industrial production and price) and the monetary variables (interest rate, exchange rate and domestic credit) we consider firstly the existence of a slow adjustment of the real variables to monetary shocks (the real sphere is influenced only with one lag by the monetary variables shocks).

Concerning the reaction function of the interest rate, we take into consideration several theoretical assumptions. We consider initially the absence of an immediate reaction of the interest rate to production and price shocks. This is based on the assumption put forward by Sims and Zha (1998) and Kim and Roubini (2000), suggesting that the information on real shocks is available only with a certain delay and thus cannot be immediately used by the monetary authorities in their economic policy decisions. Then, as our analysis is applied to small open countries, we retain also the idea developed by Kim and Roubini (2000) according to

---

3 In the recursive decomposition method à la Cholesky, the shocks identification mechanisms are conditioned by the order of endogenous variables whose instantaneous responses to different structural shocks are by consequence severely constrained.

4 This method was suggested by Bernanke (1986) and applied, inter alia, by Sims and Zha (1998), Kim and Roubini (2000), Persman and Smets (2003).

which the interest rate reacts immediately to an exchange rate shock. Finally, we consider the existence of a simultaneous response of the interest rate to a domestic credit shock.

At the same time, the identification method we used supposes that the exchange rate and the domestic credit react simultaneously to real shocks and interest rate shocks.

The estimations are carried out using monthly data over periods corresponding to stable monetary regimes because any monetary regime change is likely to affect considerably the transmission channels of the monetary policy and to affect consequently the results. Thus, we present in Table 1 the periods of analysis for each country according to various monetary regimes.

Table 1: Exchange rate regimes and analyzed time span by country

Country	Time span	Exchange rate regime
Hungary	2000:02-2007:12	Controlled floating
Poland	2001:01-2007:12	Free floating; inflation target
Romania	2000:01-2007:12	Controlled floating
Slovakia	1999:01-2007:12	Controlled floating
Slovenia	1998:01-2006:12	Controlled floating
Czech Republic	1998:01-2007:12	Controlled floating; inflation target

The data[5] is seasonally adjusted and is expressed in logarithm (except the interest rate). The order of integration of the series was studied via an ADF test which enabled us to note that the majority of the variables are integrated of order 1. The Johansen cointegration tests indicate the existence of several cointegration relations between the variables of each country. Consequently, following the example of Sims *et al.* (1990) or Coudert and Mojon (1997), we chose to carry out our estimates on variables in level.

In order to determine the optimal number of lags, we applied mainly the Akaike and Schwartz information criteria. In case of divergent indications, these criteria were supported by the log likelihood test. These tests enable us to retain a number of lags equal to 2.

---

[5] The data sources are: the IMF (International Financial Statistics), Eurostat and the national central banks.

2. Estimation results and comments

For each country, we will study the effects of an interest rate shock, of an exchange rate shock and of a domestic credit shock on the macroeconomic variables. The extent of the shocks represents one standard deviation; the impulse responses, together with confidence intervals (+/- 2 standard errors) are shown in the Figures 1 of the Appendix.

A restrictive shock which affects the interest rate (first column of the graphs in Figure 1) causes a non-significant effect on the industrial production for each of the analyzed countries, except Slovakia. After two months, this impact attains a maximum level for all the countries, but is intrinsically heterogeneous: on the one hand, in Poland, Romania, the Czech Republic and Slovakia the industrial production falls down as a result of an interest rate rise[6]; on the other hand, in Hungary and Slovenia, the industrial production reacts positively to the restrictive shock affecting the interest rate. In the latter case, the effect commonly known as the "output puzzle" is particularly persistent in Slovenia. To explain this counter-intuitive effect, we can resort to Lucas's model (1973) according to which in a relatively inflationist environment[7], the rise of the interest rate could be the sign of a future price stability, which encourages investments and stimulates the industrial production. In the case of Slovenia, this mechanism might have been reinforced by the perspective of the country's adopting the Euro, which can in itself account for this persistent effect.

An important degree of heterogeneity between CEECs is also characteristic at the price level. As a consequence of the interest rate increase, Hungary and Poland witness a rise in prices which is significant only for Hungary. This effect, which goes against the theoretical expectations, is often identified in the empirical studies using a VAR model and is called "price puzzle". The price increase occurs immediately and reaches its maximum level in five and two months' time respectively, without being however significantly persistent[8]. Several explanations have been put

---

[6] The persistent fall in industrial production is characteristic only to Slovakia, for a period of eleven months.

[7] During the period under analysis the average inflation rate was 6,4% in Hungary and 5,9% in Slovenia.

[8] The reaction of an endogenous variable is considered persistent if its accumulated responses are statistically significant at minimum 10%. The accumulated responses together with the maximum reactions of the endogenous variables are available upon request.

forward to account for this "price puzzle"[9], either methodological or structural. Thus, the methodological reasons underline the fact that the autoregressive vector is wrongly built as it doesn't allow the use either of the variables predicting the future inflation – like for instance the commodity prices (Sims (1992)) – or of the output gap as a measure of the economic activity (Giordani (2004)). The structural explanations point out that the "price puzzle" phenomenon is a temporal consequence of a specific monetary regime (Castelnuovo and Surico (2006)); it can also express the concerns of the firms to preserve their profit ratio which is threatened by the increase in financial costs as a consequence of the interest rate rise.

For the remaining countries, i. e. Romania, Slovakia, Slovenia and the Czech Republic, the interest rate rise causes, as expected, a fall in prices with an immediate effect but with a different extent and persistence. Romania and the Czech Republic are characterized by non-significant and non-persistent responses that attain the maximum level in three and eight months' time respectively. On the contrary, Slovakia and Slovenia display significant and persistent responses which last nine and twelve quarters respectively, and whose intensity is attained gradually over a longer period of time of ten and thirty-six months respectively.

Within the analysis of the impact of the interest rate increase on the macroeconomic variables, we need to underline the logical effect of the exchange rate appreciation in all the countries except Poland where the appreciation is preceded by a slight non-significant initial depreciation which lasts for two months. In this country, the depreciation of the exchange rate triggers an initial price rise and the "price puzzle" paradox could thus be accounted for by an "exchange rate puzzle".

Among the countries witnessing an exchange rate appreciation as a consequence of an interest rate positive shock, Slovenia represents again a particular case: it presents a significant response which lasts for approximately three years and whose intensity grows progressively until the thirty-sixth month. The other countries are characterized by statistically non–significant and non persistent responses that attain the maximum impact after a quarter in Hungary and Romania or later, after approximately three quarters, in Slovakia and the Czech Republic.

The responses of the domestic credit to an interest rate increase are also very heterogeneous among the six countries. Thus, the negative effect is significant and persistent in Poland but non-significant in Hungary, Romania and Slovenia, and is associated with positive responses which are

[9] See Coricelli *et al.* (2006) for a review of the literature on the various explanations of the "price puzzle" phenomenon.

equally heterogeneous: significant and persistent in Slovakia but non significant in the Czech Republic. The only common feature of these responses is that their extent tends to decrease very fast in general immediately after the first month or at the latest after a quarter. Generally, the limited or even positive impact of the interest rate shock on the domestic credit can be explained by the fact that the firms have to borrow more in order to deal with the cash-flow drop during the low growth periods (Christiano *et al.* (1994)). In the particular case of the CEECs, Creel and Levasseur (2006) consider that the disconnection between the interest rate and the domestic credit is caused on the one hand by the low level of debt of the households which are strongly inclined to consume, and on the other hand by the excess of liquidity the banking system is confronted with.

The second channel of monetary policy transmission is the exchange rate (second column of Figure 1). In general, the national responses to the depreciation of the exchange rate are more homogeneous compared to the case of the restrictive shock affecting the interest rate, and are more consistent with he theoretical expectations.

First, we notice the immediate and statistically non-significant increase in the industrial production as a result of the exchange rate depreciation for all the countries under discussion. The only discrepancies concern the persistence of these responses which are especially important in Romania and even more in the Czech Republic. The same structural responses can be identified in the case of the prices which undergo a non significant initial rise as a consequence of a positive shock affecting the exchange rate. The only exception comes from Slovakia where the prices fall down slightly during the first five months[10]. Just like in the case of the industrial production, the most persistent responses are Romania's and the Czech Republic's and in addition Hungary's. At the same time, the exchange depreciation causes a significant increase of the interest rate whose effects last during approximately one year in Hungary, Romania and Slovakia or even longer (three years) in Slovenia and the Czech Republic. The initial monetary tightening as a response to an exchange rate shock is not a feature shared by all the countries. In Poland, the interest rate increase is preceded by a non-significant fall lasting for seven months.

The most heterogeneous national responses to the exchange rate depreciation are situated at the level of the evolution of the domestic credit.

[10] The price fall could be explained by the interest rate increase caused by the depreciation of the exchange rate since Slovakia displays strong price sensitivity to an interest rate shock.

Thus, we can identify both an initial credit increase which can be statistically significant (Hungary and Romania) or very moderate (Poland and Czech Republic), and an initial credit fall of a weak extent (Slovakia and Slovenia).

The third channel of monetary policy transmission is the domestic credit (the last column of Figure 1). In general, the effects of a domestic credit increase are consistent with the theoretical intuitions, save for some exceptions, but their extent is weak and their persistence is statistically non significant. A positive shock striking the domestic credit triggers a slight increase in the industrial production with a maximum impact attained after approximately a quarter. Similarly, Romania, the Czech Republic and Slovenia witness non significant but falling effects on the industrial production. The only persistent response occurs in Hungary for a period of seven months.

The domestic credit increase causes immediate inflationist effects in all the countries under discussion except Slovenia where the price rise is preceded by a slight deflationist effect. The extent of these effects is weak, and their persistence is statistically significant only in Romania (during approximately a two-year period). At the same time, a positive shock which affects the domestic credit brings about an immediate and non significant increase in the interest rate in all the countries with the exception of Slovakia where there is a slight initial fall and of the Czech Republic. These responses are not persistent and their peak extent is generally reached during the first quarter, save for Poland and the Czech Republic whose responses are more intense during the eighth and tenth months respectively.

Finally, a domestic credit increase leads to a non significant depreciation of the exchange rate with a maximum extent during the first quarter. Two countries display particular features: the Czech Republic which is the only one with a statistically persistent response, and Slovenia which witnesses an initial exchange rate appreciation preceding the depreciation of its national currency.

If we summarize the information provided by the three channels of monetary policy transmission, there are several salient elements worth mentioning. Generally speaking, the interest rate has a very limited impact on the industrial production and at the same time the credit channel displays a striking weakness in the transmission of monetary impulses. On the other hand, according to our results, the interest rate plays an active part and represents, together with the exchange rate, the principal channel of monetary policy transmission. Thus, our study breaks with most of the literature which maintains that the exchange rate represents the main channel of monetary policy transmission for the CEECs contrary to the Euro zone countries for which the dominant channel is the interest rate (Angeloni *et al.* (2003), Creel and Levasseur (2006), Ganev *et al.* (2002)). Under these circumstances, the growing part played by the interest rate in the monetary policy transmission could show that the CEECs are gradually adopting the mechanisms of monetary policy transmission characteristic to the Euro zone countries. It is undoubtedly a sign of the structural advanced development of the economic and financial systems of the CEECs under discussion. However, the national responses to the different monetary shocks are highly heterogeneous, especially the responses brought about an increase in interest rate or in terms of the relative efficiency of the interest rate and the exchange rate as vectors of monetary policy transmission.

In addition to the information provided by the study of the response functions to the interest rate, exchange rate and domestic credit shocks, further insight into the six CEECs' heterogeneities may be underlined by the decomposition of the macroeconomic variables' variance. The Tables 2 in the Appendix present the variance decomposition of the endogenous variables at a 12-month horizon.

The information provided by the variance decomposition can be interpreted at two distinctive levels according to the predominant part played by the monetary variables. If we consider that the variables are vectors of monetary policy transmission, we can assess the relative influence of these vectors on the real variables. On the contrary, if we consider that the monetary variables are instruments of absorption of the real shocks, we can examine their capacity of responding to production or price shocks.

In the case where the monetary variables are instruments of monetary policy transmission, it appears straight away that the domestic credit plays a minor part in explaining the variance of the real variables. The only exception to this is Poland where the credit is the first channel of monetary transmission. Consequently, it is the interest rate and the exchange rate that will play the main part in explaining the variance of the real variables for the rest of the countries.

According to the relative impact of these two transmission channels on the evolution of the industrial production and prices, a distinction can be made between two groups of countries. In the first group, made up of Hungary and Poland, the exchange rate channel is stronger by far than the interest rate channel in explaining the variance of the two real variables (the industrial production and the prices). The interest rate represents 14% against 42% for the exchange rate in Hungary, and 3% against 5% in Poland. In the second group of countries, formed by the Czech Republic, Slovakia and Slovenia and partially Romania, the interest rate channel largely accounts for the real variables. Its relative efficiency in the monetary policy transmission is very marked: the interest rate represents 22% against 16% for the exchange rate in the Czech Republic, 45% against 9% in Slovakia, and 40% against 9% in Slovenia. It appears that the monetary transmission mechanisms of these countries are very close to the Euro zone mechanisms with the interest rate channel being particularly efficient. Half between these groups, Romania displays a mixed behaviour relative to the efficiency of the two monetary variables: while the exchange rate largely accounts for the variance of the industrial production, the interest rate is more apt to explain the price variance.

If we take into account the role played by the monetary variables as real shock absorbers, the distinction between the two groups of countries is confirmed again. In the case of Hungary and Poland, the exchange rate represents the main instrument for absorbing the industrial production and price shocks. Indeed, the real shocks account for 21% and 14% respectively of the exchange rate variance compared to 14% and 7% respectively of the interest rate variance. We can therefore consider that it is not likely that these countries may be integrated into the EMU very soon because of the high costs related to their giving up the exchange rate as an adjustment variable. On the contrary, for Romania and Slovakia, it is mainly the interest rate that functions as a real shock absorber[11], whereas for the Czech Republic and Slovenia, this role is played by both the domestic credit and the interest rate: the demand and supply shocks account for 35% and 20% respectively of the credit and interest rate variance in the Czech Republic, and for 23% and 8% respectively in Slovenia. According to our assessment, it is more likely for these countries to join the EMU rapidly since the opportunity cost resulting from the loss of the exchange rate as an instrument of adjustment is considerably lower than in the case of Hungary and Poland.

From a general point of view, the variance decomposition has put forward a core element which the previous analysis in terms of response functions brought about, that is the existing asymmetries between the CEECs monetary mechanisms. The integration of the CEECs into the Euro zone has to follow a multi-speed dynamic: while Slovenia has been a member since 2007, Slovakia and the Czech Republic are the most apt to join it rapidly.

---

[11] For Romania and Slovakia the real shocks account for 28% and 38% respectively of the interest rate variance.

Conclusion

In this paper, we have analyzed comparatively the channels of monetary policy transmission of the CEECs over recent periods corresponding to stable monetary regimes. We have distinguished between three specific channels - the interest rate, the exchange rate and the domestic credit - and have focussed on six CEECs which are able to make use of all of the three transmission channels.

Our study has been based on a standard VAR model and uses a structural technique of decomposition which involves short-term restrictions being applied to the monetary variables. Our analysis has shown that the interest rate has a limited impact on the dynamics of the CEECs industrial production, which is also the case in the Euro zone countries. At the same time, the domestic credit has proved to be a rather weak instrument of monetary policy transmission, which can be accounted for by an increase of the households' consumption parallel to an excess of liquidity in the banking system.

The structural VAR technique allows to grasp the large heterogeneity within the group of six countries, which may have important institutional consequences on the process of Euro zone integration. Thus, we can distinguish a first sub-group made up of the Czech Republic, Slovakia, Slovenia and partially Romania where, just like in the case of the Euro zone countries, the interest rate channel has the major influence as a mechanism of monetary policy transmission. These countries are the most apt to join the EMU in the near future which is actually confirmed by Slovenia's current situation. On the contrary, the second sub-group formed of Hungary and Poland is characterized by the high influence of the exchange rate which acts both as a mechanism of monetary policy transmission and as a supply and demand shock absorber. It would not be advisable for these countries to join the EMU in the near future, unless they manage to reinforce the relative efficiency of the interest rate channel.

References

Angeloni, I. / A. Kashyap / B. Mojon (eds.) 2003: Monetary Policy Transmission in the Euro Area, Cambridge University Press

Bernanke B. 1986: Alternative explanation of the money-income correlation, in: K. Brunner / A. Meltzer (eds): Real business cycles, real exchange rates, and actual policies, Amsterdam: North Holland, pp. 49-99

Castelnuovo, A. / P. Surico 2006: The Price puzzle: Fact or Artefact, in: Bank of England, Working Paper no. 288

Christiano L. / M. Eichenbaum / C. Evans 1999: Monetary Policy Shocks: What Have we Learned and to What End, in: J. Taylor / M. Woodford (eds.): Handbook of Macroeconomics, Amsterdam: North Holland

Coricelli, F. / B. Egert / R. MacDonald 2006: Monetary Transmission Mechanism: Gliding on a Wind of Change, in: BOFIT Discussion Papers, no. 8

Coudert, V. / B. Mojon 1997: Asymétries financières et transmission de la politique monétaire en Europe, in: Economie et Prévision, no. 128, pp. 41-60

Creel, J. / S. Levasseur 2006: Canaux de transmission de la politique monétaire dans l'UE. Le cas de trois nouveaux entrants, in: Revue économique, vol. 57, no. 4, pp. 881-898

Elbourne, A. / J. de Haan 2006: Financial Structure and Monetary Policy Transmission in Transition Countries, in: Journal of Comparative Economics, no. 34, pp. 1-23

Ganev, G. / K. Molnar / K. Rybinski / P. Wozniak 2002: Transmisssion Mechanism of Monetary Policy in Central and Eastern Europe, in: Case Report no. 52, Warsaw

Giordani, P. 2004: An alternative explanation of the price puzzle, in: Journal of Monetary Economics, no. 51, pp. 1271-1296

Héricourt, J. / I. Matei 2006: Transmission de la politique monétaire dans les Pays d'Europe Centrale et Orientale: que savons-nous vraiment, in: Economie et Prévision, no. 180-181, pp. 221-238

Kim, S. / N. Roubini 2000: Exchange rate anomalies in the industrial countries: A solution with a structural VAR approach, in: Journal of Monetary Economics, no. 45, pp. 561-586

Oros, C. / C. Romocea-Turcu 2009: The Monetary Transmission Mechanisms in the CEECs: A Structural VAR Approach, in: Applied Econometrics and International Development, forthcoming

Peersman, G. / F. Smets 2003: The Monetary Transmission Mechanism in the Euro Area: Evidence from VAR Analysis", in: Angeloni et al. (eds.) 2003

Sims, C. A. 1992: Interpreting the Macroeconomic Time Series Facts: The Effects of Monetary Policy, in: European Economic Review, vol. 36, no. 5, pp. 975-1000

Sims, C. A. / J. H. Stock / M. W. Watson 1990: Inference in Linear Time Series Models with Some Unit Roots, in: Econometrica, vol. 58, no. 1, pp. 113-144

Sims, C. A. / T. Zha 1998: Does monetary policy generate recessions? In: Federal Reserve Bank of Atlanta, Working Paper, no. 12

Appendix

Table 2: Decomposition of the variance

Hungary						
	Shocks					
	S E	*Industrial production*	*Prices*	*Interest rate*	*Exchange rate*	*Credit*
Industrial production	0.02	77.54	3.33	3.92	6.55	8.66
Prices	0.01	7.05	46.06	10.15	35.94	0.79
Interest rate	1.55	1.18	12.78	27.29	53.15	5.59
Exchange rate	0.03	4.75	16.13	10.21	64.92	3.98
Credit	0.03	4.08	8.66	12.59	17.71	56.95

Poland						
	Shocks					
	S E	*Industrial production*	*Prices*	*Interest rate*	*Exchange rate*	*Credit*
Industrial production	0.02	73.79	14.07	2.49	3.43	6.22
Prices	0.01	3.19	49.94	0.38	1.67	44.82
Interest rate	0.88	3.70	3.24	10.86	23.63	58.56
Exchange rate	0.04	2.92	11.01	2.36	18.67	65.05
Credit	0.03	1.01	10.32	51.60	1.92	35.14

Romania						
	Shocks					
	S E	*Industrial production*	*Prices*	*Interest rate*	*Exchange rate*	*Credit*
Industrial production	0.02	85.26	4.80	1.35	6.65	1.94
Prices	0.01	5.92	85.56	3.59	3.32	1.61
Interest rate	3.14	22.25	5.70	49.20	18.08	4.77
Exchange rate	0.06	16.80	0.95	22.63	58.18	1.45
Credit	0.05	14.62	1.82	3.81	10.30	69.45

Slovakia						
	Shocks					
	S E	*Industrial production*	*Prices*	*Interest rate*	*Exchange rate*	*Credit*
Industrial production	0.02	76.44	2.01	13.01	8.26	0.29
Prices	0.02	3.10	60.17	31.74	0.57	4.42
Interest rate	1.31	11.08	26.54	11.49	44.09	6.81
Exchange rate	0.02	1.35	3.09	37.52	8.09	49.96
Credit	0.08	6.54	0.23	72.56	6.59	14.09

Slovenia						
	Shocks					
	S E	*Industrial production*	*Prices*	*Interest rate*	*Exchange rate*	*Credit*
Industrial production	0.02	92.71	0.25	6.18	0.08	0.78
Prices	0.01	5.97	50.13	34.10	9.27	0.53
Interest rate	0.79	7.04	0.76	40.54	43.31	8.35
Exchange rate	0.01	9.81	22.59	42.72	22.87	2.01
Credit	0.04	0.86	22.03	12.87	2.55	61.68

Czech Republic						
	Shocks					
	S E	*Industrial production*	*Prices*	*Interest rate*	*Exchange rate*	*Credit*
Industrial production	0.02	80.42	4.98	1.39	8.05	5.15
Prices	0.01	9.81	53.55	20.73	8.46	7.44
Interest rate	0.86	13.46	6.97	7.45	66.61	5.50
Exchange rate	0.02	4.93	6.13	45.52	15.34	28.08
Credit	0.05	12.13	23.82	13.73	9.56	40.76

Time span: 12 months

Figure 1: Functions of national responses to interest rate shocks, exchange rate shocks and credit shocks

Hungary

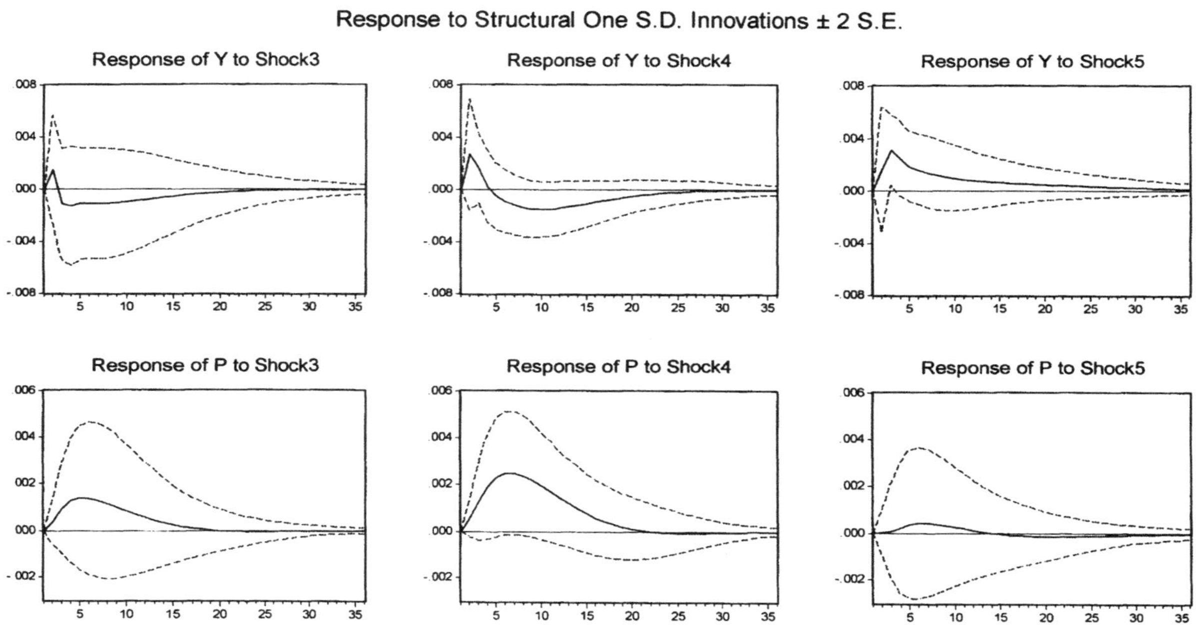

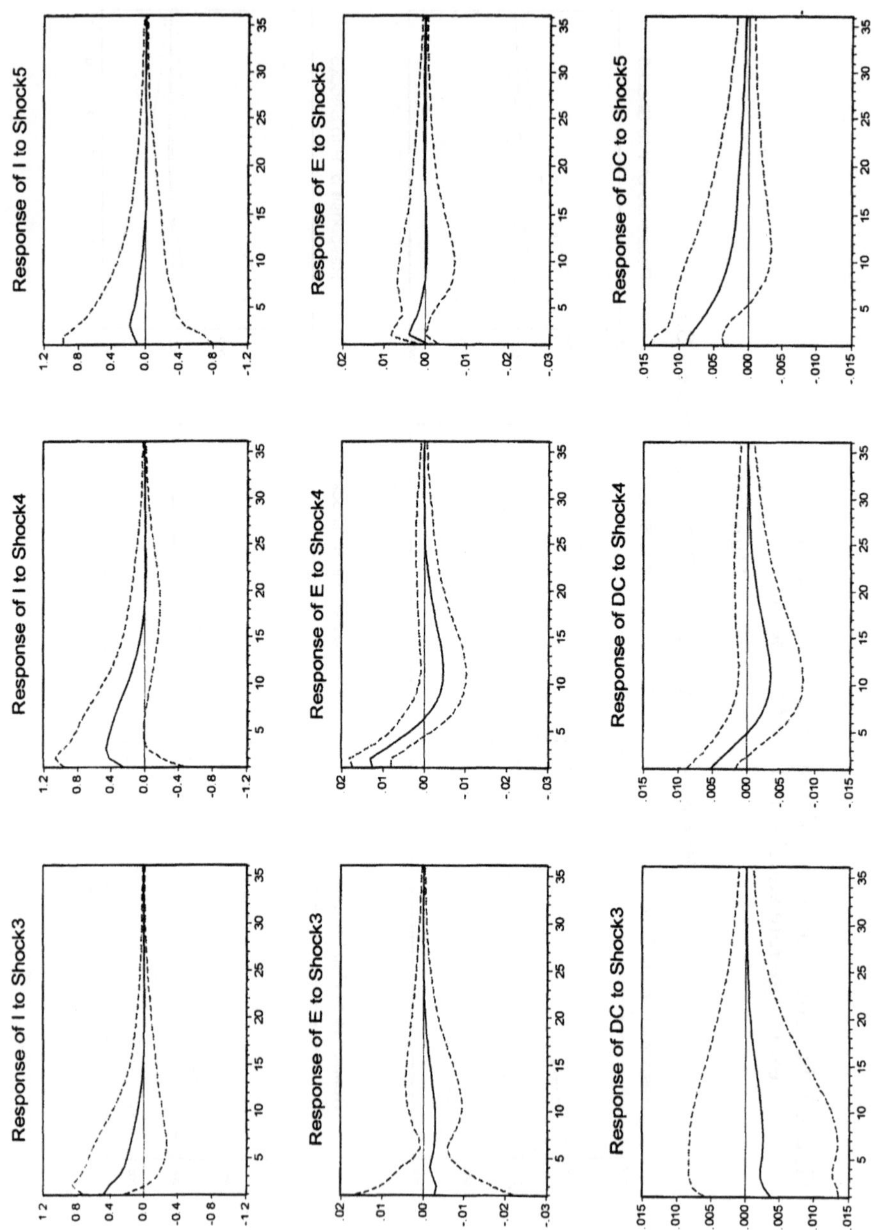
Response of I to Shock5
Response of E to Shock5
Response of DC to Shock5
Response of I to Shock4
Response of E to Shock4
Response of DC to Shock4
Response of I to Shock3
Response of E to Shock3
Response of DC to Shock3

Poland

Response to Structural One S.D. Innovations ± 2 S.E.

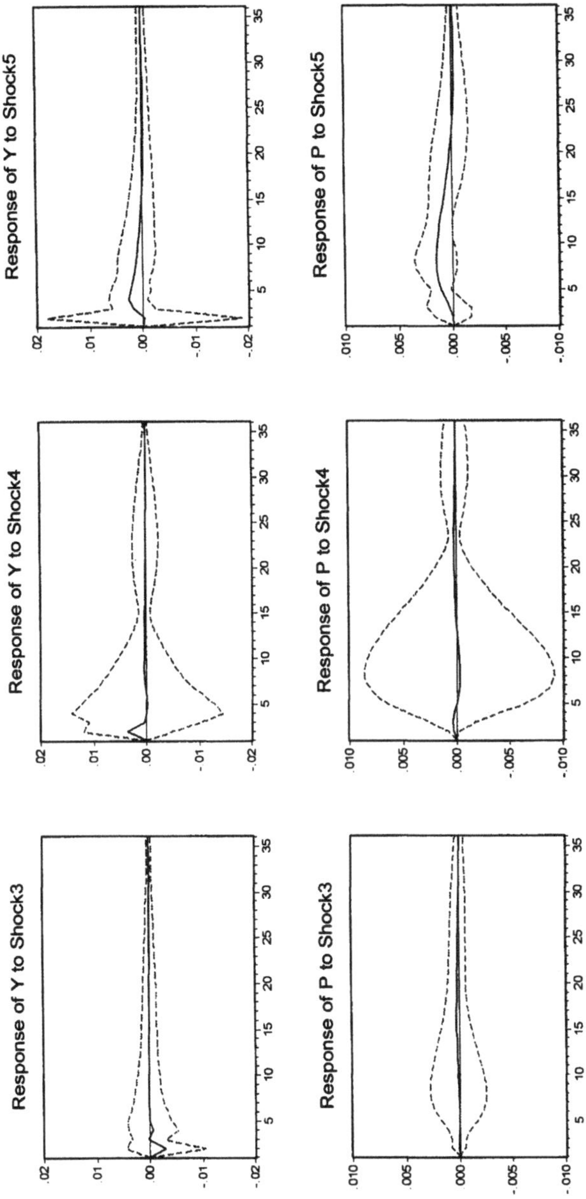

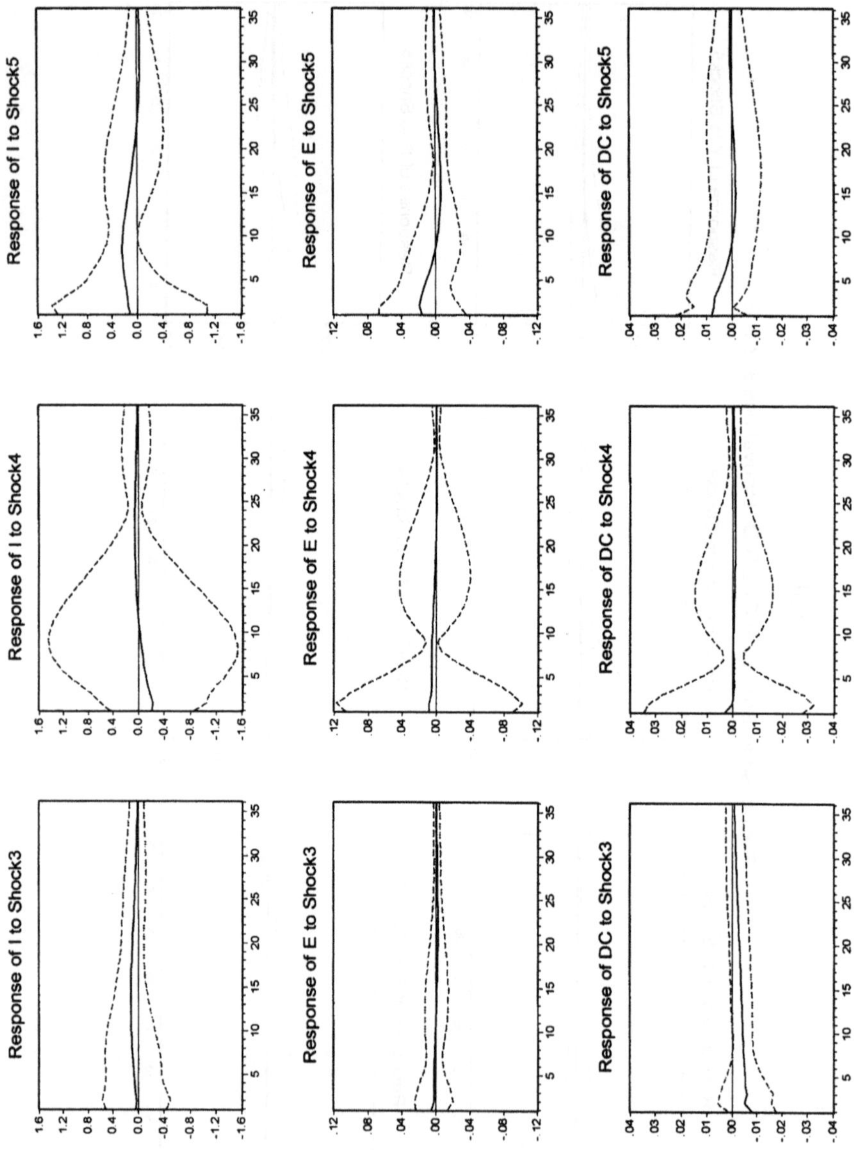
Response of I to Shock5
Response of E to Shock5
Response of DC to Shock5
Response of I to Shock4
Response of E to Shock4
Response of DC to Shock4
Response of I to Shock3
Response of E to Shock3
Response of DC to Shock3

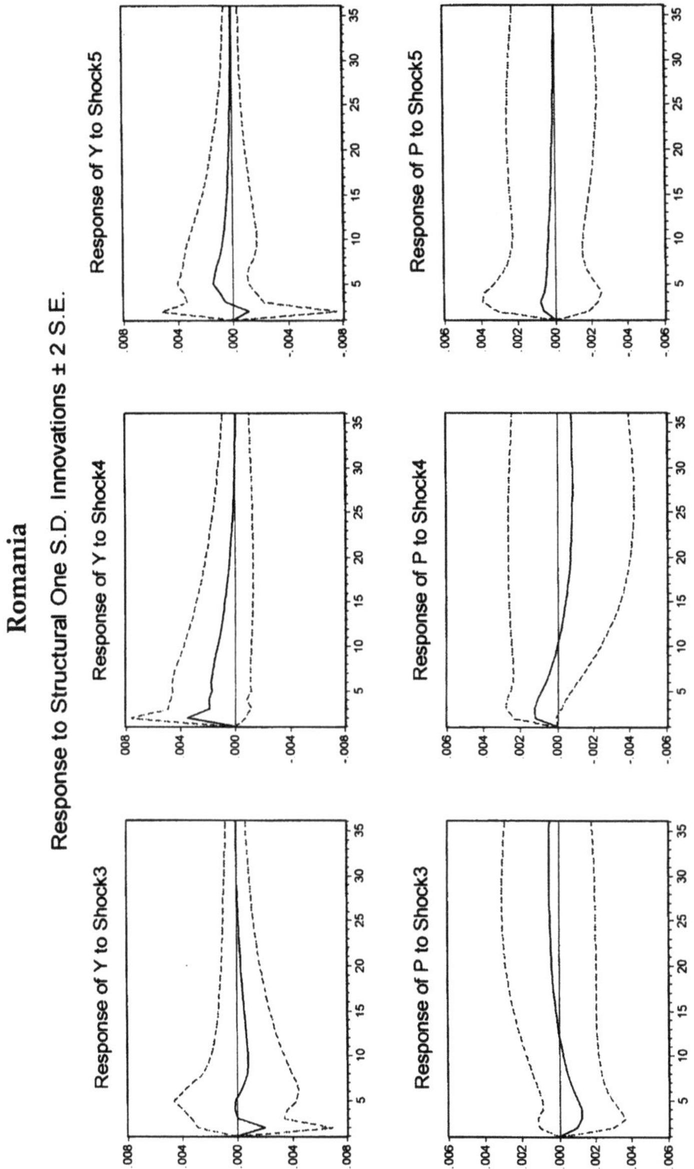
Romania
Response to Structural One S.D. Innovations ± 2 S.E.
Response of Y to Shock3
Response of Y to Shock4
Response of Y to Shock5
Response of P to Shock3
Response of P to Shock4
Response of P to Shock5

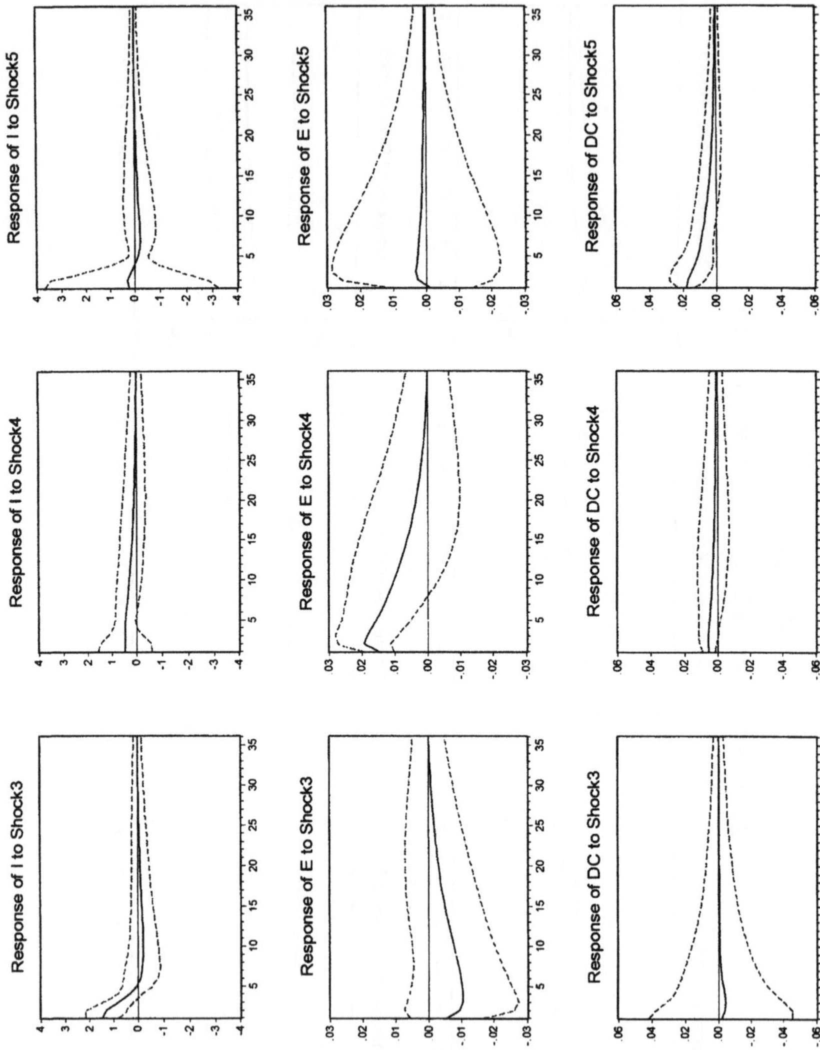
Response of I to Shock5
Response of E to Shock5
Response of DC to Shock5
Response of I to Shock4
Response of E to Shock4
Response of DC to Shock4
Response of I to Shock3
Response of E to Shock3
Response of DC to Shock3

Slovakia

Response to Structural One S.D. Innovations ± 2 S.E.

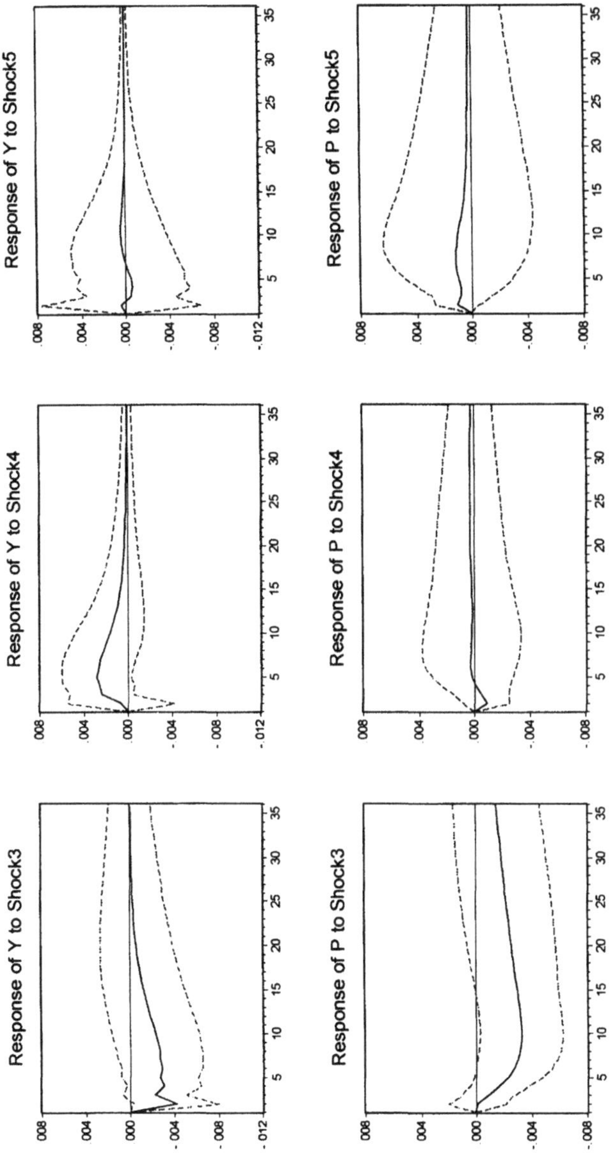

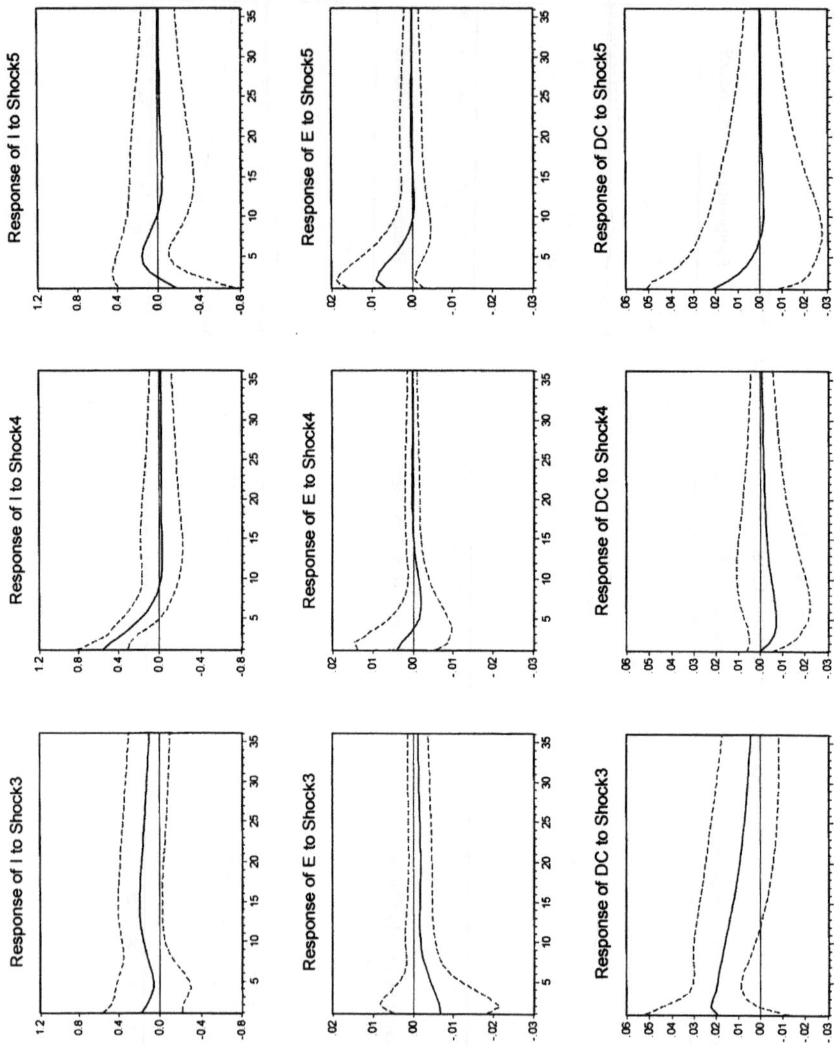
Response of I to Shock5
Response of E to Shock5
Response of DC to Shock5
Response of I to Shock4
Response of E to Shock4
Response of DC to Shock4
Response of I to Shock3
Response of E to Shock3
Response of DC to Shock3

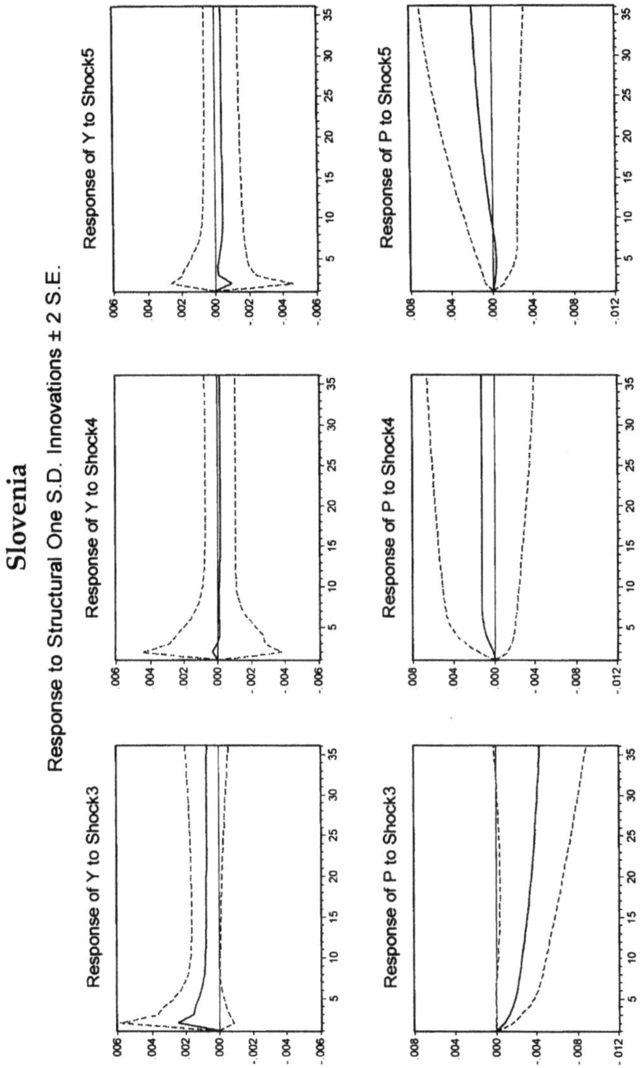
Slovenia
Response to Structural One S.D. Innovations ± 2 S.E.
Response of Y to Shock3
Response of Y to Shock4
Response of Y to Shock5
Response of P to Shock3
Response of P to Shock4
Response of P to Shock5

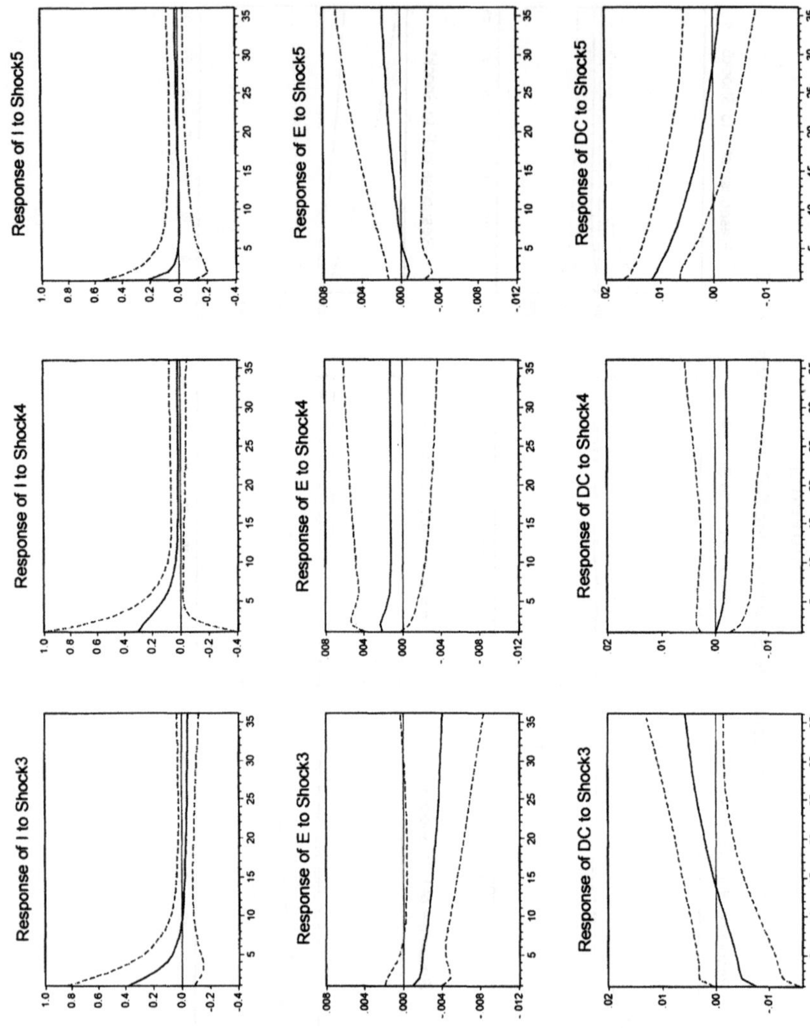
Response of I to Shock5
Response of E to Shock5
Response of DC to Shock5
Response of I to Shock4
Response of E to Shock4
Response of DC to Shock4
Response of I to Shock3
Response of E to Shock3
Response of DC to Shock3

Czech Republic

Response to Structural One S.D. Innovations ± 2 S.E.

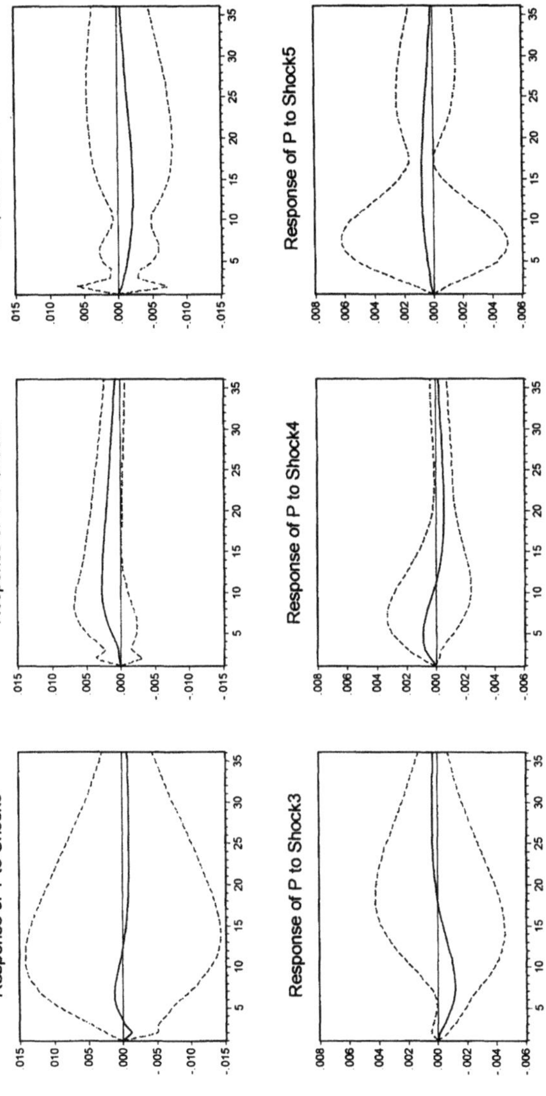

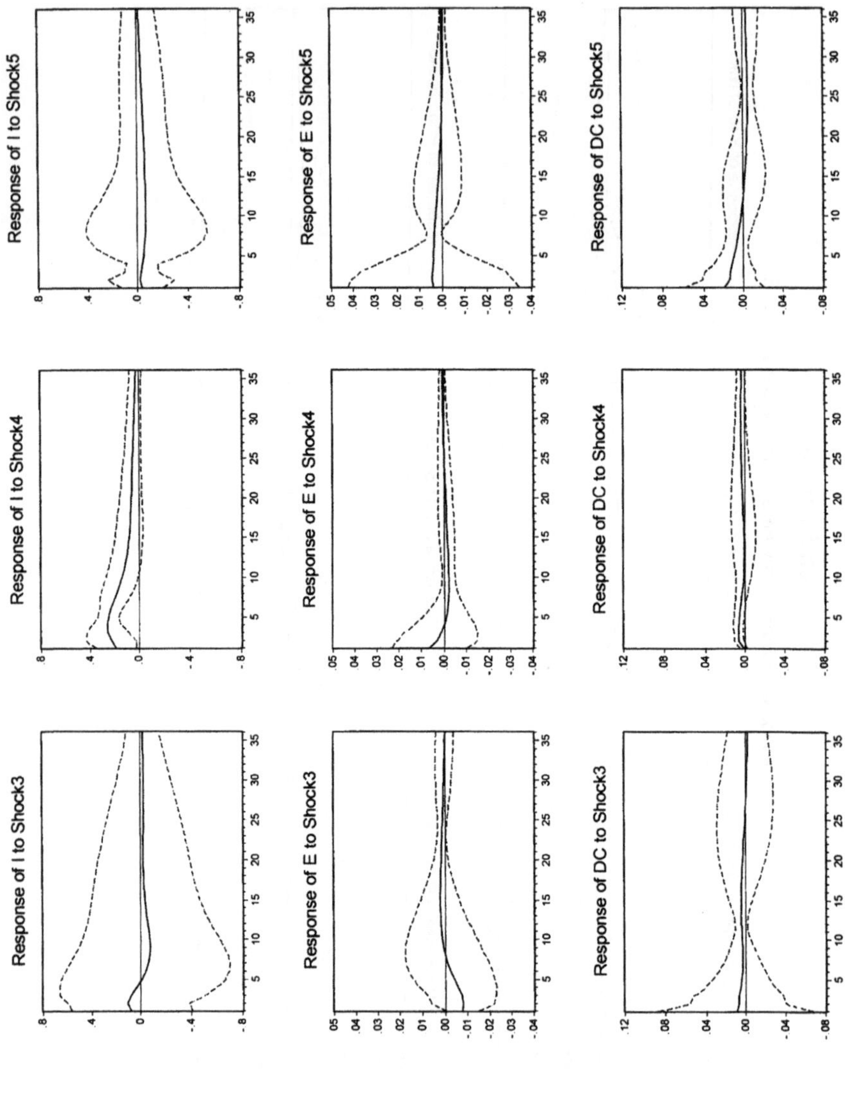
Response of I to Shock5
Response of E to Shock5
Response of DC to Shock5
Response of I to Shock4
Response of E to Shock4
Response of DC to Shock4
Response of I to Shock3
Response of E to Shock3
Response of DC to Shock3

Chapter three:

STUDIES ON SOUTHEAST EUROPE

An Assessment of the Romanian Banking System Performance. A Non-Parametric Approach

Nicolae Dardac / Iustina Alina Boitan
(Academy of Economic Studies, Bucharest, Romania)

1. Introduction

In order to characterize completely the degree of a banking system's solvability, profitability and stability at a given moment in time, two types of indicators can be assessed: *performance indicators* and *prudential indicators*. These indicators depict complementary dimensions of the efficiency and quality of the banking activity, and also of the risk exposure and of the conformity of the activities with the legislative and regulatory framework.

Without being exhaustive, the traditional indicators for evaluating the credit institutions' *financial performance* consist in: return on equity, return on assets, profit ratio, total income on total assets ratio, net interest margin, cost income ratio. The main *prudential indicators* of the banking activity are the solvability indicator, the leverage effect, the general risk rate, credit risk ratio, unperforming loans to total assets, and respectively to equity, the liquidity indicator. Their evolution over time is continuously and carefully monitored by supervisory authorities, because they indicate a rising in the exposure of the banking system to a certain risk, the quality of loans portfolio, a change in the credit institutions' risk appetite, the ability of a banking system to withstand the macroeconomic shocks and the turbulences propagated from international markets.

The information supplied by the two types of indicators has to be analyzed in an integrated and complementary manner. For instance, a high level of the indicator "interest rate margin" signals a profitable activity and therefore a good assets and liabilities management. In a more careful analysis, the indicator's high value may be the result of a significant spread of the interest rate or it can be linked to an increase in the volume of activity. In the latter case there is the suspicion that the credit institution engaged itself into riskier activities, or that it has abruptly expanded its credit portfolio. Consequently, the analysis must be completed by interpreting the information on banking risks obtained from the prudential indicators.

Our study focuses on two aspects belonging to the topic of banking sector financial performance, namely efficiency and productivity. It is the first study for the Romanian banking system that applies the two non-parametric techniques. Similar analyses were made for the Turkish banking system (Fethi, Inal, Jackson 1998; Isik, Hassan 2003), for the Estonian one (Kirikal, Sorg, Vensel 2004), for Australia's banks (Wu 2003), Indian ones (Mohan 2006) and the Singaporean banking system (Lee, Leong, Worthington 2008). The first part of the article employs the Data Envelopment Analysis (DEA) technique in order to emphasize the degree of efficiency specific to the banking activity. The second one, consecrated to productivity measurement, introduces an alternative, non-parametric technique, named Malmquist productivity index.

2. Evaluation of the banking system efficiency

Our study investigates the financial performance of the Romanian banking system between the years 2004 and 2006 through a non-parametric approach, the performance being evaluated in terms of banking activity's efficiency and productivity. The analysis comprises 16 Romanian credit institutions, which operate on a universal basis. We have excluded from the sample (1) the specialized banks, which preponderantly finance the small and medium size enterprises, the acquisition of cars or the construction of private homes, and (2) the Romanian branches of foreign banks. At the end of the year 2006, the credit institutions included in the sample summed up 75.37% of the total assets of the banking system.

In order to apply the Data Envelopment Analysis (DEA) technique, we have chosen an approach based on the intermediation function, and the selection of input and output variables reflected this criterion. The model we have proposed includes as input variables *customers deposits, operational expenses* and *equity,* whereas the output variables consist of *loans to the non-bank sector* and *net profit*. Keeping in mind that the aim of our study is to reveal the degree of efficiency of the intermediation activity and the manner how the results could be optimized, under the condition of maintaining inputs at a constant level, we have considered as adequate the implementation of an output oriented model, under the assumption of variable returns of scale. Tables 1 and 2 synthesize the most significant aspects of efficiency, obtained by applying the DEA technique.

In the year 2004 there were nine cases of inefficient banking activity, the credit institutions obtaining individual efficiency scores higher than 100%. We remind that, according to the DEA methodology, a bank is assumed to be efficient only if it reaches an efficiency score of 100%. Keeping in mind that one of the premises of the DEA technique is weighting input and output variables with a set of weights which is specific for each bank in the sample, in order to allow the maximization of the potential level of efficiency, and implicitly, its presentation in the best possible light, it means that without a significant change in the level of their activity's parameters, the banks will not become efficient.

Table 1: Efficiency scores for 2004

no. crt	*Credit institutions*	*Efficiency scores*	*Peer group banks (benchmarks)*
1	**B 1 2004**	**100.00%**	2
2	B 2 2004	117.15%	1 (0.06) 34 (0.33) 38 (0.61)
3	B 3 2004	146.08%	14 (0.55) 32 (0.15) 34 (0.06) 38 (0.25)
4	B 4 2004	139.45%	33 (0.01) 34 (0.03) 38 (0.55) 48 (0.41)
5	B 5 2004	119.96%	32 (0.75) 33 (0.00) 34 (0.25)
6	B 6 2004	111.02%	11 (0.48) 22 (0.52)
7	**B 7 2004**	**100.00%**	7
8	B 8 2004	111.49%	12 (0.74) 27 (0.16) 32 (0.04) 38 (0.06) 44 (0.01)
9	B 9 2004	286.54%	7 (0.29) 27 (0.42) 34 (0.01) 38 (0.28)
10	**B 10 2004**	**100.00%**	0
11	**B 11 2004**	**100.00%**	4
12	**B 12 2004**	**100.00%**	3
13	**B 13 2004**	**100.00%**	0
14	**B 14 2004**	**100.00%**	10
15	B 15 2004	301.82%	12 (0.59) 27 (0.09) 32 (0.09) 38 (0.21) 44 (0.02)
16	B 16 2004	111.49%	11 (0.08) 14 (0.76) 22 (0.16)

This flexibility in establishing weights has raised ample controversies among economists. Charnes, Cooper and Rhodes, the originators of the DEA model, argue that flexible weights contribute to a more accurate assessment of inefficient entities. If under this advantageous assumption banks do not obtain a score close to 100%, there is undoubtedly a case of inefficiency. Boussofiane, Dyson, Thanassoulis (1991:4) have criticized this approach, claiming that an entity can, therefore, become efficient by simply ignoring some essential input or output variables, and by weighting other variables as less important. Other authors suggest that the unsatisfactory performance of an entity, caused by a certain variable, can be neglected if the algorithm assigns the weight of "0" to that particular variable.

Credit institutions B1, B7, B10, B11, B12, B13 and B14 registered an individual efficiency score of 100%, being considered efficient and lying on the efficiency frontier. Therefore, these institutions have the ability to efficiently manage their banking activities, but we have no information about their risk appetite or their risk profiles.

The efficient credit institutions contribute to the building of the efficiency frontier towards which each inefficient bank must converge in order to maximize its financial results and to improve its efficiency. For example, the frontier for bank B6 is best described by institutions situated on the rows 11 and 22, which compose the peer group and actually represent the comparison basis. An interesting observation is that, for institutions B8 and B15, the peer group consists of the same efficient institutions (lying on the rows 12, 27, 32, 38, 44), which contribute, however, in different proportions to the building of the efficient frontier. Consequently, the two frontiers are not identical.

Table 2: Efficiency scores for the 2005-2006 period

no. crt	*Credit institutions*	*Efficiency scores*	*Peer group banks (benchmarks)*
17	B 1 2005	111.95%	1 (0.04) 34 (0.92) 38 (0.04)
18	B 2 2005	110.33%	34 (0.70) 38 (0.30)
19	B 3 2005	124.47%	7 (0.53) 14 (0.26) 32 (0.06) 34 (0.13) 38 (0.03)
20	B 4 2005	165.67%	32 (0.03) 33 (0.09) 48 (0.88)
21	B 5 2005	149.55%	32 (0.20) 34 (0.35) 38 (0.09) 48 (0.35)
22	**B 6 2005**	**100.00%**	6
23	**B 7 2005**	**100.00%**	1
24	B 8 2005	128.08%	12 (0.07) 27 (0.57) 32 (0.27) 38 (0.09)
25	B 9 2005	238.41%	7 (0.29) 14 (0.33) 27 (0.33) 34 (0.05)
26	B 10 2005	196.59%	11 (0.96) 45 (0.04)
27	**B 11 2005**	**100.00%**	5
28	**B 12 2005**	**100.00%**	0
29	B 13 2005	204.88%	39 (0.07) 43 (0.87) 45 (0.06)
30	B 14 2005	136.76%	14 (0.72) 22 (0.09) 32 (0.19) 34 (0.00)
31	B 15 2005	281.63%	7 (0.09) 14 (0.74) 32 (0.02) 34 (0.01) 38 (0.13)
32	**B 16 2005**	**100.00%**	14
33	**B 1 2006**	**100.00%**	5
34	**B 2 2006**	**100.00%**	17
35	B 3 2006	100.45%	22 (0.76) 34 (0.24)
36	B 4 2006	112.94%	32 (0.79) 33 (0.16) 48 (0.05)
37	B 5 2006	142.11%	32 (0.52) 33 (0.02) 34 (0.45)
38	**B 6 2006**	**100.00%**	15
39	**B 7 2006**	**100.00%**	1
40	B 8 2006	126.26%	14 (0.89) 22 (0.06) 34 (0.02) 38 (0.03)
41	B 9 2006	168.11%	7 (0.36) 23 (0.10) 38 (0.33) 43 (0.22)
42	B 10 2006	205.54%	11 (0.70) 14 (0.22) 22 (0.08)
43	**B 11 2006**	**100.00%**	2
44	**B 12 2006**	**100.00%**	2
45	**B 13 2006**	**100.00%**	2
46	B 14 2006	145.53%	7 (0.06) 14 (0.48) 32 (0.43) 34 (0.03)
47	B 15 2006	184.24%	7 (0.10) 14 (0.55) 32 (0.24) 34 (0.01) 38 (0.10)
48	**B 16 2006**	**100.00%**	4

In 2005 we have obtained five cases of efficiency, pertaining to banks B6, B7, B11, B12 and B16, and in the next year eight credit institutions proved to be efficient. The most performing Romanian credit institutions, in terms of efficiency, were those whose main shareholders were Greek banks.

3. Evaluation of the banking system productivity

The traditional indicators for measuring productivity consist of developing output/input ratios. Yet, they offer a static picture, at a given moment in time, and do not allow the ascertaining of leading factors that lead to a change in productivity level. In order to get an overview picture of the productivity and, by this, of the performance of the credit institutions, it is necessary to integrate a mix of several input and output variables. That has proved to be very difficult in the traditional approach. An alternative is given by the Malmquist productivity index.

To compute the Malmquist productivity index we have applied the formula proposed by Caves, Christensen, Divert (1982:1396) because it is adapted for the output oriented models.

$$M_{t,\,t+1}(y^t, y^{t+1}, x^t, x^{t+1}) = \left[\frac{D^t(y^{t+1}, x^{t+1})}{D^t(y^t, x^t)} \times \frac{D^{t+1}(y^{t+1}, x^{t+1})}{D^{t+1}(y^t, x^t)}\right]^{1/2} \quad (1)$$

where:

$M_{t,\,t+1}$ = Malmquist productivity index for a time period between t and t+1

y^t, y^{t+1} = output vectors at moment t, respectively t+1

x^t, x^{t+1} = input vectors at moment t, respectively t+1

D^t, D^{t+1} = distance function at moment t, respectively t+1. The value of distance functions is given by the individual efficiency scores obtained in the previous part of the study, by means of DEA technique.

An index value higher than "1" suggests an improvement in the productivity level, whereas a value lower than "1" indicates a deterioration. If the Malmquist index equals "1", there is no change in the productivity level in the analyzed period. According to Fare et al. (1994:71), there is an equivalent manner for writing the Malmquist index in order to stress the two components:

$$M_{t,\,t+1}(y^t, y^{t+1}, x^t, x^{t+1}) = \frac{D^{t+1}(y^{t+1}, x^{t+1})}{D^t(y^t, x^t)} \times \left[\frac{D^t(y^{t+1}, x^{t+1})}{D^{t+1}(y^{t+1}, x^{t+1})} \times \frac{D^t(y^t, x^t)}{D^{t+1}(y^t, x^t)}\right]^{1/2} \quad (2)$$

where:

$\frac{D^{t+1}(y^{t+1}, x^{t+1})}{D^t(y^t, x^t)}$ represents the technical efficiency change. It illustrates how much the distance varies between the observed production and the maximum potential production during the period t, t+1. It is also known as the *catch-up effect* and indicates the evolution of individual efficiency over the time period analyzed.

$$\left[\frac{D^t(y^{t+1}, x^{t+1})}{D^{t+1}(y^{t+1}, x^{t+1})} \times \frac{D^t(y^t, x^t)}{D^{t+1}(y^t, x^t)}\right]^{1/2}$$

reflects the technological change and indicates the *production frontier shift*, a consequence of improved technology. It is believed that technological change acts by inserting innovations and inventions into the current banking activity, favoring a change in the level of input and output variables and, implicitly, the shift of the efficiency frontier to a new equilibrium point.

Table 3 illustrates the Malmquist productivity index values, in order to reflect productivity changes over the years 2004 to 2005, 2005 to 2006 and aggregated for the entire period of time under consideration (2004-2006).

Table 3: Evolution of productivity

Credit institution	*Productivity 2004-2006*	*Productivity 2004-2005*	*Productivity 2005-2006*
B 1	0.9451	1	0.9451
B 2	0.9520	1	0.9520
B 3	0.8850	0.9573	0.9245
B 4	0.9221	1.3164	0.7005
B 5	1.0305	1.1091	0.9291
B 6	1	1	1
B 7	1	1	1
B 8	1.1063	1.0795	1.0248
B 9	0.6949	1.0490	0.6624
B 10	1.3365	1.3365	1
B 11	1	1	1
B 12	1	1	1
B 13	0.9109	1.7483	0.5210
B 14	1.3694	1.2459	1.0991
B 15	0.7716	1.1586	0.6660
B 16	0.9526	0.9526	1

Over the period 2004-2005, out of sixteen credit institutions included in the sample, eight registered an increase in productivity, the value of Malmquist index being higher than "1", whereas two banks faced a small decline in their level of productivity (Malmquist value lower than "1"). Six banks maintained a constant productivity. On average, the sample's productivity for the analyzed period of time was 1,12.

The time period 2005-2006 experienced a significant increase in the number of banks that registered a downfall in productivity. Only two had a little increase of their productivity level, but of a lesser amplitude than in the previous period. Six banks displayed no change in their productivity. The preponderant negative evolutions of the individual productivity contributed to the diminution of the sample's average productivity to 0,9015. Chart 1 illustrates the productivity's evolution over the considered period of time.

Chart 1: Productivity's trend

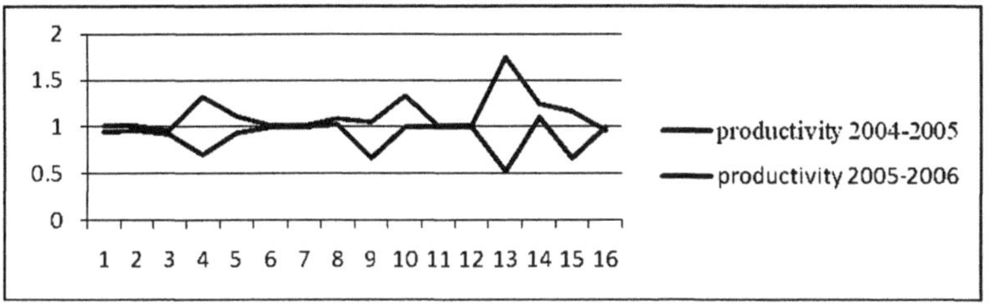

The next step consists of decomposing the productivity scores into two components, namely the technical efficiency (catching-up effect) and the technological change (frontier-shift effect), in order to establish which factor lies at the basis of a productivity increase or decrease.

Table 4: Productivity's components

	Technical efficiency		***Technological change***	
	2004 - 2005	***2005 - 2006***	***2004 - 2005***	***2005 - 2006***
B 1	1	1	1	0.9451
B 2	1	1	1	0.9520
B 3	0.9977	1	0.9595	0.9245
B 4	1.3610	0.8128	0.9672	0.8618
B 5	1.1419	1.2204	0.9713	0.7613
B 6	1	1	1	1
B 7	1	1	1	1
B 8	1.0343	0.9668	1.0437	1.0599
B 9	1.1083	0.8646	0.9465	0.7662
B 10	1	1	1.3365	1
B 11	1	1	1	1
B 12	1	1	1	1
B 13	1.7981	0.5561	0.9723	0.9368
B 14	1.1966	0.9510	1.0412	1.1557
B 15	1.0613	0.6866	1.0917	0.9700
B 16	0.9097	1	1.0472	1

As can be seen at table 4, over the 2004-2005 period the enhancement in the productivity of the 8 banks has univocally to be ascribed to an improvement in the individual technical efficiency. Of those two credit institutions whose Malmquist index is lower than "1", the bank "B3" experienced a diminution of the productivity level due, both, to the degree of inefficiency and to the technological decline. Instead, the productivity loss of bank "B16" has to be attributed to a decrease in the level of technical efficiency (-10%) which was higher than the technological progress of only 4,72%. Credit institutions whose index is equal to "1" maintained constancy on both factors.

Over 2005-2006, only the banks "B8" and "B14" registered an increase in productivity, due to the technological change (frontier shift effect). All the 8 banks that have experienced a productivity decrease had to face a diminution of the technological component. Although the technical efficiency had different evolutions (banks B1, B2 and B3 maintained their individual efficiency unchanged; B4, B9, B13 and B15 characterized themselves by a state of inefficiency; B5 was efficient), technological change played a decisive role in establishing the decreasing tendency of productivity.

In order to test whether the information provided by the Malmquist index can be interpreted as being complementary, or, contrariwise, can substitute the traditional performance indicators, we have determined the "return to assets" (ROA), the "return to equity" (ROE), the "profit ratio" and the "operational expenses/total income ratio". Moreover, we have computed the correlation coefficients between those ratios and the Malmquist index.

Table 5: Correlation coefficients between Malmquist index and standard performance indicators

	ROE	ROA	Profit ratio	Operational expenses/income
Malmquist index	0,2212	0,1968	0,2962	0,1758

There is a low correlation between all the considered indicators, therefore the information supplied by the Malmquist index reflects specific features of the banking system's productivity, distinct from the ones provided by traditional indicators. Consequently, the two alternative methods of measuring performance proved to have a complementary character.

4. Conclusions

Several authors believe that one of the effects of the liberalization process will consist in an intensification of the competition in banking systems, by the entrance of new actors, characterized by strong corporate governance and advanced technologies, being susceptible of improvements in the level of banking efficiency and productivity. At present, the Romanian banking system is dominated by private capital.

From the efficiency standpoint, the results obtained indicate that small and medium size credit institutions with foreign shareholders benefited from an emphatic dynamics of their activities between 2004-2006, deployed in a state of efficiency. Among the representative credit institutions, only the one that occupies the first place according to the value of assets proved to be efficient. From 2005 to 2006, 50% of the credit institutions in the sample faced a small decline in their productivity, relative to only 12,5% in 2004-2005. The smooth negative trend which affected productivity in 2006 was primarily due to an increase in the restrictiveness of the monetary policy, in order to consolidate the disinflations trend.

References

Boussofiane, A. / R. G. Dyson / E. Thanassoulis (1991): Invited review: Applied data envelopment analysis, European Journal of Operational Research 53, pp. 1-15

Caves, D. W. / L. R. Christensen/ W.E. Diewert (1982): The economic theory of index numbers and measurement of input, output and productivity, Econometrica, 50, pp. 1393-1414

Fare, R. et al (1994): Productivity growth, technical progress and efficiency change in industrialized countries, The American Economic Review, vol. 84, pp. 66-83

Fethi, M. D. / G. Inal / P. M. Jackson (1998): Efficiency and productivity growth in Turkish commercial banking sector: a non-parametric approach, Management Centre, University of Leicester

Isik, I. / M. K. Hassan (2003): Financial deregulation and total factor productivity change: an empirical study of Turkish commercial banks, Journal of Banking and Finance, 27

Kirikal, L. / M. Sorg / V. Vensel (2004): Estonian banking sector performance analysis using Malmquist indexes and DuPont financial ratio analysis, International Business & Economic Research Journal, 3(12), pp. 21-36

Lee, B. L. / W. H. Leong / A. C. Worthington (2008): Malmquist indices of pre and post deregulation productivity, efficiency and technological change in the Singaporean banking sector, Working/discussion paper no. 228

Mohan, R. (2006): Reforms, productivity and efficiency in banking: the Indian experience, BIS Review 15/2006

Wu, S. (2003): Productivity and efficiency analysis of Australia banking sector under deregulation, School of Accounting, Economics and Finance, Deakin University, pp. 1-40

MONETARY AND FISCAL POLICIES IN BULGARIA: LESSONS FROM THE HISTORICAL RECORD

KALINA DIMITROVA
(SOFIA UNIVERSITY "ST. KLIMENT OHRIDSKY", SOFIA, BULGARIA)

1. Introduction

There are two components by which economic policy can influence the situation of the economy: the *monetary* and the *fiscal* one. Monetary and fiscal policies have different - and sometimes controversial - *goals*, to be achieved by specific *instruments*. While the mission of the central bank is price stability, governments set their goals in the realm of economic growth and employment. Fiscal institutions, however, often use inflation in order to derive revenues (seigniorage) and finance budget deficits. Hence, inflation is viewed as a public finance phenomenon (R. Barro 1987, G. Mankiw 1987, V. Grilli 1989).

In central bankers' language, the "long-term target" of this paper is inflation and how it is influenced by fiscal policy. The study will not dare to oppose the fact that inflation is a monetary phenomenon. It would rather apply this statement as a necessary condition. The interaction between fiscal and monetary institutions, however, reflects on the price development. Hence, taking into account the role of monetary policy in setting prices, the paper will try to estimate the influence of fiscal policy on money creation, and hence on inflation.

In literature, the monetization of budget deficits resulting in inflation is known as "fiscal dominance" (King-Plosser 1985). It is, however, sometimes considered as a historical coincidence rather than as a theoretical rule (Walsh 2003: 151). Then, how should it be considered, when history repeats? And Bulgaria is an example of this, keeping recent memories of the devastating consequences of fiscal dominance on monetary policy in the first period of its transition which resulted in hyperinflation and to the introduction of the currency board in mid-1997. Therefore, it is important to know our history well and to interpret it in a modern economic language applying a quantitative analysis approach.

The time span of the study on hand is the monetary history of Bulgaria from the establishment of the Bulgarian National Bank (BNB) in 1879 until 1947 when the nationalization of the economy took place. The set-up of the BNB closely followed the political independence of Bulgaria from the Ottoman Empire in 1878. In the whole period of a centrally-planned economy since 1947, there were no budget deficits and inflation rates registered as it happens in market economies. Moreover, the "banking system" consisted of one mono-bank and the BNB functioned as a central and trade bank, financing various government structures without any limits (Avramov 1999).

The paper starts with a brief review of literature, arguing that inflation could also be classified as a "fiscal phenomenon". The third part introduces the historical background of the study, the legislation defining the relations between the central bank and the government institutions, and the research studies of that time providing evidence for the presence of a strong influence of fiscal policy on money creation. In section four, an empirical analysis is conducted and econometric estimations are derived with a view to draw some conclusions and policy implications on the interaction between monetary and fiscal policy under different monetary regimes.

2. Review of literature

As it was mentioned in the introduction, a starting point of the paper is the theory constituting inflation as a monetary phenomenon (Quantitative theory of money). Studying the behaviour of demand and supply side in the context of the quantitative equation of money, it should be recalled that the price level is determined by the money supply in the economy, given that the output and velocity of money are constant in the long-run[1]. But what determines the money supply and does the fiscal policy have some influence on this?

Several theoretical streams attempt to answer these questions by analyzing the intertemporal budget constraint. In brief, the logic of this constraint is that the sum of all government budget balances should be equal to zero at their present value. For example, a government with an issued public debt should attain budget surpluses in the future. The surplus could be generated by future extra revenues from the seigniorage or an increase of the taxes. Two representatives of the optimal seigniorage theory argue that the seigniorage originating from money creation is conditional upon the balance between budget expenditures and budget revenues (G. Mankiw 1987, V. Grilli 1989).

Robert Barro studied the impact of government expenditures on money growth and found that temporary changes in government purchases raised money growth and inflation when the gold standard was suspended (R. Barro 1987). A positive correlation between money growth and budget deficits, however, can take place in the absence of fiscal impact on money creation (R. Barro 1979, E. Joines 1985: 331). If governments were to target *real* – as opposed to nominal – values of gov-

---

[1] $M*V=P*Y$, where M is money supply, V is velocity of money, P is the general price level and Y is national output (income).

ernment debt, the nominal debt would rise in proportion to the price level; so long as money growth and inflation are positively correlated, deficit and money growth should also be positively correlated in the absence of any debt monetization by the central bank.

King and Plosser coined the term "fiscal dominance" in their seminal paper of 1985, implying the potential influence of fiscal policy over monetary policy. In other words, fiscal dominance is a situation in which fiscal policy is set a priori, while monetary policy generates enough seigniorage to satisfy the intertemporal budget constraint. Lepper (1991) generalized the case to one of active fiscal and passive monetary policy. Long-term historical studies provide different categories of evidence for the presence of fiscal dominance over money creation in Italy (Fratianni-Spinelli 2001) and in Spain from the time when the Bank of Spain was granted a monopoly of issuing banknotes to the Second World War (WW-II) (M. Sabate et al. 2004).

In the very opposite corner of the quantitative theory of money is the so called "fiscal theory of prices". It comprises of a number of studies attempting to constitute inflation as a pure fiscal phenomenon excluding the intermediation of monetary policy (Chr. Sims 1994, M. Woodford 1995, 2001). This theory focuses on a variety of prices satisfying the money market equilibrium, and on a fiscal authority as the one which sets the "equilibrium price". In contrast to other theoretical streams, the fiscal theory of prices interprets the intertemporal budget constraint as a framework rather than as a constraint which has to be met at any given price level. Yet, it has to be met only at the equilibrium price and the nominal government debt plays a crucial role in setting the price level.

This approach has its critics who seriously reject the argument that the intertemporal budget constraint is met only at the equilibrium (B. McCallum 2001, W. Buiter 2002). The increasing number of papers dedicated to the fiscal theory of prices, however, raises interesting questions not only in the fields of monetary theory, but also concerning monetary policy.

3. Bulgarian historical background and legislation

In less than a year after Bulgaria's independence the Bulgarian National Bank was established as a state trade bank, responsible for the financial intermediation of the foreign trade and for the stability of the national currency, the Lev. According to its statute, BNB was subordinated to the Ministry of Finance and most of the decisions concerning the monetary policy were subject to an agreement or permission by the Minister himself (R. Avramov 1999). Before BNB was granted the privilege to issue banknotes in 1885 (only gold-backed banknotes), different foreign currencies were allowed in circulation and the Ministry of Finance was responsible for the coinage of the Bulgarian Lev.

Although Bulgaria legally introduced a bimetallic system of the Latin Monetary Union type (1880), a silver standard was de facto in practice due to the enforced high value of silver money and particularly of the Russian Silver Ruble (N. Kiosseva, 2000). The money market was overflooded by silver coins. As a result, a difference between the legal and market price of silver coins appeared - an agio, which was moving between 4% and 9%. BNB efforts to manage the money in circulation were in vain; it accumulated losses since it was obliged to respect the legal parity of silver to gold at the ratio 15.5:1 and did not have any instrument to limit the silver coins minted by the financial authority upon budget needs (Dimitrova-Fantacci 2009a). Several years after its neighbouring countries, Bulgaria demonetized the Russian Silver Ruble in 1887 and prohibited the circulation of foreign coins which lead almost to the disappearance of the agio.

In 1891 BNB got the legal right to issue silver-backed banknotes in order to have a better control of the money in circulation, but instead of activating this privilege, the Ministry of Finance preferred to put a new volume of Bulgarian silver coins into circulation. Only in 1899 BNB was de facto allowed to start issuing silver-backed banknotes against providing more credit to the government.

As it had been put into law in 1885: "BNB credit to the government could not exceed more than 1/5 of its capital", which equaled 1,824 thousand levs, expressed in an absolute term. Until 1889 the Bulgarian government obtained money from BNB sporadically and against government securities (BNB 1929: 132). Upon the outbreak of the economic crisis at the end of the XIX century, Bulgaria's fiscal authorities began to receive regular direct credits from the central bank for its short-term needs. The treasury, however, kept some deposits at the bank at the same time for some fiscal transactions.

Since 1902 BNB loans to the government increased and became a permanent item on the asset side of its balance sheets, apart from the credits received from abroad. This was a period of huge efforts in the construction of public goods like railways and motorways, financed both by local and foreign resources (BNB 1929: 138). In spite of the fact that the law in 1906 did not put any qualitative constraint on the central bank's financing of the budget, it stated that the central bank could extend credit to the government only for short-term (up to 3 months) needs. In 1911 a new amendment of the law clarified that BNB was allowed to provide financial support to the budget for "less than its nominal capital", i.e. 20,000 levs.

From 1912 until 1922 BNB did not have any limit on the credits provided to the government for war financing as Bulgaria entered a long period of wars - the Balkan wars and World War One (WW-I). As a consequence, the public finances were completly destroyed. Moreover, being defeated in WW-I, Bulgaria faced the heavy burden of war debts and it had to provide huge sums for debt services. This resulted in the inability of the MF to put public finance into order for almost a decade.

In 1924 radical efforts for monetary stabilization were enforced, among them harder budget constraints on public finance. Direct credit of BNB to the government was stabilized at a certain limit, because according to the new law "the overall credit to the government should not exceed 4,700 million levs" The fiscal extra needs, however, were met by credits from abroad and negotiated with the League of Nations. In 1926 Bulgaria obtained the so called refugees' loan which was provided for covering the expenses of Bulgarian refugees from neighbouring countries because of the change of the boundaries after WW-I. Two years later the government was granted a stabilization loan for the implementation of the monetary stabilization in compliance with the international agreements. Although the stabilization in Bulgaria started de facto in 1924, it was legalized in 1928 when the gold exchange standard was introduced (R. Avramov 1999, 152).

According to the new statute, BNB should act like an independent central bank. After a short time, however, the first signs of the Great Depression appeared. The world liquidity crisis worsened the balance of the budget and the government was in need of more extra financing (seigniorage). At the end of 1928 a legislative provision had been enacted according to which the government should repay its debt to the central bank, but that clause was never put into practice and, by permission of the Financial Committee of the League of Nations, it was dropped shortly thereafter. Furthermore, the amendment stated that "BNB net profit and seigniorage should not be used to pay back the government debt to the central bank, but for current expenses of the Treasury".

At the outbreak of WW-II the government did not provide any sums in the budgets to redeem its debt to the BNB. The new law dating back to 1937 seemed to put some obligations on the government to pay off its debt to the central bank by requiring that the Treasury should buy back government securities from the BNB at the value of 1 billion levs. At the same time the government was allowed to get direct credit from the monetary authorities. Therefore, this was simply a balance sheet transaction between two components of the government debt to the central bank, without producing any decrease of its total stock. Moreover, there was no limit for BNB to credit the budget.

One of the latest amendments of the BNB law for the period under study said that "BNB will extend an additional amount of money not exceeding 140% of the capital and reserves against government securities provided by foreign companies for government purchases, which have to be cleared in less than 7 years" (1940). These purchases were mostly from German companies in the period of the clearing agreements and compensation deals in the 1930s[2].

4. Evidence of fiscal influence on money creation

The analysis of the long-term record of the fiscal influence on money creation in Bulgaria and hence on inflation will incorporate an interdisciplinary approach. First, we will provide a descriptive evidence of the interaction between the fiscal and monetary authorities according to the literature. Then we will proceed with empirical evidence showing the development of the indicators of interest in different periods of time characterized by specific monetary arrangements. The last piece of evidence will be generated by the application of econometric tools to the respective variables.

4.1 Evidence in the literature

The dependence of the central bank on fiscal policy has been in the focus of the Bulgarian economic critics. There are a lot of studies which provide evidence for the influence of the fiscal policy on the inflation rate by the central bank's financing of the budget.

D. Yordanov provided a critical research of BNB balance sheets arguing that since its establishment the central bank financed the government in various ways and did not keep proper records of this financing (D. Yordanov 1910). His thorough analysis was based on weekly balance sheet data. He came out with the finding that for some periods of time the item "current account of the government" (which usually had a credit balance) was merged with the item "current non-interest bearing accounts" (ending with a debit balance); thus, BNB balance sheets did not allow for the precise evaluation of the overall credit to the government. Moreover, Yordanov found out that among the credits extended to companies and individuals, some "were guaranteed by the Ministry of Finance or the Minister of Finance himself". (D. Yordanov: 1910: 26).

Another study provides a longer record of the influence of fiscal policy on money creation (St. Bochev 1924). The author came out with an evaluation of the overall credit to the government based on information from the text of the annual report, analyzing the purposes of various

[2] For more details on the exchange rate control in Bulgaria in the interwar period see Nenovsky and Dimitrova (2007).

credits extended by the central bank. It turned out that his figures were quite different from the ones reported in the balance sheets, because apart from the direct credit, they include also financing of various public funds, i.g. financing provided for public foreign debts. Stoyan Bochev concluded his study on BNB as an emission institute with the argument that "the state financial policy dominates BNB emission policy" (St. Bochev 1924: 29).

In his "Course on banking in Bulgaria" at the Economic Department of Sofia University, Assen Christophoroff stated that George Knapp's book "State Theory of Money" played a crucial role in the collapse of the gold standard and the occurrence of the fearful inflation in the world (A. Christophoroff 1946: 26). Studying different episodes of the Bulgarian banking system with BNB playing the central role, he argued that the central bank's almost constant financing of the government reached its peak in the war years. Even in periods of time when BNB was forced to limit its emission of banknotes (during the stabilization), the government enhanced coinage in order to provide the necessary extra revenues from the seigniorage (K. Nedelchev 1940); hence the fiscal policy again interfered with the creation of money, which was no longer under the control of a monetary authority.

Summarizing various studies dedicated to the interaction between the Bulgarian monetary, banking and financial institutions, on the one hand, and the governments on the other hand, a recent publication argues that the creation and development of the financial system in Bulgaria has been dominated by the state, fiscal policy and municipal needs of financing (R. Avramov 2007).

4.2 Empirical evidence

As mentioned by some contemporaries, there were various ways in which BNB financed the government or public projects and municipal initiatives (St. Bochev 1924). Apart from the conventional direct credit to the government and purchases of treasury bonds, there were also credits extended to state institutions and funds. Moreover, there were credits granted to companies and even to individuals who were qualified as "guaranteed" by the Ministry of Finance (D. Yordanov 1910). Last but not least, we should mention also the high share of BNB profit (around 70% on average) generated predominantly from seigniorage which was designated to the fiscal authorities[3].

Among all elaborated channels of BNB financing to the government, for the sake of the objectivity and reliability of the data we will study

---

[3] The share is calculated based on information from various issues of BNB Annual reports.

only items explicitly recorded in the central bank's balance sheets. Being aware of the fact that this classification will not be exhaustive, only direct credit to the government and treasury bonds together will serve as a proxy for the overall BNB credit to the government. In the framework of the balance sheet analysis (chart 1), partially similar to the one employed in the money growth accounting textbook by Cagan (1965), we will try to estimate the relationship between the monetary base and the overall financing of the government. The monetary base comprises only of banknotes in circulation for the period until 1927 when no requirement for the banks' reserves was in place and they were not reported in the BNB's balance sheets. Since 1927 the monetary base consists of banknotes in circulation and the banks' demand deposits when trade banks started to maintain deposits at the central bank as a part of the stabilization package. Classifying the other components of the domestic credit and monetary base is no simple task because BNB acted as a trade bank as well and only in the late 1920s it took over its typical central bank functions to guarantee the monetary stabilization.

Figure 1: Balance sheet framework

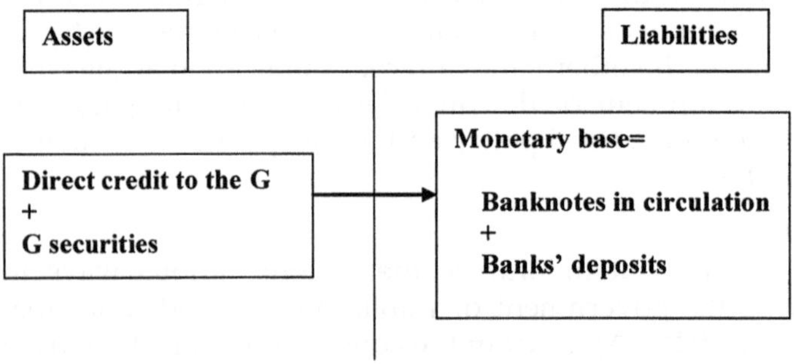

The first piece of empirical evidence for the relationship between the monetary base and the credit to the government and its impact on inflation is supposed to be underlying in the development of the respective variables (table 1). Studying the annual growth rates of the monetary base (on the liabilities side), the credit to the government (on the asset side), and the inflation rate as a resulting variable, we can observe a similar behaviour of the three indicators under different periods of time. During the classical Bulgarian gold standard started in 1906 and ended with the outbreak of the Balkan wars in 1912, the credit to the government and the emission of banknotes as a cheap source of financing budg-

budgetary needs, experienced high average growth rates of 84.53% and 35.60% respectively, due to their very low starting levels in absolute terms. Inflation, however, seemed to be moderate on average (2.79), but speeded up at the end of the period.

Table 1: Monetary base, credit to the government and inflation (annual average growth rates, in percent)

Indicators/periods	Monetary base	BNB credit to government	Inflation
Bimetallism and Gold Standard	35.60	84.53	2.79
Stabilization	2.07	-0.27	-2.13
War years	74.64	64.84	37.45
Whole period	44.61	46.30	9.28

Stabilization is an interesting, although short, period of time for which we can provide a qualitative estimation of the deflation which was very painful for the economy - monetary contraction, resulting in agrowth rate of 2.07% on average, leading to a *deflation* of 2.13%[4]. The efforts to put the hard budget constraints on the government into practice became obvious in the decrease of the overall BNB credit to the fiscal authorities of 0.27%.

As expected, the war years scored the highest growth rates of money creation (74.64%) as well as of the credits extended to the government for war and other extraordinary needs (64.8%) - and consequently of inflation (37.5%). Unfortunately, Bulgaria had more than the two world wars, and as a defeated country in WW-I and WW-II, it accumulated huge war debts which turned out to be a heavy burden for the budget for a long period of time.

Summarizing the development of the three indicators for the whole period, it is easy to see that the monetary base and BNB's credit to the government grow with close rates of 44.61% and 46.3% respectively. In other words, we can argue that both were in close interdependence and that there is some relation between fiscal and monetary policy. The average growth rates, however, are static estimations which do not necessarily characterize every point in time under study.

Another piece of evidence we can look at is the application of statistical correlations. The cross-correlation matrix (table 2) provides us with high degrees of correlation coefficients for the development of all three vari-

[4] The growth rate of banknotes in circulation only was negative of 1.5% on average. Nenovsky and Dimitrova (2006) provide more details on the stabilization in Bulgaria.

ables. If we look at these estimates more closely, we can see that the correlation between money creation and the credit to the government is – not surprisingly – the highest: 0.98. The correlation between inflation and the monetary base is also very high (0.89), but, interestingly, the inflation follows closely (0.93) the development of the credit to the government.

Table 2: Correlation matrix of monetary base, credit to the government and inflation

Correlation coefficient	Monetary base	BNB credit to the government	Inflation
Monetary base	1	0.98	0.89
BNB credit to the government	0.98	1	0.93
Inflation	0.89	0.93	1

One explanation for this observation might be the fact that we look only at banknotes in circulation for the period until the deposits of commercial banks appear as a separate item in the BNB's balance sheets, while the behaviour of the overall money supply is likely to be transmitted more thoroughly to the price development. In this case, the high correlation coefficient could be interpreted in the way that the credit extended to the government reflects the overall monetary base more precisely. There are supporting statements for this assumption in some studies (D. Yordanov 1910, St. Bochev 1924), which argue that for a certain period of time the central bank extended credit to the government from deposits at its disposal. Unfortunately, the BNB's balance sheets before 1927 do not allow us to study different components of the aggregatedly reported demand deposits.[5] Although this piece of evidence has the characteristics of the dynamic statistical analysis, the correlation is not enough to draw a conclusion that there is a strong fiscal influence on money creation and hence, on inflation (R. Barro 1979, E. Joines 1985, 331).

4.3. Econometric estimation

The econometric estimation of the influence of fiscal policy on inflation though public deficits monetization starts with the determination of the direction of causality between inflation on the one hand, and BNB credit to the government and the monetary base, on the other hand. We will apply the Granger test according to which the causality relationship implies that A causes B, if lagged values of A improve the forecast of B (C. Granger 1969).

[5] Since 1927 demand deposits are reported into three components: banks' deposits, government deposits and private deposits with average shares in the aggregate indicator of 35.7%, 23.3% and 50% respectively.

Table 3: Granger causality test

Null Hypothesis	F-statistics	Probability
Inflation does not Granger cause monetary base	2.48663	0.09481
Monetary base does not Granger cause inflation	3.47398	0.03973
Inflation does not Granger cause credit to the Government	2,02119	0,14462
Credit to the Government does not Granger cause inflation	3,40013	0,04236

According to the rule of thumb, the first pair of the Granger causality test tells us that the monetary base is the determinant of inflation. The second pair of the test also suggests that the credit extended by the central bank to the national and subnational governments is determining the development of inflation. Therefore, we could summarize the results in the following way: Granger causality tests with respect to inflation suggest that BNB loans to government have an impact on inflation through the creation of money.

The last piece of evidence will be generated by an econometric estimation of the interaction between fiscal and monetary policy. For that purpose we will apply Ordinary Least Squares (OLS) regressions to estimate the simple equation:

$$MB = \beta_0 + \beta_1 GDebt + \upsilon_t,$$

Where MB stands for the monetary base (in logarithm), GDebt for the BNB's financing of the government (in logarithm), β_o and β_1 are coefficients, and υ_t are the residuals. The coefficient of interest is β_1, which characterizes the relationship between the overall credit to the government and the money creation. All variables have undergone the necessary stationarity transformations before entering the regressions (table 4).

The econometric results confirm the existence of the fiscal impact on the increase of the monetary base for the whole period and hence on inflation. The coefficient is not very high (0.14), most probably reflecting the fact that the proxy for the credit extended by the central bank to the government is not exhaustive. The comparatively high adjusted R-squared suggests, however, that there was some monetization of fiscal debt and central bank dependence on fiscal authorities (R. Avramov 2007).

Table 4: Econometric results

Period		β_1
Whole period (1889 - 1947)		0,14
	t-statistic	2,46
	Adj. R-squared	0,71
Bimetallism and gold standard (1889-1913)		-0,26
	t-statistic	-2,06
	Adj. R-squared	0,30
War and interwar years (1913-1947)		0,18
	t-statistic	2,69
	Adj. R-squared	0,59

For the first sub-period of bimetallic and gold monetary standards, we generate a negative coefficient of -0.26 suggesting that BNB loans to the budget were not a determinant of the development of the monetary base, and thus an inflationary factor. One explanation for this might be the comparatively small sums received by the government through these two channels or the comparatively small amount of the overall financing under these monetary arrangements (A. Christophoroff 1946, 34). Another possible explanation for this negative relationship between budget financing and money creation could be the limited creation of money through the emission of banknotes. In fact, until 1914 74% of the whole money in circulation were represented by silver coins. Coinage, however, was a privilege of the fiscal authorities, hence not presented in central bank's liabilities, and it was often exercised to derive an average of 50% seigniorage to finance the budget directly (Dimitrova-Fantacci 2009b). As a result of this high supply of silver coins together with the high supply of silver-backed banknotes since 1899, a persistent agio (a difference between the market and the official silver-to-gold ratio) appeared (Dimitrova-Fantacci 2009a). It was not until 1906 when the gold standard was de facto introduced and the banknotes in circulation became a true means of money creation.

As expected, the highest coefficient (0.18) is attained during the war years. War years are usually characterized by a stronger interaction between fiscal and monetary authorities and even experiencing fiscal dominance in some cases (Fratianni-Spinelli 2001). For the sake of having higher numbers of observations, the time series also covers the interwar years (stabilization) and the depression years. Therefore, the observed deflation during the stabilization most likely turns the coefficient of interaction downward, although it was short enough and smaller by degrees relative to war financing to turn the relation from positive to negative.

5. Conclusion and policy implications

Applying different research approaches - historical, statistical and econometric ones - we have found various kinds of evidence (descriptive and empirical) for the fiscal impact on money creation, and hence on inflation. The general outcome of the study could be interpreted in the following way: any degree of fiscal interferences with money creation is translated into inflation.

Studying the interaction between fiscal and monetary policy in different periods of time, characterized by specific monetary arrangements, this impact turned out to be higher during times of war and probably negligible, during the classical gold standard. Our results suggest that different monetary regimes allow for the presence of fiscal interferences in money creation to different extents. Therefore, not surprisingly, the fiscal impact on the monetary base is weak during the bimetallic and gold standard, and during the monetary stabilization in the 1920s when the international monetary system was based on national currencies fixed either to the gold parity or to a gold exchange ratio. Assuming that the parallel between the gold standard mechanism and the currency board arrangement was appropriate (Desquilbet-Nenovsky 2004), we could argue that the latter one is a regime generating the low "fiscal" inflation by putting hard budget constraints on financing the government.

Although it is still disputable whether and how the fiscal dominance concept could be presented as a theoretical postulate (C. Walsh 2003), it has been into practice for a long time. Unfortunately, it does not only belong to the past. Fratianni and Spinelli (2001) argue that the whole monetary history of Italy until its joining the Euro zone is characterized by a constant monetization of budget deficits. Blanchard (2004) provides recent evidence from Brazil for fiscal dominance under an inflation targeting regime. Bulgaria also experienced the consequences of fiscal dominance over money creation at the beginning of its transition period, forgetting its monetary history of the pre-centrally-planned economy. The result was hyperinflation which was solved by the introduction of the currency board, enabling the central bank to act as an independent monetary institute and with the hard budget constraint as a first principle.

References

Avramov, R. 1999: 120 Years Bulgarian National Bank, Sofia: BNB

Avramov, R. 2007: Komunalniat kapitalizam (Communal capitalism), volumes I, II and III, Sofia: Bulgarian science and culture Foundation (in Bulgarian)

Barro, R. 1979: On the Determinants of the Public Debt, in: Journal of Political Economy, vol. 87, pp. 1095-1117
Barro, R. 1987: Government Spending Interest Rates, Prices, and Budget Deficits in the United Kingdom, 1701-1918, in: Journal of Monetary Economics, vol. 20, pp. 221-247
Blanchard, O. 2004: Fiscal Dominance and Inflation Targeting: Lessons from Brazil, NBER Working Paper No. 10389 (May 2004)
BNB 1929: Jubileen sbornik 1879-1929 (Jubilee Book 1879-1929), Sofia: BNB
Bochev, St. 1924: Balgarskata narodna banka kato emisionen, kambialen I krediten institut (Bulgarian National Banks as an emission, exchange rate policy and credit institute) Sofia: AL. Paskalev Publication (in Bulgarian)
Buiter, W. 2002: The Fiscal Theory of the Price Level: A Critique, in: The Economic Journal, vol. 112, pp. 459-480
Cagan, P. 1965: Determinants and Effects of Changes in the Stock of Money, 1875-1960, New York: Columbia University Press
Christophoroff, A. 1946: Kurs po Balgarsko bankovo delo (Course on banking activities in Bulgaria), Sofia: n.a. (in Bulgarian)
Desquilbet, J./N. Nenovsky 2004: Credibility and Adjustment: Gold Standards versus Currency Boards, BNB Discussion Paper No. 39, Sofia: BNB
Dimitrova, K./L. Fantacci 2009a: The establishment of the gold standard in Southeast Europe: convergence to a new system or divergence from an old one?, in: P. Baubeau / A. Ögren (eds.): Convergence and divergence of national financial systems during the gold standards, 1871-1971, London: Pickering & Chatto Publishers Ltd (forthcoming)
Dimitrova, K./L. Fantacci 2009b: Financial stability, monetary autonomy and fiscal interference: Bulgaria in search of its way 1879-1913, in: Economic and Financial Stability in Southeastern Europe in a Historical and Comparative Perspective, National Bank of Serbia Conference Proceedings' Volume, Belgrade: NBS (forthcoming)
Fratianni, M./F. Spinelli 2001: Fiscal Dominance and Money Growth in Italy: The Long Record, in: Explorations in Economic History, vol. 38, pp. 252-272
Granger, C. 1969: Investigating Causal Relations by Econometric Methods and Cross-spectral Methods, in: Econometrica, vol. 37, pp. 424-438
Grilli, V. 1989: Exchange Rates and Seigniorage, in: European Economic Review, vol. 33, pp. 580-587
Joines, D. 1985: Deficits and money growth in the United States 1872-1983, in: Journal of Monetary Economics, vol. 16, pp. 329-351
King, R./C. Plosser 1985: Money, Deficit, and Inflation, in: Carnegie-Rochester Conference Series, vol. 22, pp. 147-196
Kiosseva, N. 2000: Istoria na parichnite krizi w Balgaria, 1879-1912 (History of the monetary crises in Bulgaria, 1879-1912), Sofia: Economic University Press (in Bulgarian)
Leeper, E. 1991: Equilibria under 'Active' and 'Passive' Monetary and Fiscal Policies, in: Journal of Monetary Economics, vol. 27, pp. 129-147
Mankiw, G. 1987: The Optimal Collection of Seigniorage: Theory and Evidence, in: Journal of Monetary Economics, vol. 20, pp. 327-341
McCallum, B. 2001: Monetary Policy Analysis in Models Without Money, Review of the Federal Reserve Bank of St. Louis (July/August), pp. 145-160

Nedelechev, K. 1940: Parichnoto delo v Balgaria, 1879-1940 (Monetary activities in Bulgaria, 1879-1940), Sofia: Knipegraph Printing House (in Bulgarian)

Nenovsky N./K. Dimitrova 2006: Exchange Rate and Inflation: France and Bulgaria in the Interwar Period, in: R. Avramov /S. Pamuk (eds.): Monetary and Fiscal Policies in South-East Europe. Historical and Comparative Perspective, Sofia, BNB

Nenovsky, N./K. Dimitrova 2007: Exchange Rate Control in Bulgaria in the Interwar Period: History and Theoretical Reflections, BNB Discussion Paper No. 61, Sofia: BNB

Sabate, M./M. Gadea/R. Escario 2004: Does fiscal policy influence monetary policy? The case of Spain, 1874-1935, in: Explorations in Economic History, vol. 43, pp. 309-331

Sims, Chr. 1994: A simple model for the study of the determination of the price level and the interaction of monetary and fiscal policy, in: Economic Theory, vol. 4, pp. 381-399

Walsh, C. 2003: Monetary Theory and Policy (Second edition), London: MIT Press

Woodford, M. 1995: Price Level Determinacy without Control of a Monetary Aggregate, in: Carnegie-Rochester Conference Series on Public Policy, vol. 43, pp. 1-46

Woodford, M. 2001: Fiscal Requirements for Price Stability, in: Journal of Money, Credit and Banking, vol. 33, pp. 669-728

Yordanov, D. 1910: Balgarskata Narodna Banka 1879-1908 (Bulgarian National Bank, 1879-1908), Sofia: Liberalni klub Printing House (in Bulgarian)

NEW DATA ON THE BULGARIAN TRANSACTION SECTOR: 1997 TO 2006

HENRIK EGBERT / MARIA IVANOVA / GEORGE CHOBANOV
(JUSTUS-LIEBIG-UNIVERSITY GIESSEN, GERMANY /
SOFIA UNIVERSITY "SV. KLIMENT OHRIDSKI", BULGARIA)

1. Introduction

Transaction costs are a feature of every economic system. They exist because institutions, like markets and firms, do not work in a frictionless way. The complexity and the number of institutions increase in the process of development. This is due to the division of labour and the specialization within an economic system. As a consequence, the transaction costs in the system rise in absolute numbers as well as with respect to their inherent share of the national output. Wallis and North (1986) articulate these ideas and they describe the concept of the transaction sector. This sector provides the share of GDP, which is necessary to run a national economy. Wallis and North (1986) show that the transaction sector has grown over time in the USA. To put it in different words, economic development requires a growing share of GDP to facilitate production in the system of a national economy.

A growing transaction sector does not necessarily constitute a problem for a national economy *if* the rising transaction sector goes hand in hand with productivity gains. Then, the increased productivity of the non-transaction activities compensates the rising transaction costs reflected in the transaction sector.

We assume that every national economy has an optimal size of the transaction sector. This optimal size is represented by the relation transaction cost/output as a percentage of GDP. Since the transaction sector is not a concept that the official statistics computes, its size has to be calculated before it can be related to productivity gains. The aim of this paper is to provide a database for one transition country, i.e. to outline the calculation of the transaction sector.[1]

Some researchers followed Wallis and North (1986) and measured the transaction sector for several national economies.[2] Only three studies have addressed transition countries. We outline the methodology and the data for the transaction sector of Bulgaria for the decade 1997 to 2006.

---

[1] The correlation between productivity growth and size of the transaction sector is not the topic of this paper. For attempts in Germany compare Löchel (1995), Reichhardt (1995), Bischoff and Bohnet (2000), Bischoff (2002).

[2] Van Dalen and van Vuuren (2005) developed an alternative way of calculating the transaction sector.

In general, we follow the idea of Wallis and North (1986) and our first attempt for Bulgaria (Chobanov and Egbert 2007). However, in this article we improve the existing data: we include more precise calculations and new data provided by official statistics. The result of our study confirms the trend of a rising transaction sector in the country within a decade. This general result does not exclude that the data in sub-sectors are different if compared with the previous study.

The paper is structured as follows: Section two provides a brief review of the literature. In section three we outline the methodology of calculations. Section four draws attention to the results. Finally, a conclusion follows.[3]

2. Review of the Literature

The computation of the transaction sector can be achieved by focussing on aggregated data from official statistics or by empirical research at the micro level.[4] Here we follow the approach of Wallis and North (1986). It has been criticised by Davis (1986: 152-155), who outlines several problems related to the measuring and the conceptualization of the transaction sector (cf. additionally Wallis and North 1988). Parker (1988: 432-433) and Löchel (1995) added further critical comments. It may well be due to this critique that the original approach was replicated not before 1998. Then, Dollery and Leong (1998) adapted the concept to the system of national accounting of Australia. Hazledine (2001) replicated the method for New Zealand. In conference papers Ghertman (1998) introduced a comparative approach and Dagnino-Pastore and Farina (1999) used the concept for Argentina. Recently Datta *et al.* (2004) provided results for India.

Eissrich (2001) applied the concept to transition countries but only for a couple of years. In a conference paper Sulejewicz and Graca (2005) calculated the transaction sector in the Polish economy. One of their major contributions is the adaptation of the classification used by Dollery and Leong (1998) to the Classification of Economic Activities in the European Community (NACE), thus allowing a replication of their study in other EU countries with identical classifications of industries and activities. In a first replication of the approach for Bulgaria (Chobanov and Egbert 2007), the results have been compared with the results for Poland.

---

[3] For conceptualization of the transaction sector and a detailed discussion of the literature compare Chobanov and Egbert (2007).

[4] For a micro approach compare Chobanov, Egbert and Giuredzheklieva (2006) and Chobanov, Egbert and Sedlarski (2007).

All studies show that the transaction sector increases over time in various countries. In the transition countries Bulgaria and Poland this increase seems to be dynamic, probably due to the implementation of markets and accompanying institutions.

3. Methodology of Calculations

In this section we outline how we adapted the data from the National Statistical Office (NSI) and the Ministry of Finance to compute the Bulgarian transaction sector.[5] Dollery and Leong (1998) used the logic of Wallis and North (1986) to define sectors in order to replicate the calculations for a country with similar institutions. In table 1 we present a variation of this classification which consists of changing the places and the headings of the columns. Like Dollery and Leong (1998), we do not dispute the reasoning of Wallis and North (1986) to place an industry in the transaction sector or in the non-transaction area (but see Davis 1986) because our aim is to provide a comparative study for a post-socialist country.

Table 1: Classification of economic activities

Private sector		Public sector	
Sub-sector I	Sub-sector II	Sub-sector III	Sub-sector IV
Transaction industries	Non-transaction industries	Transaction services	Non-transaction services
Finance Insurance Real estate Wholesale trade Retail trade	Agriculture Construction Mining Manufacturing Transport / Storage Services	Public administration Public order Defence Postal services	Education Health Rail/Air transport Public utilities Social welfare Communications

Source: Based on Dollery and Leong (1998: 209, table 1).

Due to specificities in the official statistics, it is impossible to replicate the calculations with the same particularity for Bulgaria. In the following paragraphs we list some of the main specificities of the Bulgarian data set. Data for GDP are from the NSI statistical yearbooks: for 1997 from Statistical Yearbook 2002, for the period 1998 to 2001 from Statistical

[5] We are grateful to the National Statistical Institute of Bulgaria and the Bulgarian Ministry of Finance for their kind support and the provided data.

Yearbook 2003, and for the period 2002 to 2006 from Statistical Yearbook 2007.

In sub-sector I "finance" and "insurance" have merged in "financial intermediation". "Wholesale trade" and "retail trade" are combined with "repair of motor vehicles", "motorcycles" and "personal" and "household goods". "Real estate" includes renting and other business activities such as computer services, research and development, legal, accounting, advertising, etc.[6]

Data for sub-sector III are provided by the Ministry of Finance in its annual consolidated fiscal programmes. We slightly changed the names of the items in table 1 to make them correspond more closely to the budget classification of the Ministry of Finance. "Public administration" is divided into two parts: "justice system" and "state administration". The latter consists of executive and legislative bodies and common services, such as general economic and social programming and planning, control of foreign investments, services that are connected with foreign affairs. "Public order" is named public security and fire protection. It sums up the expenditures for two items in the consolidated fiscal programmes, i.e. police public order and security, which includes fire protection, and the administration of prisons. "Defence" remains unchanged as a name in our classification. Data for "postal services" are neither provided in the consolidated fiscal programmes, nor can they be extracted from NSI publications, due to a problem that is set forth in the next paragraph.

Calculating sub-sectors II and IV, Sulejewicz and Graca (2005) used the Polish classification of economic activities *Polska Klasyfikacja Działalności* (PKD) to classify economic activities as belonging to the non-transaction industries or services and to use official statistical data for their measurement. Like the Bulgarian classification of economic activities, PKD is based on NACE and thus provides a good base for comparative studies. One common problem of Polish and Bulgarian statistics is that the data are published only at the level of sections. For some economic activities this level of aggregation confronts with the definitions for transaction and non-transaction activity. We have summarized these problems in table 3 (appendix).

In table 3 the names of sections A, B, C, D, F, M and N show into which category they fall. For instance, "hotels and restaurants" stands for "services" in table 1, "electricity, gas and water supply" stands for "public utilities". Sections I, L and O are problematic. NSI publishes data at the level of sections. At the level of divisions and groups we see a mixture of

---

[6] For a more precise listing see NACE Rev. 1.1 (2002).

public vs. private and transaction vs. non-transaction activities. For sections I (transport, storage and communication) and O (other community, social and personal service activities) we propose to take advantage of the fact that NSI publishes data on salaries and the number of employed separately for state and for private companies. Instead of calculating labour costs for a whole economic activity and classifying it solely as a non-transaction industry or a non-transaction service, we add the labour costs of private companies for sections I and O to the sum for non-transaction industries and, by analogy, the labour costs of state companies go in the non-transaction services. The group 64.1 (post and courier activities) cannot be subtracted and thus it underestimates the transaction services and overestimates the labour costs for type-one-occupations in the non-transaction sector. This special type of occupations is defined below. The last problem concerns section L (social welfare). Group 75.3 (compulsory social security activities) could present this problem, but since data for it are not available, it underestimates the non-transaction services.

The tasks that are performed in type-one-occupations are dominantly related to transaction activities (Wallis and North call them type I professions). As a measure of labour costs in the non-transaction industries and services we define the sum of wages and salaries of the employees under employment contract according to the Labour Code or to the Law of State Officials for occupations that are considered to fit type-one-occupations. According to the National Classification of Professions and Occupations, which is harmonized with the International Standard Classification of Occupations, ISCO - 88, these are managers, analytical specialists, technicians, clerical support workers, and service, sales and security workers. The rest are agricultural, forestry, fishery and hunting workers, skilled manufacturing workers, equipment, machine and transportation operators, and elementary occupations, which are considered to perform transformation tasks. The sum of wages and salaries is a product of the average number of employees and the average annual wages and salaries. The data are provided by NSI.

4. Results

Table 2 provides a survey of the results (for details see appendix). The size of the transaction sector has increased more than 15% points in one decade. This is mainly the result of an increase in the sub-sector II, i.e. transaction industries (see table 1 and 2).

Table 2: Transaction sector as a percentage of GDP

Year	1997	1998	1999	2000	2001	2002	2003	2004	2005	2006
Transaction industries	24.33	21.07	24.18	26.64	27.16	27.99	28.84	31.86	36.12	37.53
Non-transac tion industries	2.98	3.2	3.05	2.89	2.83	2.88	3.03	3.21	3.25	3.34
Total private sector	**27.31**	**24.27**	**27.23**	**29.53**	**29.99**	**30.87**	**31.87**	**35.07**	**39.37**	**40.87**
Transaction services	5.3	7.15	7.63	8.49	7.66	7.84	7.99	7.55	7.51	7.39
Non-transac-tion services	3.66	4.28	4.41	4.27	4.09	4.26	4.4	4.05	3.92	3.67
Total public sector	**8.96**	**11.43**	**12.04**	**12.76**	**11.75**	**12.1**	**12.39**	**11.6**	**11.43**	**11.06**
Total private + public sector	**36.27**	**35.7**	**39.27**	**42.29**	**41.74**	**42.97**	**44.26**	**46.67**	**50.8**	**51.93**

Source: Own calculations.

There are differences from the results in Chobanov and Egbert (2007). These are explained by four reasons.

1. The NSI recalculated the data on the GDP for the years 2002, 2003 and 2004.
2. We add "Financial Intermediation Services Indirectly Measured" (FISIM) to GDP for the years before 2002. The NSI data for GDP before 2002 do not include FISIM in the gross value added and consequently it is not calculated in the GDP. After 2002 FISIM is distributed among the economic activities and is included in the GDP. To keep consistency, we add FISIM to GDP for the period 1997 to 2001.
3. The imputed rent of owner occupied dwellings is now subtracted from the gross output of the economic activity real estate, renting and business activities. Wallis and North (1986: 140) do not include rental income in the transaction industry real estate.
4. In the calculation of labour costs for type-one-occupations in the two sub-sectors of non-transaction industries and non-transaction services, now we sum up for all companies – no matter whether they are public or private. The only exception is made for sections I (transport, storage and communication) and O (other community, social and personal service activities). Chobanov and Egbert (2007) calculated labour costs for type-one-occupations in the non-transaction industries only for private companies and in the non-transaction services they used data only for state companies. Since ownership structure in transitional periods is often unclear and sometimes not fully reported to statistical offices, this approach

seemed to be justified especially for the categories of these sub-sectors. Thus, in this follow-up study we revised the calculations. To sum up, the present paper does not only provide a longer time series, but it also relies on an improved data source provided by the NSI and clarifies the data of the two sub-sectors which have been calculated by Chobanov and Egbert (2007) in a rather cautious way. The trend of the results remains the same.

5. Conclusion

In this paper we showed that the size of the transaction sector could be measured with regularly gathered official statistics in a satisfactory way. We recalculated the data from a previous study. This became necessary because GDP as our main references point had been adjusted in official statistics. Furthermore, we prolonged the time series for three years. Our result, a growing transaction sector, supports the hypothesis that the emergence and development of markets and related institutions influence transaction costs. In the described case they increase. So we confirm results of previous studies for other countries, and also for Bulgaria. In a follow-up study we will relate the data to the development of productivity in order to come closer to the aim of defining the optimal size of the transaction sector in a national economy.

References

Bischoff, I. 2002: Transaction Activities, Labor Productivity and Economic Growth, in: Jahrbuch für Wirtschaftswissenschaften, vol. 53, pp. 161-179

Bischoff, I./A. Bohnet 2000: Gesamtwirtschaftliche Transaktionskosten und wirtschaftliches Wachstum, in: Jahrbücher für Nationalökonomie und Statistik, vol. 220, pp. 419-437

Chobanov, G./H. Egbert 2007: The Rise of the Transaction Sector in the Bulgarian Economy, in: Comparative Economic Studies, vol. 49, pp. 683-698

Chobanov, G./H. Egbert/A. Giuredzheklieva 2006: Предложения за измерване на Транзакционния сектор от официалната статистика (Suggestions for Measuring the Transaction Sector by the Official Statistics), in: Statistics (Journal of the National Statistical Institute of Bulgaria), vol. 2, pp. 49-62

Chobanov, G./H. Egbert/T. Sedlarski 2007: Методи за статистическо извличане на данни за транзакционните операции на микро ниво (Methods for Data Collection on Transaction Tasks: a Micro-level Analysis), in: Statistics (Journal of the National Statistical Institute of Bulgaria) vol. 1, pp. 5-14

Dagnino-Pastore, J. M./P. E. Farina 1999: Transaction Costs in Argentina, Paper presented at the 3rd Annual Conference of the International Society for New

Institutional Economics, Washington, 16-18 September, http://www.isnie.org/ISNIE99/Papers/pastore.pdf (November 7th, 2008)

Dalen, H. van/A. van Vuuren 2005: Greasing the Wheels of Trade: a profile of the Dutch Transaction Sector, in: De Economist, vol. 153, pp. 139-165

Datta, C./A. Yadwadkar/S. Madheswaran/ S. Datta/R. Nilakantan 2004: Implications of Transactions Sector Growth for the Indian Economy: 1950-2003, Working Paper Centre for Management in Agriculture, Indian Institute of Management, Ahmedabad, http://www.iimahd.ernet.in/download.php?downloadid=307 (November 7th, 2008)

Davis, L. 1986: Comment, in: S. Engerman/R. Gallman (eds.) Long-Term Factors in American Economic Growth, Chicago and London, University of Chicago Press, pp. 149-161

Dollery, B./W. Leong 1998: Measuring the Transaction Sector in the Australian Economy 1911 - 1991, in: Australian Economic History Review, vol. 38, pp. 207-231

Eissrich, D. 2001: Systemtransformation aus Sicht der Neuen Institutionenökonomik, Frankfurt and New York, Campus

Ghertman, M. 1998: Measuring Macro-economic Transaction Costs: A Comparative Perspective and Possible Policy Implications, Paper presented at the 2nd Annual Conference of the International Society for New Institutional Economics

Hazledine, T. 2001: Measuring the New Zealand Transaction Sector, 1956-98: with an Australian Comparison, in: New Zealand Economic Papers, vol. 35, pp. 77-100

International Standard Classification of Occupations, ISCO-88, International Labour Organization, http://www.ilo.org/public/english/bureau/stat/isco/index.htm (November 7th, 2008)

Löchel, H. 1995: Institutionen, Transaktionskosten und wirtschaftliche Entwicklung, Berlin, Duncker and Humblot

NACE 2002: Statistical Classification of Economic Activities in the European Community, NACE Rev. 1.1 (2002)

National Statistical Institute (NSI) 2002-2007: Statistical Yearbook of the Republic of Bulgaria, Sofia, National Statistical Institute

Parker, W. 1988: Old Themes and New Techniques, in: Journal of Economic History, vol. 48, pp. 428–435

Reichhardt, M. 1995: Der Beitrag des Transaktionskostenansatzes zu einer Theorie der Transformation von Wirtschaftsordnungen, Frankfurt, Lang

Sulejewicz, A./P. Graca 2005: Measuring the Transaction Sector in the Polish Economy, 1996 - 2002, Paper presented at the 9th Annual Conference of the International Society for New Institutional Economics, Barcelona, 22-25 September, http://www.isnie.org/ISNIE05/Papers05/Sulejewicz_Graca.pdf (November 7th, 2008)

Wallis, J./D. North 1986: Measuring the Transaction Sector in the American Economy, 1870-1970, in: S. Engerman/R. Gallman (eds.) Long-Term Factors in American Economic Growth, Chicago and London, University of Chicago Press, pp. 95-148

Wallis, J./D. North 1988: Should Transaction Costs be Subtracted from Gross National Product? in: Journal of Economic History, vol. 48, pp. 651-654

Appendix

Table 3: Statistical Classification of Economic Activities in the European Community

Type	Code	Name	By function	By sector
section	A	Agriculture, hunting and forestry	non-transaction	private
section	B	Fishing	non-transaction	private
section	C	Mining and quarrying	non-transaction	private
section	D	Manufacturing	non-transaction	private
section	E	Electricity, gas and water supply	non-transaction	public
section	F	Construction	non-transaction	private
section	H	Hotels and restaurants	non-transaction	private
section	I	Transport, storage and communication		
• division	60	Land transport; transport via pipelines	non-transaction	public
• division	61	Water transport	non-transaction	private
• division	62	Air transport	non-transaction	public
• division	63	Supporting and auxiliary transport activities; activities of travel agencies	non-transaction	private
• division	64	Post and telecommunications		
○ group	64.1	Post and courier activities	transaction	public
○ group	64.2	Telecommunications	non-transaction	public
section	L	Public administration and defence; compulsory social security		
○ group	75.1	Administration of the State and the economic and social policy of the community	calculated in transaction services	
○ group	75.2	Provision of services to the community as a whole	calculated in transaction services	
○ group	75.3	Compulsory social security activities	non-transaction	public
section	M	Education	non-transaction	public
section	N	Health and social work	non-transaction	public
section	O	Other community, social and personal service activities		
• division	90	Sewage and refuse disposal, sanitation and similar activities	non-transaction	public
• division	91	Activities of membership organizations n.e.c.	non-transaction	private
• division	92	Recreational, cultural and sporting activities	non-transaction	private
• division	93	Other service activities	non-transaction	private

Source: Own presentation.

Table 4: Transaction industries as a percentage of GDP

Year	1997	1998	1999	2000	2001	2002	2003	2004	2005	2006
Financial inter- mediation	3.93	3.5	4.06	4.17	4.33	4.76	5.14	6.1	7.31	6.83
Real estates, renting & business activities	4.89	5.98	6.62	7.41	7.77	8.31	8.63	9.62	9.73	10.79
Trade and repair	15.51	11.59	13.5	15.07	15.07	14.92	15.06	16.13	19.08	19.9
Total	24.33	21.07	24.18	26.65	27.17	27.99	28.83	31.85	36.12	37.52

Source: Own calculations.

Table 5: Non-transaction industries as a percentage of GDP

Year	1997	1998	1999	2000	2001	2002	2003	2004	2005	2006
Agriculture, hunting and forestry; Fishing	0.28	0.33	0.27	0.25	0.21	0.20	0.20	0.18	0.16	0.14
Construction	0.26	0.30	0.35	0.29	0.28	0.26	0.28	0.29	0.32	0.36
Mining and quarrying	0.18	0.17	0.15	0.13	0.12	0.12	0.12	0.12	0.11	0.11
Manufacturing (ind.)	1.94	2.00	1.81	1.64	1.57	1.59	1.61	1.56	1.54	1.53
Transport, storage, communication	0.06	0.10	0.14	0.22	0.24	0.28	0.33	0.56	0.59	0.65
Hotels & restaurants	0.18	0.19	0.19	0.19	0.21	0.21	0.26	0.26	0.28	0.31
Services: municipal, social, personal, other	0.08	0.10	0.14	0.17	0.18	0.21	0.23	0.23	0.24	0.24
Total	2.98	3.19	3.05	2.89	2.81	2.87	3.03	3.20	3.24	3.34

Source: Own calculations.

Table 6: Transaction services as a percentage of GDP

Year	1997	1998	1999	2000	2001	2002	2003	2004	2005	2006
State administration	1.33	2.52	2.58	3.31	2.85	2.57	2.82	2.54	2.65	2.77
Justice system	0.24	0.34	0.33	0.38	0.36	0.45	0.51	0.58	0.62	0.67
National defence	2.55	2.56	2.72	2.77	2.43	2.56	2.38	2.25	2.16	2.01
Public security and fire protection	1.18	1.74	1.99	2.03	2.02	2.27	2.27	2.18	2.08	1.94
Total	5.30	7.16	7.62	8.49	7.66	7.85	7.98	7.55	7.51	7.39

Source: Own calculations.

Table 7: Non-transaction services as a percentage of GDP

Year	1997	1998	1999	2000	2001	2002	2003	2004	2005	2006
Education	1.31	1.60	1.72	1.80	1.66	1.77	1.80	1.72	1.64	1.55
Health and social security	0.91	1.12	1.11	1.04	1.01	1.10	1.21	1.22	1.19	1.06
Transport, storage, communication	1.01	1.01	0.98	0.85	0.84	0.81	0.79	0.52	0.51	0.49
Services: municipal, social, personal, other	0.16	0.21	0.22	0.21	0.20	0.20	0.20	0.20	0.21	0.20
Electricity, gas and water supply	0.27	0.35	0.39	0.37	0.38	0.38	0.40	0.39	0.37	0.37
Total	3.66	4.29	4.42	4.27	4.09	4.26	4.40	4.05	3.92	3.67

Source: Own calculations.

SOCIAL EFFECTS OF GOVERNMENT SUBSIDIES TO LOCAL PUBLIC GOODS

IVAN IVANOV / JULIA DOBREVA
(SOFIA UNIVERSITY "ST. KLIMENT OHRIDSKI", BULGARIA)

1. Introduction

In Europe the initiative for fiscal decentralization has been undertaken during the last decade as a revolutionary approach towards a better public financial management and an increased social awareness of public policy. It is not just an alternative instrument for economic development, rather it is an outcome of the growing need for active participation of the various communities within a given country in the social, economic, environmental and political life in their regions.

It is well-known that the state fiscal policy is a union of two, mutually dependent policies - a policy of public expenses directed towards the provision of strictly defined public goods and a tax policy that serves as a source for financing these costs. Since 1989 (the threshold year which marks the end of communism and the beginning of democracy) there has been a political trend in Bulgaria to reform the tax policy, but the structure and effectiveness of the public expenses have often been neglected and underestimated. This has caused an imbalance in the policy making and has in its turn led to the realization that the old system of centralized budgets should be replaced by fiscal decentralization. The moment is marked by an important historical event - the accession of Bulgaria to the EU in the beginning of 2007. By the end of 2006 only 5% of the tax income was transferred to the municipality budgets (while the average for Europe was 20-30%).

In the beginning of 2007, with the fourth amendment in the Constitution of the Republic of Bulgaria, the municipalities were given the right to determine the rates of their local taxes and also one or two other taxes. This has caused a remarkable increase in the municipality income of more than 10% for the last two years with about 21% of capital expenditure. Along with the change in the Constitution, the Bulgarian government adopted the so called *Strategy for Fiscal Decentralization*, which is an important programming document, laying down the basic principles for improvement in the standard of life and in the quality of the provided local public goods and services. The process is further accelerated by the new opportunities for financing investment projects through EU funds. Thus, there has been a remarkable increase in the levels of responsibilities of the local governments with regard to the choice of local public goods provided, starting from schools, kindergartens, health and social services centres on the one hand, and, on the other hand, improvements in the basic infrastructure like roads, sewage and water supply networks.

The provision of local public goods and the effect of subsidies for their supply have been subject to a number of recent studies such as we find in Akai and Ihori (2002: 227-239) as well as in Greenberg (1983: 17-33, 1977: 137-150). This subject matter is further treated in the comparative analyses of local public goods and clubs presented by Scotchmer (2002: 1998-2042) and the studies on the provision of central public goods such as in the works of Faguet (2004). These publications excel in their approaches at treating the problem of government financing schemes and the benefit of local communities as an outcome of the instruments applied. Furthermore, in the mid 1980s and early 1990s, the scientific interest was focused on the private supply of public goods, with the most outstanding examples in Andreoni and Bergstrom (1996: 295-308) and in Bergstrom, Blume and Varian (1986: 25-49).

However, there are other authors in whose analyses, like, for example, the analysis we find in Triesman (1999: 488-517), a decentralised provision of public goods lead to a higher redistribution of income, economic inefficiency, and political instability. It is often a more global question which instigates the analysis of this problem and which is mainly concerned with the idea of whether a decision in favour of a decentralised economy by providing independence to the local governments is preferable and whether there are any unique advantages of such a policy.

In this paper we try to briefly propose a comparison between centrally financed and locally provided public goods in a Nash equilibrium model, considering also the consumption and financing of private goods. The results of our study will be pointing towards the efficiency attained in providing government transfers for the production of public goods on the local level. Moreover, we will propose a classification of the goods which will help in differentiating them in any further analyses on consumption choice and the measurement of social welfare.

2. Model

The model which we propose in this paper is entirely based on the optimization model, derived from the consumption theory and applied to the study of public goods, in particular, the choice between locally and centrally provided public goods and the degree of social effects attained in this process. in the first place, we consider the function $u(c,G)+H$, which is continuous, monotonically increasing, twice differentiable, quasi-concave and homogeneous of degree one. In our model the function $u(c,G)+H$ is the objective function which we want to maximize under a certain linear constraint. The model takes the following form:

$$\max u(c,G)+H$$
$$\text{s.t. } \langle p^1,c\rangle + \langle p^2,G\rangle \le I-T$$

where $c=(c_1,c_2,...,c_s)$ is private consumption, $G=(G_{s+1},G_{s+2},...,G_n)$ is the vector of local public goods, which are entirely financed through the private donations of local residents, and H - a constant -, is the aggregate quantity of centrally provided pure public goods (central public goods); $p^1=(p_1,p_2,...,p_s)$ is the vector of prices paid for the consumption of the private goods and the vector $p^2=(p_{s+1},p_{s+2},...,p_n)$ represents the private contribution to the supplied local public goods, I defines consumer income before taxation, which is designated by T.

For the purposes of our analysis we shall introduce the value function $v(p,B)$, which takes the following form:

$$v(p,B)=\max_{c,G,\ge 0} u(c,G)+H \qquad (1)$$
$$\text{s.t. } \langle p^1,c\rangle + \langle p^2,G\rangle \le B$$

where B is income after taxation. By using the first order condition, the solution to equation (1) is the vector $x^*(p,B)$ with coordinates $x^*_k = x^*_k(p, B)$, for $k = 1, 2, \ldots, n$. To describe the Nash equilibrium we shall use the dual approach by defining the following expenditure function:

$$E(p,U)=\min_{c,G\ge 0}\langle p^1,c\rangle + \langle p^2,G\rangle \qquad (2)$$
$$\text{s.t. } u(c,G)+H \ge U$$

The function $h^*_k = h^*_k(p,U)$, for $k=1,2,...,n$ forms the vector $h^*(p,U)=(h_1(p,U),...,h_n(p,U))$ which is a solution to the problem. According to the properties of consumption theory found in Mas-Collel, et al. (1995: 5-127) and in Varian (1992: 85-102) and their generalization, considered in Ivanov and Dobreva (2007: 161-163), the point of minimum coincides with the point of maximum, i.e. the solution to equations (1) and (2) is one and the same vector. Based on this we derive the following equation:

$$\frac{\partial x_i(p^*,B^*)}{\partial p_j} = \frac{\partial h_i(p^*,U^*)}{\partial p_j} - x_j(p^*,B^*)\frac{\partial x_i(p^*,B^*)}{\partial B} \qquad (3)$$

for $i,j=1,2,...,n$.

Equation (3) is the Slutsky equation, well-known from consumption theory, describing the total effect on optimal consumption choice as a result of the impact of the substitution and income effect.

Depending on the changes in the value of the price p and the constraint B, the local public goods and the private goods which comprise the optimal vector x^* can be classified as *normal/ordinary goods, luxurious, necessary, inferior or Giffen goods.* Local public and private goods could be also classified as *substitutes* or *complements.* It is then the two basic elements – price and income – which determine the type of the private and local public goods being consumed, based on the consumption level within a given community.

3. The social effect of consuming local public goods

In this part of our analysis we focus our attention on the process of consuming local public goods, discussed by Bergstrom, Blume and Varian, 1986: 25-49), as well as by Faguet (2004), Greenberg (1983: 17-33, 1977: 137-150), and Scotchmer (2002: 1998-2042). By applying our dual model in the form presented in section 2, we will support their claim that local communities are better off under a decentralised provision of public goods than under a centralized one.

In the first place, it should be noted that it is mainly the decentralised provision of public goods that takes into account the preferences of local residents. Therefore, the utility maximization problem for the locally provided aggregate public good G and, respectively, for the consumed aggregate private good c can be presented in the form:

$$\begin{aligned} & v(p,\tau,I) = \max u(c,G) \\ & \text{s.t. } p_1 c + G(\tau + p_2) = I \end{aligned} \qquad (4)$$

Here, in contrast to equation (1), we consider that there is an additional financing of the local public goods through the collection of taxes. In (4), τ is taxes paid by local residents and p_2 is the amount of private contribution for the financing of local public goods. It is clear that equation (4) excludes the provision of centrally provided public goods but at the same time it most realistically represents the optimal level of social utilities obtained from the consumption of locally provided public goods. The residents within a given community consume as much of the local public goods G as they are willing to pay directly (through their private contribution p_2) and indirectly through taxation τ. Hence, the local residents have to solve the following problem as well:

$$\begin{aligned} & E(p,U) = \min p_1 c + G(\tau + p_2) \\ & \text{s.t. } u(c,G) = U \end{aligned} \qquad (5)$$

The decision on whether to consume a certain combination of private and public goods is taken on the basis of available income and preferences. Therefore, consumption is confined to specified and clearly defined income groups, so that in case of governmental transfers to the local budget in the form of subsidies, as presented in the following section of this paper, there is no leakage of resources to other non-contributing communities. These claims lead us to the conclusion that the indirect utility function of decentralised, locally provided public goods most genuinely designates optimality in consumption and marks the social effect of public goods on a local level. The main idea lying behind this fact is that local residents maximize their utility by consuming as much of the public goods as they prefer and also make private contributions to provide for their financing. Thus, the goods provided (1) impact the level of maximum utility at minimum expenditure and (2) are consumed on a local level by certain pre-defined income groups, who are willing to contribute to the supply of these goods through private contributions or who benefit from the local public goods as a result of the government's decentralization policy.

Figure 1: Social effect of local public goods

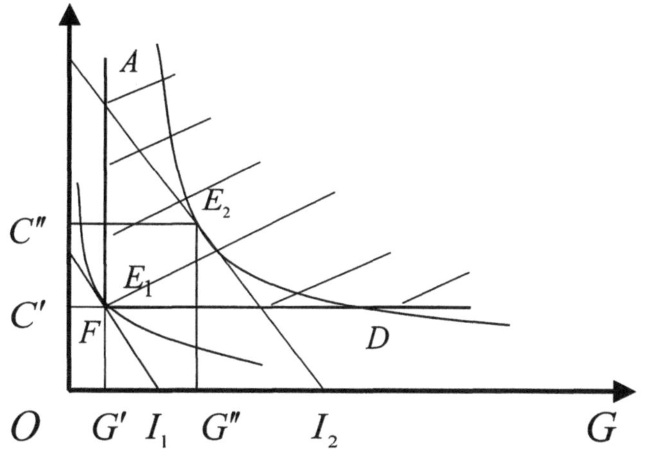

In fig. 1 the initial point of optimality $E_1(G',c')$ should be considered as a solution to the dual problem formulated through equations (4)-(5) under budget I_1 so that the Pareto efficient allocation is found in the shaded area, more precisely in the triangle *AFD*, considering the budget lines I_1 and I_2. This means that all consumption bundles in this area represent combinations of private and local public goods which increase in quantity and respectively bring about an increase in utility. Secondly, fixing the price vector p to a constant level causes an increase only in the budget levels, i.e. $I_2 > I_1$ and thus we have the point $E_2(G'',c'')$ which is a solution to the equations (4)-(5) under budget I_2. Hence, the local residents are in any case better off at point $E_2(G'',c'')$ than at the initial point of optimality $E_1(G',c')$, which demonstrates an increased social welfare effect. Then it follows from equation (3) that the effect on the change in consumption is a result of the income effect only. Our claim is that in equations (4)-(5), representing locally provided public goods, it is mainly the income effect that impacts the level of consumption.

With the isolation of the substitution effect it becomes clear that the quantities of both goods C and G can either remain constant at the initial point of the Nash equilibrium or increase. Therefore, we can claim that fixing the price of private goods to constant, the local public goods can be either normal, ordinary or luxurious goods. Rarely could it be the case for these goods to fall below the initial optimality levels, i.e. become Giffen or inferior goods. Again, it should be pointed out that the local provision of goods (be they private or public) takes into consideration the precise measurement of preferences of the local residents. Therefore, we can reach the conclusion that social welfare and Pareto improvement are possible only with decentralised provision of public goods rather than with centralized one.

To provide a further proof to this statement we shall now look at the case where we have centrally financed public goods and private goods. The central public good has one major advantage - it can be accessed by everyone and, in most of the cases, free of charge. However, it does not always bring about utility to the consumers and often it may be easily given up and replaced by a private equivalent. Certainly, in this case the reasons for this could be various but the most common ones are bad quality of the good which causes zero utility and lack of personalised elements in the supply process. In this case, in contrast to the previous one, when $\tau = const$ and both p and I change, we have the substitution effect along with the income effect and the consumption bundle is very likely to be positioned outside the Pareto efficient shaded area. Thus, the precise positioning of the point of optimality is hard to be defined and at the possibility of having such a level of consumption that classifies the central public goods or the private goods as Giffen or inferior leaves serious doubts as to the positive social effect in supplying such goods.

4. The social effect of subsidies on the optimal supply of local public goods

The social effect of subsidies on the optimal supply of local public goods has been discussed by a number of recent studies such as we find in Akai and Ihori (2002: 227-239) and Andreoni and Bergstrom (1996: 295-308). According to the theoretical analysis in Jackson and Brown (1995), depending on the decision of the local self-government, there are three main directions for the allocation of the government transfer: for financing new public goods, to cover the costs for the provision of new as well as existing public goods, and entirely for financing the currently supplied local public goods.

The maximization problem in the supply of public goods takes the following form:

$$v(\tau, B_G) = \max_{G \geq 0} u(G) \qquad (9)$$
$$\text{s.t. } \langle \tau, G \rangle = B_G$$

where the objective function $u(G)$ is the utility function, $G = (G_1, G_2, ..., G_m)$ is the amount of local public goods, $\tau = (\tau_1, \tau_2, ..., \tau_m)$ is a vector, representing the amount of taxes paid by the local consumers and used for financing these goods, and B_G is the available budget of the local government. Hence, the solution to problem (9) is the Marshallean demand function $x^*(\tau, B_G)$, which represents the optimal choice of locally supplied public goods.

Formulating the dual to this problem, we get the expenditure minimization problem:

$$E(\tau, U) = \min_{G_i \geq 0} \langle \tau, G \rangle \qquad (10)$$
$$\text{s.t. } u(G) \geq U$$

where the function $E(\tau, U)$ is the expenditure function for the supplied local public goods.

When transferring government grant ζ, the available budget constraint becomes $\langle \tau - \zeta, G \rangle = B_G$, and it should be further redistributed among the existing local public goods and those planned to be provided. The government grant $\zeta = (\zeta_1, ..., \zeta_m)$ is a vector attributable to each particular local public good, where *m* equals the number of public goods supplied.

In equations (9)-(10) it is the substitution effect that influences, as a result of the government transfer, the change in the consumption levels for the supplied local public goods. This is a proof that the subsidies to the decentralised budgets have the same consumer demand effect as the collection of taxes – the greater amount of subsidies reduces the tax rates and this consequently leads to an increase in the available consumer income and also in the quantities of goods consumed. Hence, it is either the reduction of taxes or the transfer of government grants that changes the budget levels and influences local consumption as a result of the substitution effect.

Therefore, the overall effect from subsidizing public goods on a local level results in a reduction in the level of local taxes and respectively increases the available consumers' budget. Based on the results of our equations (4)-(5), (7)-(8), and (9)-(10), we can draw the conclusion that the social effect of government transfers to local public goods is attained through two major instruments - the amount of grants in combination with any private donations provided by the local community representatives. It is predictable to postulate that the substitution effect in the analysed equations (9)-(10) actually measures, through the application of the Slutsky equation (3), the social effect of public goods supplied on a local level and the aggregate welfare effect on a national level. In this sense, we put forward the notion that the decentralised management of the state budget is better in terms of social effectiveness than the centralized allocation of resources for the provision of public goods as it closely monitors and takes into consideration the utility level of the local residents and most effectively controls the allocation of the grants by targeting them at particular local public goods. Thus, through the management of grants, collected taxes and donations, the local self-governments actually make more precise decisions on the quantities of the supplied local public goods and most effectively redirect the quantities from private consumption to public and vice versa to achieve a better social impact and a higher equilibrium level.

6. Conclusion

The aim of this paper was to provide a model of comparison between centrally and locally provided public goods and to argue in favour of the decentralised approach in this supply process. It was mainly inspired by the recent changes in the Bulgarian fiscal policy, aiming at full decentralisation and thus entrusting the local authorities with the responsibilities to define the levels of local public goods provided within the communities. The positive social effect of the fiscal decentralisation in the case of Bulgaria is clearly proven by the doubled increase in the municipal budgets and the growing interest in the implementation of investment projects that are co-financed by the government and by EU funds. Our conclusions made it evident that social welfare is possible in most of the cases only when we have a local distribution of public goods due to the respect of preference levels, the stability of income groups and the absence of leakage of government transfers to goods, which are provided to residents with zero utility from their usage. We claimed that the opposite is true for the centrally supported public goods.

Our contribution to the available literature treating this topic is the use of the dual problem and its results in the examples that support our claims. We applied the Slutsky equation to define, as in our previous works, the type of local public goods consumed, depending on the Marshallean and the Hicksian demand functions. Furthermore, we postulated that the social effect in the supply of local public goods is achieved through the income effect which changes the level of optimality and, along with this, the type of goods consumed according to the proposed classification. Our contribution is that in addition to these conclusions, the social effect of local public goods is further increased through the provision of government subsidies and in this case it is measured by the substitution effect. We further explained that local governments make better and more reasonable decisions on the allocation of the available financial resources than the central government. They target it at particular public goods that are socially effective, taking into account any changes that might occur in price and quantity, and this is largely based on the fact that they have more precise information on the utility attained by the local residents and respectively the behaviour of the income groups which are direct consumers of these goods.

References

Akai, N. / T. Ihori 2002: Central government subsidies to local public goods, in: Economics of Governance, vol. 3, pp. 227-239

Andreoni, J. / T. Bergstrom 1996: Do government subsidies increase the private supply of public goods, in: Public Choice, vol. 88, pp. 295-308

Bergstrom, T. / L. Blume / H. Varian 1986: On the private provision of public goods, in: Journal of Public Economics, vol. 29, pp. 25-49

Faguet, Jean-Paul 2004: Why so much centralization? A model of primitive centripetal accumulation: Working Paper, in: Suntory and Toyota International Centres for Economics and Related Disciplines, London School of Economics and Political Science, London, UK

Greenberg, J. 1983: Local public goods with mobility: Existence and optimality of a general equilibrium, in: Journal of Economic Theory, vol. 30, pp. 17-33

Greenberg, J. 1977: Existence of an equilibrium with arbitrary tax schemes for financing local public goods, in: Journal of Economic Theory, vol. 16, pp. 137-150

Ivanov, I. / J. Dobreva 2007: Application of the optimization model and the Slutsky equation in the supply of public goods, in: University of Rousse Conference Proceedings, vol. 46, book 4 – Economics and Management, pp. 161-165

Jackson, P. M. / C. V. Brown 1995: Public Sector Economics, 4th ed., Blackwell, Oxford UK & Cambridge USA

Mas-Collel, A. et al. 1995: Microeconomic Theory, Oxford University Press

Scotchmer, Suzanne 2002: Local Public Goods and Clubs, in: Alan Auerbach / Martin Feldstein (eds.): Handbook of Public Economics. vol. 4, Amsterdam, pp. 1998-2042

Triesman, Daniel 1999: Political Decentralization and Economic Reform: A Game-Theoretic Analysis, in: American Journal of Political Science, vol. 43, No 2, pp. 488-517

Varian, Hal R. 1992: Microeconomic Analysis, W. W. Norton & Company, New York, NY

Chapter four:

STUDIES ON THE EUROPEAN UNION AND GERMANY

Challenging Budgetary Situations – Municipal Management

Thomas Lenk / Oliver Rottmann / Tatsiana Makarevich
(Leipzig University, Germany)

1. Introduction

Traditionally, most European countries have a relatively well developed public sector whose tasks and services were continuingly expanded in past decades both at the state and municipal levels. In a large number of countries, including Germany, this development led to an increase of public expenditures, which could not be covered by appropriate revenues, thus causing a persistent deficit financing. Due to the resulting interest and redemption payments, municipalities have an ever decreasing financial room for manœuvre. The debt itself causes further expenditures such as costs of borrowing, interest payments (depending on the key interest rate and the national or municipal debt management) and thereby incurring opportunity costs.

After the new EU Member States from Central and Eastern Europe faced difficult social transformation processes in the 1990s, state and local bodies are facing intense fiscal pressure. At the same time, they are confronted with an infrastructure in dire need of repair. Furthermore, efforts to meet the accession criteria of the European Monetary Union within the Treaty of Maastricht place strong pressures on governments to enforce budget discipline. The recent economic downturn has additionally complicated the compliance with international obligations (GÖW 2003: 94).

Many European regions are affected by demographic trends such as a declining and ageing population, i.e. changes in the population age structure at the expense of the economically active population (inter alios Deutsche Bundestag 2002). A lot of municipalities are confronted with shrinking population figures and decreasing revenues, therefore they have to adapt the provision of the public services to changing demands and conditions.

On the one hand, there is a wide range of support instruments for regional development at the European level; on the other hand, however, the development objectives of the structural and cohesion policy of the EU often do not meet the needs of regional development, as issuing policy guidelines in the EU multi-level system is not an area falling within the competence of the regional level, but of the European Commission instead.

The following article examines the consequences of the above mentioned facts and developments on the municipal policy within the European Union. Firstly, we will consider the framework conditions of public or municipal management. In doing so, we will put particular emphasis on services of general interest (i. e. the qualitative and quantitative assurance of service provision by public bodies) and their framework conditions changed by the implementation of EU-legislation. Secondly, demographic and regional political planning implications of services of general interest are discussed and the possibilities for the use of the EU-support policy are outlined. Finally, the option of privatisation of public services and, especially, the role of Public-Private-Partnerships (PPP) are to be discussed.

2. Characteristics of Public/Municipal Management

2.1 Characteristics of Public Management

For the most part, public and especially municipal management follows a different premise than private enterprise management. While private enterprises are subject to market forces and competition, municipal management is obligated to the EU-competitive policy as well as to provide services of general interest, i.e. fulfilling public service obligations. Within the framework of this interdependence between competition and services of general interest, the municipal debt situation plays a major role in the possible room for manœuvre of budgetary policy. Furthermore, public enterprises must act within the framework of the strategic objectives of the municipality.

2.2 The Concept of Services of General Interest

Services of general interest include those services that exceed the benefits for a single citizen and aim to secure the standard of living of all citizens and to enhance the social development. Therefore, the concept reflects the duty of the regional authorities to provide the most necessary infrastructure services. Originally, services of general interest were within responsibilities of the Member States and became only an issue at the European level with the Treaty of the European Union (Treaty of Amsterdam) in 1997. Furthermore, according to the European Commission (2000: 4) services of general interest are a key element in the European model of society. By this, the tradition of the Member States is taken up to provide high-quality public services. National jurisdictions in this area are also recognized. In addition, in Green and White Papers as well as in guidelines it was stated that the Member States had the right to define these services and to determine quality, amount, method and price regulation (European Commission 2003: 3, 9).

The concept of services of general interest applies in particular to goods and services which are essential to the existence of the citizens, thus must be offered nation-wide and at politically – i.e. publicly – controlled prices for all users. Especially, it implies those goods whose technical production conditions foster the monopolisation of the supply-side (the so-called natural monopoly). A natural monopoly is a situation where one company can supply the desired output for a good or service at a lower cost than two or more companies can.[1] The following areas fall under the heading of "general interest":

- sewage disposal,
- waste management,
- water and energy supply,
- hospitals,
- local public transport,
- museums,
- theatre,
- retirement homes,
- schools (inter alios Otto 2002: 23), etc.

As a rule, the performance of services of general interest must fulfil the following criteria according to the Treaty of Lisbon: a high level of quality, safety and affordability, equal treatment and the promotion of universal access. Beyond that, the incorporating of social, cultural or environmental aspects (Budäus 2003: 25) are widely discussed in literature.

2.3 Historical Development of the Concept of Services of General Interest

The EU term *"services of general interest"* corresponds to the German term *"Daseinsvorsorge"*[2] which goes back to Ernst Forsthoff (1938). However, it has changed its original character in the course of the years. Forsthoff's intention was to demonstrate the dependence of the urban citizens on public services and, thus, to clarify the responsibility of the state to provide these services (Püttner 2003: 1). As an example, he discusses energy and water supply. However, the concept of competition is not included into Forsthoff's scheme, as it did not play any significant role in the economic policies at that time.

---

[1] It is motivated by the subadditivity of the cost function, i.e. the production costs of a single supplier are lower than the sum of the costs of multiple suppliers together producing the same amount of services. In the majority of relevant cases, decreasing average costs were observed, i.e. the growing production volume results in decreasing average costs per unit (the economies of scale).

[2] Literal translation: provision for existence.

From our point of view, however, Forsthoff's definition falls short as it does not explain the existing interaction of services of general interest and competition. Nowadays, competition is used as *one instrument* for the implementation of services of general interest. The competitive thought can be traced back to the liberal trends and influences from the USA which gained ground in post-war (Western) Europe. However, the idea of public services cannot be found in the minds of the economic-liberal competitive theorists (Püttner 2003: 3).

The concept of *services of general interest* is neither an idea exclusively related to the welfare state philosophy, nor does it possess an illiberal character. Rather, it encompasses those services essential to the implementation of basic rights (Ronellenfitsch 2005: 201). Services of general interest are regulated by public law and imply a certain *guarantor position of the state*. The government *has to* provide the respective services either itself or to let a third party provide them. The government *can* provide services either itself or generate a competition.

Competition is not an end in itself; it helps to secure public services in an efficient and effective way and hereby to save costs of the public sector. That is why the municipality must have the choice of structures for the performance of public tasks. In cases of distorted competition (e.g. by cross subsidisation), public companies might have trouble competing with private enterprises (inter alios Ronellenfitsch 2005: 202).

In the Treaty of Lisbon, the concept of services of general interest is motivated by the goals and aims of article 14[3], article 106[4] TFEU in con-

---

[3] Article 14 TFEU (ex Article 16 TEC):

„Without prejudice to Article 4 of the Treaty on European Union or to Articles 93, 106 and 107 of this Treaty, and given the place occupied by services of general economic interest in the shared values of the Union as well as their role in promoting social and territorial cohesion, the Union and the Member States, each within their respective powers and within the scope of application of the Treaties, shall take care that such services operate on the basis of principles and conditions, particularly economic and financial conditions, which enable them to fulfil their missions. The European Parlament and the Council, acting by means of regulations in accordance with the ordinary legislative procedure, shall establish these principles and set these conditions without prejudice to the competence of Member States, in compliance with the Treaties, to provide, to commission and to fund such services.", in: Official Journal C 115, 9.5.2008, p. 54.

[4] Article 106 TFEU:

"(1) In the case of public undertakings and undertakings to which Member States grant special or exclusive rights, Member States shall neither enact nor maintain in force any measure contrary to the rules contained in the Treaties, in particular to those rules provided for in Article 18 and Articles 101 to 109.

nection with the principle of the free and undistorted competition (art. 119 TFEU[5]) (Schwintowski 2003: 283). Article 14 TFEU specifies the legislative competence of the EU for services of general economic interest and presents a fundamental revision of the corresponding Article 16 of the Maastricht Treaty which stated a certain exemption provision to the competition rules (Püttner 2003: 4). Thus, it emphasizes much stronger the idea of competition. At the same time, the Treaty of Lisbon as well assumes that market imperfections represent inevitable by-products of a market economy, for example, within the scope of public goods, external effects, natural monopolies, asymmetries of information or distorted preferences. Therefore, the special position of the public services will continue to be protected. Article 106 TFEU refers explicitly only to services of general economic interest and, in doing so, excludes non-

---

(2) Undertakings entrusted with the operation of services of general economic interest or having the character of a revenue-producing monopoly shall be subject to the rules contained in the Treaties, in particular to the rules on competition, in so far as the application of such rules does not obstruct the performance, in law or in fact, of the particular tasks assigned to them. The development of trade must not be affected to such an extent as would be contrary to the interests of the Union.

(3) The Commission shall ensure the application of the provisions of this Article and shall, where necessary, address appropriate directives or decisions to Member States.", in: Official Journal of the European Union C 115, 9.5.2008, pp. 90/91.

[5] Article 119 TFEU:

"(1) For the purposes set out in Article 3 of the Treaty on European Union, the activities of the Member States and the Union shall include, as provided in the Treaties, the adoption of an economic policy which is based on the close coordination of Member States' economic policies, on the internal market and on the definition of common objectives, and conducted in accordance with the principle of an open market economy with free competition.

(2) Concurrently with the foregoing, and as provided in the Treaties and in accordance with the procedures set out therein, these activities shall include a single currency, the euro, and the definition and conduct of a single monetary policy and exchange-rate policy the primary objective of both of which shall be to maintain price stability and, without prejudice to this objective, to support the general economic policies in the Union, in accordance with the principle of an open market economy with free competition.

(3) These activities of the Member States and the Union shall entail compliance with the following guiding principles: stable prices, sound public finances and monetary conditions and a sustainable balance of payments.", in: Official Journal of the European Union C 115, 9.5.2008, pp. 96/97.

economic activities from the principle, i.e. those tasks that are reserved to the state (inter alios Cox 2002: 331; Schwintowski 2003: 285).

2.4 European Internal Market Integration and Municipal Services of General Interest

The welfare of the citizens as well as economic and social progress are considered as original objectives of the EU. Concerning the economic system, *an open market economy with free competition* is brought into focus (art. 119 TFEU). The EU argumentation defines competition respectively as a possibility for the enforcement of efficiency and the lowest possible prices. However, at the same time in article 3 (3) of the EU Treaty the EU is classified as a *competitive social and ecological market economy.*

Community law puts emphasis on the position of public enterprises. Besides the special protection in the area of the competition law (art. 106 (2) TFEU), services of general interest are also of great importance. Article 14 TFEU applies to the Community and the Member States within the scope of their competence to take care of the conditions for the functioning of services of general interest, which are to be formed in such a way that they can carry out the particular tasks assigned to them. Wieland (2005: 55) argues that because of the growing of services of general interest into the area of communal objectives and because of the consequent duty of the Member States to protect services of general interest, the status quo is not merely updated, instead, there is a shift of the rule-exception in favour of public welfare-oriented services.

The Member States are free to define public welfare and to provide public welfare-oriented services (Ambrosius 2007: 103). Article 345 TFEU basically gives the freedom to the Member States to choose their ownership structure. This regulation guarantees the autonomy of action. Accordingly, the municipalities of the Member States can freely choose how to provide or guarantee public services. After the municipalities have determined a certain structure (self-production, production by a third party), the EU Commission applies certain rules which must be kept (Koman 2003: 9). The EU Internal Market strategy leads to the fact that all institutions have to undergo an EU law-compatibility test.

The EU Commission as "guardian of the Treaty" sees its duty in inspecting the compatibility of the national practices of the Member States with the Internal Market and, if powers were granted, also to control it, in this case in particular the competitive law, state aid and public procurement would be employed as instruments (GÖW 2007: 2). On the municipal level it means that municipalities in being responsible for services of general interest have *the option of appointing* a third party to carry the provision of the services. However, the public enterprises *are obliged to* eliminate their monopoly position on the basis of EU law (Rottmann/Bretschneider 2007: 30). At the same time, this implies that other objectives which the municipality pursued up to now with the operation of its municipal enterprises can be at risk.

The privatisation proved to be a significant instrument for the enforcement of efficiency and competition in the public sector. However, it has to be emphasized that *internal efficiency* generated by private service production (i.e. service production at minimal costs) does not result per se in *allocation efficiency* (i.e. the transfer of minimal cost production to low prices for the consumer) (Mankel/Schwarze 2000: 424). Besides, internal efficiency does not emerge by itself; instead, it is dependent on the interdependent structures of management, supervisory board and shareholders. The new interrelation between public and private interests has to be harmonised. This involves the risk of rising conflict potential (Lenk/Rottmann 2007: 5).

Already in the 1980s and 1990s, liberalisation led to large-scale changes in the area of public management in the Member States. The process was accelerated to a varying degree in the different areas. Its progress was most noteworthy in the energy market. On the other hand, only a few changes have been observed in the areas of water supply and wastewater disposal as well as in local public transport (Bogumil/Holtkamp/Kißler 2004: 66).

2.5 Interdependence of Services of General Interest and Competition: the Example of Germany

Given the indicated interdependence between national developments and the EU legislation, the practice of services of general interest in a number of Member States is under pressure and needs adjustment (Schulz-Nieswandt 2005: 12). In the following the German practice will be regarded as an example.

Beside the regulation and provision of obligations, financing remains a key issue for services of general economic interest and, especially, for the service providing public companies. Cox (2002: 337) distinguishes between two financing levels:

- the financing of the business activities by equity as well as
- the financing of services of general economic interest by various methods of funding.

Public enterprises, which are mostly financed by borrowed capital, lose their sole supplier rights due to the intensified competition and are increasingly in need of an injection of equity capital. The possibility to finance services through monopoly pricing has dropped widely and because of competitive pricing the financial room for manœuvre is considerably restricted. Today, due to intensive competition, a significant number of public enterprises are undercapitalised.

An achievable solution lies in the (partial) privatisation of public enterprises which in the meantime has been implemented by various municipalities. Cox (2002: 338) notes in view of this process that the admission of private co-owners has changed the enterprise structures, which up to now were purely public enterprises; thus leading to changes in the interest structure, development of objectives and decision-making processes in the enterprise. Before municipalities consider privatisation it must be carefully examined, to what extent potential private partners are

- strategic investors with a long-term objective or
- pure finance investors who may have only very short-term objectives.

In principle, two reasons for privatisation are to be distinguished:

- competition policy reasons (regulatory measures in connection with the higher efficiency of private management, incentives for innovations),
- financial policy reasons (reduction of a structural deficit, debt relief).

Should a municipality decide on a privatisation of services of general interest areas, different objectives need to be taken into consideration. In particular,

- the question of a sufficient coincidence of the partner's goals (long-term approach, sustainability),
- the guarantee of cross subsidisation, jobs and training positions, as well as
- a mutual exchange of know-how has to be considered.

In requiring a compulsory competitive tender, in the recent years the European Commission has pursued a consistent extension of the free market philosophy to the public service area in order to implement the fundamental freedoms of the EC Treaty. However, this implementation is in conflict with the fact that the public service area represents an exception to the competition, due to its public welfare connections and the natural monopoly characteristics which exist in connection with the net character and the net restraint of these services. Theoretically, procurement through competitive tender is not an optimal solution, rather it is considered to be a second-best solution. The model-theoretical first-best solution of market self-regulation must fail on this occasion, - at least partially - due to the already mentioned market imperfections.

Cox (2003: 19) considers this strategy of the EU Commission as an attempt to avoid competitive exception regulations and "to put through tendering the positive effects of a dynamic free competition in the provision of the public goods with the competition around the market (...). In the process, the principle of competition is adopted as a means of pressure and as an incentive system in connection with the economic acquisition principle as its core element."

The in-house contract presents one of the possibilities for the municipalities to avoid the compulsory contract procurement. On January 11, 2005 a trendsetting judgment of the ECJ was delivered as to when the question of an in-house business is existent. Respectively, a contract has to be tendered if a private enterprise is involved in a potential contractor under company law - then an in-house procurement is discarded - the public contract procurement must take place, this means the enterprise has to participate in the tendering process (Schwintowski 2007: 92).

At the moment, it can be stated that the inter-municipal cooperation or municipal cooperation associations are not acceptable to the Commission, if:

- there is private participation,
- the municipality does not exercise sufficient control over the 100-percent subsidiaries,
- a few months after the award of a public works contract a private person takes a share in the municipal enterprise (Schwintowski 2007: 94).

The EU Commission (2007: 8) argues in this frame as follows:

> *"During the allocation of contracts below the threshold for the application of the Procurement Directive, public bodies in general have to comply with the principles of transparency, equal treatment and non-discrimination derived from the EC Treaty. However, under certain conditions small local service contracts may even be awarded without complying with the above-mentioned principles as they have no relevance to the Internal Market. This applies if, in view of their particularly low value (well below the threshold for application of the Procurement Directive which amounts currently to 211 000 EUR) and of the characteristics of the social service and the market concerned, it cannot be assumed that there is any potential interest by economic operators from other Member States to provide the service in question.*
>
> *For instance, the Commission assumed that in cases involving contracts for legal services with an average value around 5 000 EUR or planning services with a value between 6 000 EUR and 26 500 EUR (...) the contracts in question were not relevant to the Internal Market."*

For the enterprises which depend on the reliability of orders from the respective municipalities the recent legislation is difficult. Herrmann (2007: 86) points out the fact that for private enterprises the participation in semi-public companies is not very profitable if this enterprise cannot receive follow-up orders without participation in the tender procedure. Accordingly, municipalities consider the foundation of a semi-public enterprise unsuitable, if the execution of the tasks for which it was founded is to be tendered anyway.

As a result of the described developments, in future cities and municipalities must increasingly put contracts out to tender. Particularly smaller orders become more expensive, due to Europe-wide tendering (Rühle 2008: 8). However, competitive tenders cause general transaction costs (inter alios Lenk/Rottmann 2008: 23). For the preparation of the tender and the tender itself the municipalities have to provide facilities. Additional costs emerge due to the contracts, for instance, pre-contract costs, contract conclusion costs, ongoing control costs, or, where necessary, contract dispute costs. All these components are transaction costs of the tender which can have serious consequences for municipal enterprises.

Another area of problems is whether and to what extent tenders can guarantee a functioning parallel competition in the long run. The functioning of the tender depends to a large extent on the following factors:

- How many and what kind of bidders eventually participate in the tender?
- Are there any structural barriers to a market entry and, if so, how high are they?
- How high are the economic incentives of the tendered object?
- How far do the larger oligopolists, who are partially multinational or global enterprises, successfully get into the municipal markets and establish themselves there (Cox 2003: 29)?

Moreover, the danger of the "winner's curse"[6] has to be considered, as it may endanger the sustainability of the production of the services.

During the last years, due to the negative demographic development in many European regions, the implementation of the competitive philosophy has faced another problem: the remaining population in scarcely populated and structurally-weak areas does not create sufficient demand, which could potentially lead to a market establishment. Hence, the public procurement law as a competitive tool is of no help if the provision of public services in such areas is at stake. These problems are the topic of the following section.

---

6 In general, the phenomena of "winner's curse" refers to the situation when "the bidder wins the auction only because, of all the bidders, he overestimated to the greatest extent the real unknown value of the auctioned object" (Kräkel 1992: 84).

3. Demographic and Regional Planning: Political Implications of Services of General Interest

Although EU policy with its huge number of programmes aims at the elimination of regional disparities, the existing imbalances often turn out to be persistent. They form an essential cause for the partially drastic decline in population in numerous European regions, particularly in the new Member States and in Eastern Germany. Besides the decline in population, a substantial change of the population's age structure is observed resulting in changing demands in the society. Thus, elderly households are the only growing group of customers in many structurally-weak regions. These consumers have a partially high purchasing power (Böllhoff 2007: 20).

The public infrastructure as a component of services of general interest, which up to now is geared towards strengthening its performance in the first line, is oversized in the light of this background. Some services of general interest (for example, water supply and energy supply, local public passenger transport or schools) have to be reduced, due to the lack of demand. "... [I]n total, less people will be using the infrastructures and they will not utilize the whole capacity, besides, they will be paying less fees and taxes" (Junkernheinrich/Micosatt 2005: 44). This entails serious consequences for the balance between the municipal task fulfilment and financing requirements (Jakubowski 2006: 237). In the affected areas, the task is to ensure a minimum standard and to prevent the reduction of the infrastructures (Winkel 2007: 41). As public services have often been produced with a high proportion of fixed costs, the capacity adjustment can react at the changing demand only with a time delay. The costs will not reduce proportionally to the shrinking population (Lenk 2005: 9). This phenomenon is known as cost remanence or cost lag; which makes it clear that the adjustment of the offer to the sinking demand is more expensive than the growing demand.

The only way to guarantee acceptable costs of the quantitative equipment adaptation and, at the same time, guarantee a qualitative development of the infrastructural offer of services of general interest in areas with shrinking populations is by applying innovative concepts (Winkel 2008: 44). With respect to the adaptation of the infrastructure, Thrun (2003: 715) suggests six options of actions which can modify the present form of the provision of services:

(1) Enhancement of the accessibility: improvement of the transport connection, leading to an increase of capacity utilization, for instance, with the help of optimized local public transport networks, demand-oriented intervals;

(2) minimization: proportional reduction, for instance, reduced bus networks of an establishment;
(3) decentralization: fragmentation into smaller efficient units (with high connection costs), such as several organic waste management centres instead of one large waste management centre, local public offices instead of a central administration;
(4) centralization (with an accessibility strategy): centralization of those units that are not working at full capacity and complementary accessibility improvement, for instance, merging of schools and a complementary school bus system;
(5) temporary mobile approaches: provisional institutions available only at certain times (instead of closing down or not establishing these institutions), for instance, weekly markets, mobile libraries;
(6) new structuring/substitution: the goal can be achieved due to a novel way of task fulfilment, e.g. internet orders instead of shopping, merging of classes, adopting new pedagogical concepts, taxi service instead of local public passenger transport working at intervals.

The character of the demographic change depends on the region and its effect is different in every municipality. In order to be able to regard it as a chance and not only as a handicap, it is helpful to know how demography impacts other areas. Then it might be possible to react to the current processes with a structured municipal policy at an early stage (Lenk 2005: 19).

4. Support Policies

EU funding is one possible course of action to improve the financial situation of the municipality. The support options of the European Community are divided into two categories:

- the so-called Structural Funds which aim to implement a common structural policy, as well as
- the so-called action programs, which arise from the policies and objectives of various EU support programs.

4.1 Structural Funds of the EU

The Structural Funds are the most significant EU funding instruments, which help to reduce the economic and social divergences between the European regions. The cohesion policy 2007-2013 consists of three priority objectives: convergence, regional competitiveness and employment, and European territorial cooperation. In particular (European Union 2007):

1. Funded by the European Regional Development Fund, the European Social Fund and the Cohesion Fund, the convergence objective aims at the stimulation of growth and employment in lesser developed regions. This objective also highlights: innovation and knowledge-based society, adaptability to economic and social changes and the quality of environmental and administrative efficiency.
2. Also funded by the ERDF and ESF, the regional competitiveness and employment objective covers all the areas of the European Union not eligible for the convergence objective. The regional competitiveness and employment objective aims at the reinforcement of the regions' competitiveness and attractiveness as well as at employment, by anticipating economic and social changes.
3. The European territorial cooperation objective which is funded by the EDRF, aims at the reinforcement of cooperation at cross-border, transnational and inter-regional levels. It acts as a complement to the above-mentioned objectives, as the regions eligible for the convergence and regional competitiveness and employment objectives are automatically eligible for the European Territorial Co-operation objective.

National authorities used these objectives as guidelines for drafting their national strategic priorities and planning for 2007-2013 known as National Strategic Reference Frameworks (NSRF), which serves as a benchmark for the planning of funds. The national operational programs must be approved by the EU Commission. The support through EU funding happens in the way of national support programs, which must be co-financed by national (also partly regional) means. The maximum support is based on the respective support programs and varies between 50% and 85% of the eligible project costs. However, not all support programs are directed at municipal applicants. Thus, as a rule, public applicants can only access a part of the accorded funding.

4.2 Action Programs

The action programs of the European Union are support programs which are issued by the European Union to support certain political aims. They consist of the following political fields:

- education, training and youth,
- culture,
- freedom, security and justice,
- economic and financial affairs,
- environment,
- energy,

- information society,
- transport,
- research and innovation, etc.

The funds are usually granted for projects which are best suited to achieve the political objectives of the European Union because of there innovative approach. An EU support occurs in general only if other public or private funding providers take part in the whole financing. The participation percentages vary mostly between 20-70%. The decision for or against a particular project lies with the European Commission or with European or national agencies, which have been instructed in the management of certain funding. Applicants can be enterprises, federations, associations, universities, research facilities or regional and local governmental units. The project funds are awarded through Europe-wide grants which are published in the Official Journal and, depending on the program or year, there are different calls for proposals - and application modalities. Applicants do not have an entitlement to the funding, therefore support cannot be guaranteed. Rather, the applications must be conceived innovatively and attempt to reflect the respective objectives of the EU Commission.

Different Member States of the EU compete frequently with a number of project proposals for the restricted funds. To increase the chances of proving to the EU the right to a grant, the application should be planned in time and the requirements for the tender should be carefully followed. There are several agencies in Brussels and other European centres that can assist with the application process.

5. Privatisation in the Area of Services of General Interest: an Example of Public-Private Partnership

In the past, apart from complete privatisation, municipalities were applying the model of public-private partnership as an instrument of improvement in efficiency of services of general interest. The notion of public-private partnership (PPP) is not defined across the Community. "The notion generally refers to the forms of partnership between the public authorities and private enterprises for the purpose of financing, construction, renovation, operating and maintenance of an infrastructure or provision of a service" (European Commission 2004: 3). "The essence of a PPP is that the public sector does not buy an asset; it is purchasing a stream of services under specified terms and conditions." (Grimsey/Lewis 2007: 6) The central point is the synergetic effect they expect from their interaction: more effectiveness and/or efficiency than would be the case if they acted independently. PPP also distinguishes itself

from comparable organisations by the preservation of the respective identities of the parties involved (Kouwenhoven 1993: 120).
Budäus (2004: 14) describes the possible goals of the public activities of PPP projects as follows:

- the exploitation of private resourses for public functions,
- the transfer or sharing of risk with the private partner,
- the use of markets and competition structures including,
- exploitation of innovations by the public sector,
- a generally efficient fulfilment of public functions,
- politico-economic effects, particularly in form of employment and
- economic growth.

On the other hand, the goals of private enterprises participating in PPP are the following:

- a possibility to develop new areas of capital investment,
- the transfer of risk to the public sector or the sharing of risk,
- the creation and development of new markets and
- the use of PPP as the first step of the enterprise strategy towards a complete privatisation of services which had been regarded as public until now. This issue is particularly relevant if complete privatisation is not possible in the first phase due to reasons of political opportunity.

Public authorities are generally committed to specific rules or laws, such as the general principles of proper administration, whereas market parties follow the rules of the market. As a result, the objectives of the different parties are not identical (Kouwenhoven 1993: 125). These different goals result in corresponding consequences when it comes to the determination and embodiment of an enterprise's objectives; they have to be harmonised or compromised in the process of negotiation. Budäus describes the situation of the partners in this negotiation process as follows:

> "The private partner can precisely calculate the effect that different measures and actions have on his formal goal 'profit'. The public partner has to keep in mind that the perspective goals have to conform to the existing complex action and legal framework. In other words, the public partner is satisfied with the PPP only when he manages to conform the objectives to the public procurement law, spatial planning law, budget law, municipal law, subsidiary law, tax law and the contractual structure emerging with the PPP" (Budäus 2004: 20).

The problem areas, which originate from the regulation of services of general interest with the help of PPP have to be differentiated between the macroeconomic and microeconomic problem areas. With regard to the macroeconomic level, there is a danger that single marketable areas of services of general interest can develop into global oligopolistic markets. There is a danger of the development of monopolist supply structures on the regional level as well. Finally, there is a risk that in the course of the liberalisation of single markets, a substitution of the former public regional monopoly by a private monopoly will occur (Budäus 2003: 33-35).

A further complication can occur in the distribution of risks. Theoretically, risks can be classified into three categories, stated by Miller and Lassard (2001: 78-83) in the following:

- "market-related" risks (structure of demand, interest rates, exchange rates),
- "completion" risks (related to the technical realisation or applied technologies, implementation costs, failure to observe the time-limit, etc.),
- "institutional" risks (legal situation and regulation, social acceptability, likelihood that a responsible decision-making body will renegotiate contracts or property rights).

Most of these risks are common to any project-financing activity; however, there are some peculiarities of how the distribution and evaluation of risks takes place in the case of PPP. Grimsey and Lewis (2007: 176/177) show: "... [T]he risk allocation between the government and the private party in a PPP project is governed by three things: specified service obligation, the payment/pricing structure and express contractual provisions adjusting the risk allocation implicit in the basic structure". "The question for government is whether the risk premium is good value for money or whether it is more cost-effective to accept the risk itself, taking into account the likelihood of a particular risk occurring and how government bodies may be able to mitigate the impacts." (Grimsey/Lewis 2007: 179)

The interdependency of competition and political and institutional control in the area of services of general interest considered at the beginning of the article is clearly reflected in the discussed types of risk distribution and risk evaluation in the case of PPP. In the first case control is executed virtually through commodities and factor markets. Such control is only executable, if negative sanctions are applied to inefficiency and controlling errors. In case of private ownership structures, the functioning of competition results as a rule due to the risk of bankruptcy. The competition at the commodities and capital markets without any risk of bankruptcy could hardly fulfil the above mentioned functions of the competition. The same is true for institutional arrangements with public ownership structures, where the risk of bankruptcy is virtually excluded due to public ownership. The function of economic control over markets is replaced by political control (Budäus 2003: 27) with different tools and effects.

On the level of individual economic units, an essential role is played
- by transparency (the extent to which all shareholders have the same access to information and can gain the same level of understanding of the situation), related to it:
- by the quality of communication (symmetry of power, trust, cultural distance between enterprises, politics and administration) and,
- finally, by information behaviour (willingness of public enterprises to disclose information, motivation and competence of stakeholders to search, absorb and process information) (Theuvsen 2008).

An asymmetric distribution of information can cause a serious problem between the partners. According to the principal-agent theory, the actors are strongly inclined to conceal their opportunistic behaviour. Following Spremann (1990: 566) three types of opportunistic behaviour can be differentiated: "hidden characteristics", "hidden intentions" and "hidden action".[7]

Budäus (2003: 35) emphasizes that in order to resolve the conflicts and related behaviour difficulties resulting from such information asymmetry and to get protection against related negative consequences, PPP needs a professional contract, information and conflict management. Such a management can guarantee that interests of each participant, and especially of public partners, will be taken into consideration. The arising transaction costs should not be underestimated. Moreover, in a written charter or a framework document the partners should formulate and make transparent the reasons of their participation in the PPP, their goals and expectations (particularly in cases of a high formal organizational level). Finally, the partners should contractually define the respective roles, specific competences, an acceptance of risks, and the process of conflict resolution (for instance, in the articles of partnership).

As a rule, the information policy correlates with public acceptance of PPP.

The experiences in German municipalities indicate that partial privatisation or PPP can be a suitable solution to provide an efficient supply of

---

7 „Hidden characteristics refer to the characteristics of performances which are known only by the agent.(...) Hidden actions result from the deficit of information from the principal's side sourcing from the actions of agent targeted to profit from this deficit by shifting the cost to the principal and is called "moral hazard". Finally, hidden intentions are the secret intention of the agent through which the agent profits during the production of services." (Schneider/Coskun 2007: 8)

services of general interest; however, this is not necessarily the case. It is essential to take into account whether a private partner is a strategic investor, as such a partner knows the market and can strategically and functionally support a public enterprise. A financial investor, on the other hand, has the goal of rapidly getting a return on the capital investment. Thus, there is a danger of a resale of the shares in the short or medium term. Moreover, unprofitable branches can be closed down thus endangering existing workplaces.

6. Conclusion

The municipal policy has to choose the way of providing municipal services and, specifically, services of general economic interest. It has the responsibility to offer high quality services of general interest at affordable prices. The way of service delivery chosen by the municipality plays only a minor role in the context of the Ensuring State. As it follows from the above-presented analysis, a blanket recommendation is not justified.

References

Ambrosius, G. (2007): Die Europäisierung des Gemeinwohls und die Entwicklung der öffentlichen Dienstleistungen in Europa, in: D. Bräuning / D. Greiling (eds.): Stand und Perspektiven der Öffentlichen Betriebswirtschaftslehre II, Berlin, pp. 99-110

Bogumil, J. / L. Holtkamp / L. Kißler (2004): Modernisierung lokaler Politik - Auswirkungen auf das kommunale Entscheidungssystem, in: J. Werner et al., Status-Report Verwaltungsreform - Eine Zwischenbilanz nach 10 Jahren, Berlin, pp. 64-74

Böllhoff, C. (2007): Demografischer Wandel in Deutschland - Herausforderungen für die öffentliche Wirtschaft, in: Gesellschaft für öffentliche Wirtschaft (eds.): Die Zukunft der öffentlichen Dienstleistungen, Beiträge zur öffentlichen Wirtschaft, vol. 24, Berlin, pp. 7-20

Budäus, D. (2003): Die Gewährleistung der Daseinsvorsorge durch Public Private Partnership, in: U. Kirchhoff / G. Thrilling (eds.): Öffentliche Wirtschaft, Sozialwirtschaft und Daseinsvorsorge im Wandel. Zum Spannungsfeld von europäischer Wettbewerbsordnung und Allgemeininteresse, Regensburg, pp. 23-38

Budäus, D. (2004): Public Private Partnership - Ansätze, Funktionen, Gestaltungsbedarfe, in: Gesellschaft für öffentliche Wirtschaft (eds.): Public Private Partnership: Formen - Risiken - Chancen, Berlin, pp. 9-22

Commission of the European Communities (2000): Communication from the Commission - Services of General Interest in Europe, in: COM(2000) 580 final, 20.9.2000, Brussels

Commission of the European Communities (2003): Green paper on services of general interest, in: COM(2003) 270 final, 21.5.2003, Brussels.

Commission of the European Communities (2004): Green Paper on Public-Private Partnerships and Community Law on Public Contracts and Concessions, in: COM(2004) 0327 final, 30.4.2004, Brussels

Commission of the European Communities (2007): Frequently asked questions concerning the application of public procurement rules to social services of general interest, in: SEC(2007) 1514, 20.11.2007, Brussels

Consolidated versions of the Treaty on European Union and the Treaty on the Functioning of the European Union, in: Official Journal C 115, May 9, 2008, pp. 1-388

Cox, H. (2002): Dienstleistungen von allgemeinem wirtschaftlichen Interesse in Europa, Regulierung, Finanzierung, Evaluierung, gute Praktiken, in: Zeitschrift für öffentliche und gemeinwirtschaftliche Unternehmen, vol 25/3, pp. 331-339

Cox, H. (2003): Obligatorischer Ausschreibungswettbewerb bei öffentlichen Dienstleistungen - Garant für optimale Marktergebnisse?, in: Gesellschaft für öffentliche Wirtschaft (eds.): Ausschreibungswettbewerb - obligatorisch für alle Dienstleistungen, Beiträge zur öffentlichen Wirtschaft, vol. 20, Berlin, pp. 19-38

Deutscher Bundestag (2002): Schlussbericht der Enquête-Kommission „Demographischer Wandel - Herausforderungen unserer älter werdenden Gesellschaft an den Einzelnen und die Politik", Dt. BT Drs. 14/8800, March 28, 2002

European Union (2007): Cohesion Policy 2007-13 Commentaries and Official Texts, Luxemburg

Grimsey, D. /M. K. Lewis (2007): Public Private Partnerships: The Worldwide Revolution in Infrastructure Provision and Project Finance, Cheltenham

Herrmann, B. (2007): Der Einfluss der Europäischen Union auf die Zukunft der öffentlichen Dienstleistungen, in: Gesellschaft für öffentliche Wirtschaft (eds.): Die Zukunft der öffentlichen Dienstleistungen, Beiträge zur öffentlichen Wirtschaft, vol. 24, pp. 84-90

Jakubowski, P. (2006). Stadt ohne Infrastruktur heißt Stadt ohne Zukunft. Zur Agenda kommunaler Infrastrukturpolitik, in: Bundesamt für Bauwesen und Raumordnung (eds.): Zukunft städtischer Infrastruktur, Informationen zur Raumentwicklung, vol 5.2006, pp. 237-248

Junkernheinrich, M. / G. Micosatt (2005): Kommunale Daseinsvorsorge im Ruhrgebiet bei rückläufiger Bevölkerung: einnahmeseitige Handlungsspielräume, aufgabenbezogene Bedarfsverschiebungen, kommunalpolitische Handlungsoptionen, Essen

Koman, A. (2003): Szenarien für die Vergabe öffentlicher Dienstleistungen, in: Gesellschaft für öffentliche Wirtschaft (eds.): Ausschreibungswettbewerb - obligatorisch für alle Dienstleistungen, Beiträge zur öffentlichen Wirtschaft, vol. 20, pp. 8-18

Kouwenhoven, V. (1993): Public Private Partnership: A Model for the Management of Public-Private Cooperation, in: J. Kooiman (ed.): Modern Governance: New Government-society Interactions, London, pp. 119-130

Kräkel, M. (1992): Auktionstheorie und interne Organisation, Wiesbaden

Lenk, T. (2005): Gemeindefinanzbericht Sachsen 2004/2005, in: Sachsenlandkurier 9/05

Lenk, T. / O. Rottmann (2007): Öffentliche Unternehmen vor dem Hintergrund der Interdependenz von Wettbewerb und Daseinsvorsorge am Beispiel einer Teilveräußerung der Stadtwerke Leipzig, in: Arbeitspapier Nr. 36

Lenk, T. / O. Rottmann (2008): Grundlegende transaktionskostenökonomische Analyse öffentlicher vs. Privater Leistungserstellung, in: Wirtschaftswissenschaftliches Studium, vol. 1/2008, pp. 21-26

Mankel, B. / R. Schwarze (2000): Wettbewerb in der Wasserversorgung - Konzepte, Modelle, Effekte, in: Zeitschrift für öffentliche und gemeinwirtschaftliche Unternehmen, vol. 23/4, 2000, pp. 418-427

Miller, R. / D. Lessard (2001): Mapping and Facing the Landscape of Risks, in: R. Miller / D. Lessard / S. Floricel (eds.): The Strategic Management of Large Engineering Projects: Shaping Institutions, Risks, and Governance, Cambridge, pp. 75-92

Otto, R. et al., BBVL (2002): Beteiligungsmanagement in Kommunen, Stuttgart

Püttner, G. (2003), Daseinsvorsorge: Eine Idee mit Zukunft?, in: U. Kirchhoff / G. Trilling, (eds.): Öffentliche Wirtschaft, Sozialwirtschaft und Daseinsvorsorge im Wandel - Zum Spannungsfeld von europäischer Wettbewerbsordnung und Allgemeininteresse, Regensburg, pp. 1-10

Ronellenfitsch, M. (2005): Daseinsvorsorge ist originär Staatliche Aufgabe, in: Gesellschaft für öffentliche Wirtschaft (eds.): Öffentliche Dienstleistungen zwischen Eigenerstellung und Wettbewerb, Beiträge zur öffentlichen Wirtschaft, vol. 22, pp. 201-202

Rottmann, O. / W. Bretschneider (2007): Kommunales Wirtschaften in Leipzig, in C. Kunze, T. Lenk (eds.): Großstädte im Transformationsprozess vor dem Hintergrund europäischer Integration und internationalen Strukturwandels, Transformation, Leipziger Beiträge zur Wirtschaft und Gesellschaft, vol. 21/22, pp. 29-38

Rühle, H. (2008): Die Zukunft der Daseinsvorsorge nach dem Reformvertrag. Zwischen Binnenmarkt und Gemeinwohl: „Dienste von allgemeinem Interesse", http://www.heide-ruehle.de/heide2007/media/doc/1208883496118.pdf

Schneider, H. / B. Coskun, (2007): Significance and specifics of Communication in the service sector, in: F. Keuper / B. Hogenschurz (eds.): Sales & Service: Management, Marketing, Promotion und Performance, Wiesbaden, pp. 1-21

Schulz-Nieswandt, F. (2005): Daseinsvorsorge und europäisches Wettbewerbsregime, in: Gesellschaft für öffentliche Wirtschaft (eds.): Öffentliche Dienstleistungen zwischen Eigenerstellung und Wettbewerb, Beiträge zur öffentlichen Wirtschaft, vol. 22, pp. 12-24

Schwintowsi, H.-P. (2003): Gemeinwohl, öffentliche Daseinsvorsorge und Funktionen öffentlicher Unternehmen im europäischen Binnenmarkt, in: Zeitschrift für öffentliche und gemeinwirtschaftliche Unternehmen, vol. 26/3, 2003, pp. 283-310

Schwintowsi, H.-P. (2007): PPP, Inhouse und Ausschreibungswettbewerb, in: Gesellschaft für öffentliche Wirtschaft (eds.): Die Zukunft der öffentlichen Dienstleistungen, Beiträge zur öffentlichen Wirtschaft, vol. 24, pp. 91-98

Spremann, K. (1990): Asymmetrische Information, in: Zeitschrift für Betriebswirtschaft, vol. 5/6, pp. 561-586

Theuvsen, L. (2008): Public (Corporate) Governance - eine neue Chance für gute Verwaltungsführung? Paper presented at the Conference of the University of Leipzig „Institutionelle Vielfalt und neue Unübersichtlichkeit: Zukunftsperspektiven effizienter Steuerung öffentlicher Aufgaben zwischen Public Management und Puclic Governance", Leipzig 14. November 2008

Thrun, T. (2003): Handlungsansätze für ländliche Regionen mit starkem Bevölkerungsrückgang, in: Bundesamt für Bauwesen und Raumordnung (eds.): Demographische Wandel und Infrastruktur im ländlichen Raum von europäischen Erfahrungen lernen?, Informationen zur Raumentwicklung, vol. 12.2003, Bonn, pp. 709-718

Wieland, J. (2005): Neue rechtliche Rahmenbedingungen für die kommunalen Unternehmen, in: Gesellschaft für öffentliche Wirtschaft (eds.): Öffentliche Dienstleistungen zwischen Eigenerstellung und Wettbewerb, Beiträge zur öffentlichen Wirtschaft, vol. 22, pp. 54-70

Winkel, R. (2008): Öffentliche Infrastrukturversorgung im Planungsparadigmenwandel Infrastruktur und Daseinsvorsorge in der Fläche, in: Bundesamt für Bauwesen und Raumordnung (eds.): Infrastruktur und Daseinsvorsorge in der Fläche, Informationen zur Raumentwicklung, vol. 1/2.2008, pp. 41-47

Wissenschaftlichen Beirats der Gesellschaft für öffentliche Wirtschaft (2003): Wandel und Perspektiven der öffentlichen Wirtschaft, Positionspapier des Wissenschaftlichen Beirats der Gesellschaft für öffentliche Wirtschaft, in: Zeitschrift für öffentliche und gemeinwirtschaftliche Unternehmen, vol. 26/1, pp. 93-98

Wissenschaftlichen Beirats der Gesellschaft für öffentliche Wirtschaft (2007): Ausschreibung oder Direktvergabe öffentlicher Dienstleistungen - Plädoyer für ein Wahlrecht der Gebietskörperschaften - Stellungnahme des Wissenschaftlichen Beirats der Gesellschaft für öffentliche Wirtschaft zur Notwendigkeit einer gesetzlichen Regelung des Inhouse-Begriffs in der Europäischen Union, in: Zeitschrift für öffentliche und gemeinwirtschaftliche Unternehmen, vol. 2, pp. 207-229

FROM UNEMPLOYMENT TO SELF-EMPLOYMENT. POLITICAL CONCEPTS, ECONOMIC REALITIES, AND SOCIAL EFFECTS IN GERMANY

JÜRGEN PLÖHN / ALEXANDER PENIUK
(MARTIN-LUTHER-UNIVERSITY, HALLE / ESSEN, GERMANY)

1. Introduction: Economic growth and unemployment in Germany

Unemployment, the lamentable fate of more than 5.6 million Germans in the annual average of 1932 and again of 1.9 million in 1950, seemed to have evaporated during the so-called "economic miracle" of the 1950s. The situation on the German labour market remained favourable in the 1960s and early 1970s (Petzina/Abelshauser/Faust 1978: 119; Schäfers 2002: 224).

Graph 1: German GDP: annual rate of change since 1971 (until 1991 FRG, since 1992 re-united Germany)

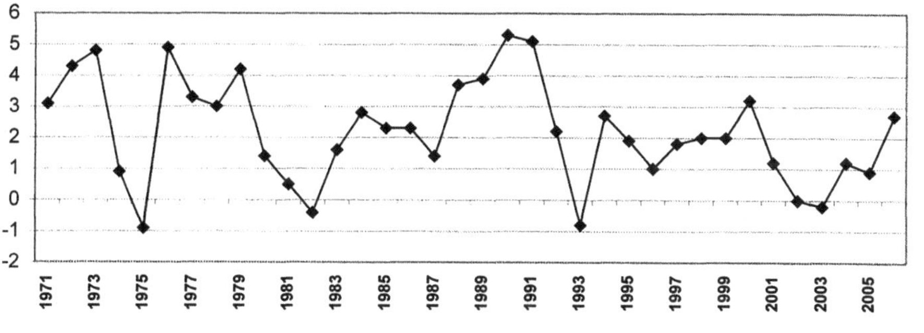

Data: Statistisches Bundesamt (ed.) 2007: 634-5 (own graph).

But in 1973 the first oil crisis initiated the end of a period of universal employment for those, who wanted and needed to make their living by working. The growth rate of the GDP declined dramatically (see graph 1). In 1975 for the second time after World War II the rate became negative. Within two years, the number of unemployed persons jumped to more than one million. Federal Chancellor *Helmut Schmidt*, who had a reputation for his economic knowledge, could not change much until after the second oil crisis (1979) the figures on unemployment went up again to the next level (see graph 2).

Graph 2: Unemployed members of the labour force in Germany, 1971-2006 (annual averages)

Data: Statistisches Bundesamt: 1987: 89 / 2006: 98-99 / 2008: 118-119; Statistisches Bundesamt (ed.) 1979: 106 / 1992: 127 / 1996: 123; Bundesagentur für Arbeit: 2006: 2 / 2009: 57 (own graph).

Since that time the two major political forces in Germany, the Social Democrats (SPD) and the Christian Democrats (CDU and CSU), quarrelled with each other about the possibilities to improve the situation on the labour market. The article in hand is dedicated to

- presenting the changing alternative concepts for the labour market and, because of their obvious shortcomings,
- the allegedly new approach of the *Schröder* government's so-called *"Hartz reforms"* in the first decade of the 21st century.

2. Labour market policies according to German party platforms

The first national election after the economic depression of 1975 was held in 1976. Being the party in power, the SPD pointed to the global economic situation as the main reason for the problems on the labour market. Nevertheless, the party insisted on everyone's "right to work". Besides fostering a new economic upward trend, the SPD advocated the establishment of part-time jobs and intensified attempts in the professional qualification of younger people (SPD 1976: 13, 18-20).

The parliamentary opposition perceived of the problem as a consequence of the trade cycle. Investments and moderate wage agreements were seen as major parts of the necessary answer. General education for the youth and a special counselling in combination with alternative career opportunities for grammar school students should complement the economic approach (CSU 1976: 24-26).

Four years later the Christian Democrats, still in opposition, recognized unemployment as a permanent problem in Germany. The central element of their counter strategy was encouraging private investments. Special attention was given to the problems of young, old, female and physically handicapped members of the labour force (CDU 1980: 18). The opposition's assertion that not only politicians, but also trade unions and management bear responsibility for the rate of employment was fiercly attacked by the Social Democrats, who, nevertheless, entered a new element into the labour market policy: They advocated a reduction of working hours as a result of collective bargaining. Moreover, the SPD insisted on the success and, therefore, a further development of auxiliary measures by the Federal Authority of Labour (*Bundesanstalt für Arbeit*). Though the party confirmed its support for the modernization of the German economy by entrepreneurial initiative, now the Social Democrats wanted to strengthen the political influence on the economy, especially by conditioned support programmes for special regions and branches (SPD 1980: 18-20).

In effect, the party's approach was not sufficient in order to avoid the next crisis or to cope with it two years later. Instead, due to problems in the area of economic policy as well as in foreign and defence policy, the coalition government broke apart and a new coalition formed by CDU, CSU and FDP came into office in October 1982 (Plöhn 2001: 703-744).

In the 1983 electoral campaign *Helmut Kohl's* government perceived of the existing unemployment as a heritage of the SPD which could not be overcome immediately. But self-assured the CDU claimed to have a superior economic programme. The new coalition wanted to fight unemployment by economic growth, which should be induced by investments and innovations (CDU 1983: 5-8). Additional aspects of the labour market programme consisted of

- fighting bureaucracy,
- enhancing flexibility,
- "job sharing", and
- inducing young people to take regionally remote positions.

The Social Democrats, now in opposition, entered a lengthy chapter on labour market policy into their electoral platform: Contrary to their formerly positive attitude towards technical innovations, now they showed skepticism with respect to the possible social and environmental effects. Thus the party's approach was centered on re-distributive measures: higher taxes on dividends of corporations and on higher-than-average incomes, public work programmes financed by public debts, public investments into selected economic branches and public subsidies provided under strict conditions and controls. On the international as well as on the national level the SPD recommended a coordinated strategy with strong expansionist incentives and elements of public planning of the economy. Remarkably, with respect to public work programmes, the party programme indicated that there were employment chances in the social services sector and mentioned "new forms of self-employed economic activities" which should be supported on the local level (SPD 1983: 15-27, esp. pp. 22-23).

The Christian Democrats' platform for the next election pointed to

- incentives for foreign workers to return to their home countries,
- an early retirement programme,
- enhanced possibilities for labour contracts limited in time,
- intensified programmes in further education, and
- a higher degree of flexibility concerning the working hours and the span of working in life (CDU 1986: 20-21).

What they did *not* mention was the beginning of public support for the attempts of unemployed persons to become entrepreneurs in 1986 (based on the new paragraph 55a in the law on the promotion of labour, *AFG*; Oschmiansky/Ebach 2009: 16 (15-20)).

Meanwhile the Social Democrats admitted that no strategy for the struggle against mass unemployment could promise a quick success. Alongside with aspects of German and European economic policies which had been advocated before, the party envisaged an improvement of the instruments of labour market policy and a more even distribution of labour, especially by supporting a reduction of the working hours to only 35 per week. The prosecution of illegal employment and a precise targeting of labour market instruments in combination with other economic and social goals should improve the situation gradually. On the other hand, demanding a new wave of foundations and innovations in business was a rather broad and sweepy approach, representing an attempt to overcome the pessimistic redistribution of labour (SPD 1986: 10-17).

After the German re-unification of 1990, the CDU tried to win the confidence of the voters by past successes in the creation of 2 million additional jobs – nearly totally absorbed by the growth of the labour force because of the baby boomers – and by

- a commitment to investments,
- a tax reform on the EU level,
- new technologies and high quality products and, again,
- an increase of human capital by a further professional qualification of workers (CDU 1990: 5-7).

Contrary to this optimistic approach dominated by economic assumptions and projects, the Social Democrats repeated their reliance on a reduction of working hours, explicitly assuming that this measure in combination with curbing overtime would create an additional demand for manpower. On that base the party favoured intensified endeavours in professional qualification, advocated a combination of programmes for labour and the protection of the environment and stressed the importance of unproductive corporations (employment firms, "*Beschäftigungsgesellschaften*") guiding unemployed members of the labour force to new jobs by counselling and offering further qualification (SPD 1990: 13-14).

In the following years, the immediate positive effects of the German reunification on the demand of goods and services withered away. The shut down of inefficient East German production sites produced extremely high degrees of unemployment in the German *New Länder* (Plöhn 1996: 11-13; Geißler 2002: 270-276; Sahner 2005: 49-55, 59-63, 72-78; Statistisches Bundesamt (ed.) 2008: 117-118).

For the 1994 election, the still governing CDU stuck to their concepts by stressing corporate taxes, growth and investments. The party added factors of location, the goal of further de-regulation, and the importance of small and middle size enterprises for innovations and adaptations to its electoral platform (CDU 1994: 12-20). Once more, the changes in the programme to further self-employment, which became effective in 1995 (Wießner 1997: 1), were not mentioned at all.

The oppositional SPD asserted that *Kohl's* cabinet had given up the goal of universal employment, whereas the Social Democrats could offer a comprehensive programme, again linking incentives for the labour market to ecological goals and, more explicitly than before, to gender policy. Now some specific Socialist aspects became obvious: The party set the goal to include the whole working force into social security. Private enterprises as well as public authorities should be urged to offer qualified part-time work with a pay to make a living. Moreover, all professional training positions should be evenly divided among male and female applicants. On the other hand, the SPD claimed the necessity of a new wave of foundations in business which should be fostered by risk capital. The support for self-employment of unemployed persons was repeated and degressive benefits for employers, who provided jobs for long-term unemployed workers, were recommended (SPD 1994: 10-22).

Only in 1998, after the gradual extension of the allowances for unemployed founders in 1995, the Christian Democrats passed a platform with more detailed provisions for the labour market, including a more efficient employment authority, local public work programmes, a combination of wages and public transfers, public incentives for the start to work and special low level professional training programmes (CDU 1998: 3-8).

In a complete exchange of the parties' basic attitudes, now the Social Democrats chose an optimistic, business-oriented approach, endorsing a market based economy and its dynamic development considering the globalized markets. Demand was recognized as the basic cause of production and investment. Despite a comprehensive perception of social security, the costs of labour should be reduced by a reduction of income taxes. Special attention was given to private services which were regarded as a promising field for new employment possibilities. Whereas self-employment, share holding and an enhanced supply of venture capital were endorsed by the SPD, specific programmes in order to turn unemployed workers into entrepreneurs were lacking (SPD 1998).

Now *Gerhard Schröder's* success for his envisaged red-green coalition was complete. *Helmut Kohl's* party suffered major losses and went out of office.

Conclusions of the first part:

1) The dominant attitude towards the problems on the labour market was an economic one. The demand for manpower was adequately regarded as a function of the demand for and production of goods. This perception of the Christian Democrats was accepted by the Social Democrats prior to the election of 1998.
2) The economic approach appears to be an optimistic one. It was pursued by all electorally successful parties, especially in those elections which followed or introduced a political change (1983, 1990, 1998). The alternative concentration on improvements for the narrowly defined labour market itself was electorally unsuccessful for both, the SPD as well as the CDU.
3) The first incentives for unemployed workers to become entrepreneurs themselves entered the auxiliary programmes without having been advocated before or propagated afterwards by one of the major political parties. Therefore in the beginning of the 21st century it was possible to present the additional measures as a brand new approach.

3. Conceptual changes and the reform by Gerhard Schröder's red-green coalition

After a scandal and a re-structuring of the administration of Labour, the "red-green" coalition under Chancellor *Gerhard Schröder* tried to intensify the use of the possibility to turn unemployed persons into entrepreneurs. The rationale of that approach was the following:

Graph 3: Self-employed persons as percentage of the labour force in Germany 1882-2004 (1950-1970: West Germany)

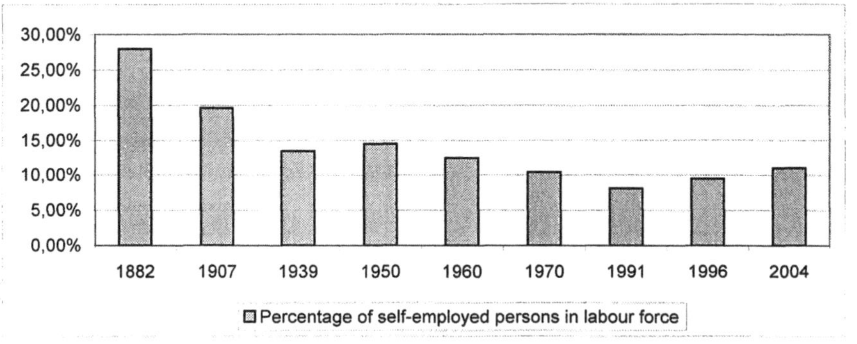

1882	1907	1939	1950	1960	1970	1991	1996	2004
28.0%	19.6%	13.4%	14.5%	12.4%	10.4%	8.1%	9.5%	11.0%

Data: Bernhard Schäfers 2002:192; Statistisches Bundesamt (ed.) 2006: 94. – Own graph.

The share of self-employed persons in the labour force has been shrinking for decades. Despite *Joseph Schumpeter's* positive attitude towards the dynamic entrepreneur (1976: 81-86; 2006) this development has been regarded as a consequence of mergers and thus as an element of the necessary modernization of the economy. But in the 1990s, the role of entrepreneurs, which was emphatically stressed by research for the *Global Entrepreneurship Monitor* (Sternberg/Otten/Tamásy 2000), had become recognized also by some politicians like, for instance, German Federal President *Roman Herzog* who pointed to the innovative potentials of founders (Herzog 1997: 13-28, 61-73; 2000: 198-211; Plöhn (ed.) 2008: 26-30). In public, successful individuals like *Bill Gates* (USA), *Henning Kagermann* (Germany) or *Joanne Rowling* (UK) were used - vastly exaggerated - as models for possible dynamic future developments.

Moreover, whereas the *Kohl* government had wanted to support industrial production and expected the services sector to develop alongside the production of goods, the councillors of the *Schröder* government, headed by *Peter Hartz*, saw chances to push the services sector directly.

Graph 4: German labour force: shares of economic sectors (1800-2006)

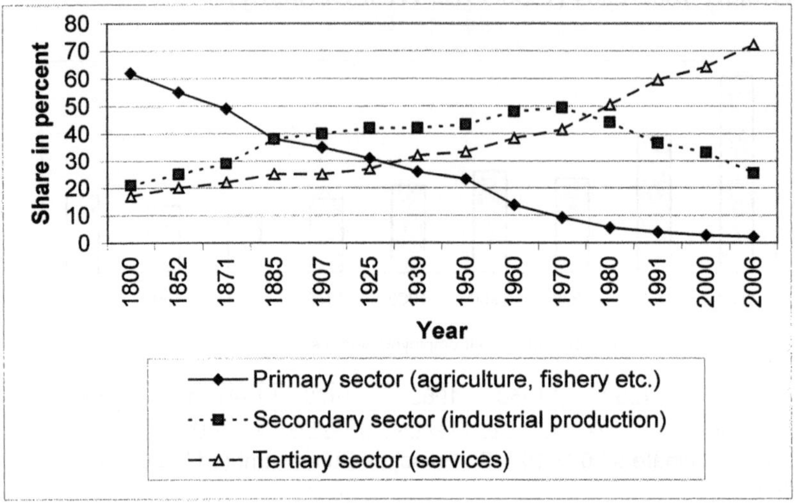

Data: Geißler 2002: 29; Schäfers 2002: 177; Statistisches Bundesamt (ed.) 1987: 83; 2006: 92 / 2008: 115 (own graph).

As it had been the longest growing sector in Germany and other developed economies (see graph 4), its positive trend should be used for the establishment of new enterprises. Explicitely the commission pointed to services related to private households, especially for elderly people, due to the aging of the population in general. Though the difference between the *Schumpeter*-like, innovative "*high tech*" approach of enterprises which were founded as an offspring of technical universities on the one hand and the generally "*low tech*" approach of individual service suppliers on the other hand (Sternberg/Brixy/Hundt 2007: 5; Kohn/Spengler 2008: 101-104) was rather obvious even for the commission, the assumption of the so-called "*Hartz II* reform" was that the growing services sector was suitable to employ a major part of the unemployed labour force (Kommission "Moderne Dienstleistungen am Arbeitsmarkt" 2002: 165).

Based on the suggestions of the "*Hartz* commission", the *Schröder* government added a new instrument to the existing labour market tools: the self-employment grants or, in popular language, the so-called "*Ich-AG*" ("Me plc.") - though that corporation was neither a corporation nor had it any stock owners. Thus, from January 1, 2003 to June 30, 2006 two separate instruments were used side by side by the Federal Agency of Labour which both aimed at the self-employment of short-term unemployed persons. From August 1, 2006 onward, the different tools were combined and transformed into one new instrument ("*Gründungszu-*

schuss" (start-up grants)) according to paragraph 57 in Book III of the Social Code (Bundesagentur für Arbeit 2008a; Redel 2007: 58-59; IHK Limburg 2008). Additionally, in 2005 a small fund was established, providing support for long-term unemployed at the local agency's discretion (see table 1).

4. The design of the empirical research and the structure of the support programmes

For the article in hand, the empirical research on the effectiveness of the instruments to foster self-employment was carried out from December 2003 to March 2006 (Peniuk 2008: 21-22). The goal was to identify *reasons* for decisions of intelligible human beings and *to understand the situation* they were in before and after their decision for an attempt to establish their own business. For that purpose, the social conditions under which the founders had made an attempt to overcome their unemployment had to be described and the situation they found themselves in after their decision for self-employment had to be assessed.

Two series of structured in-depth interviews were conducted:

- The first one was focused on unemployed *going-to-be entrepreneurs*. The necessary contacts to and personal confidence of the founders could be established through several networks as well as by participation in workshops for unemployed persons in the city of Essen, in the center of the Ruhr area.
- The second series was directed at a subgroup of the first one, namely, *formerly unemployed founders* after at least six months of self-employed business activities.

Because of its qualitative approach, it was the contents of those answers which mattered most.

Due to the state of the labour market policy, the specific construction of the two major instruments mentioned above had to be taken into consideration for the survey conducted. Differences can easily be recognized with respect to in the hight and the duration of the allowance (Lampert/Althammer 2004: 195-196).

Graph 5: Bridging allowances (for recipients of unemployment benefits of 1200 € per month) and self-employment grants in comparison (2003-2006)

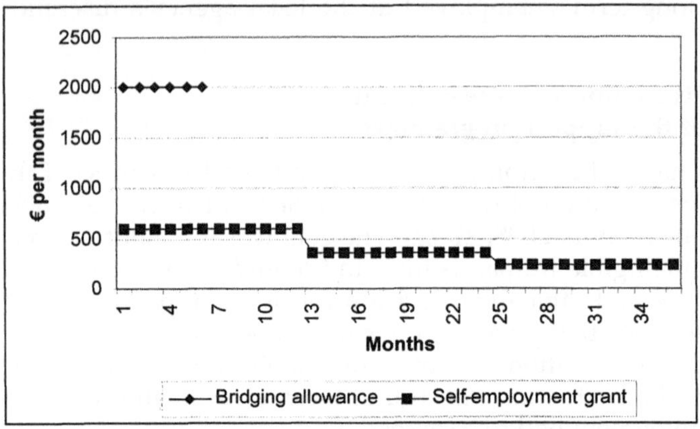

Data: Koch/ Wießner 2003: 2; Lampert/Althammer 2004: 195-196 (own graph).

The *bridging allowance* was relatively high but it was available only for a short period of time - up to 6 months. The *self-emploment grant* was paid much longer - up to 36 months -, but its height could only serve to cover basic insurances, not to make a living from it (see graph 5). Though both of the instruments have had some desired outcomes, quite obviously, their respective specific goals have not been achieved.

Since August 1, 2006 the readjusted start-up grants require a professional business plan. If such a plan can be shown - actually that is not very difficult - the new law provides for a 9-months-subsidy. Its height is given by the personal unemployment benefit and an additional lump sum of 300 €. The local employment agency may grant the lump sum - not the unemployment benefit - for another period of 6 months, if the business activities have intensified sufficiently (see graph 6).

Graph 6: Start-up grants for recipients of unemployment benefits of 1200 € (since 2006)

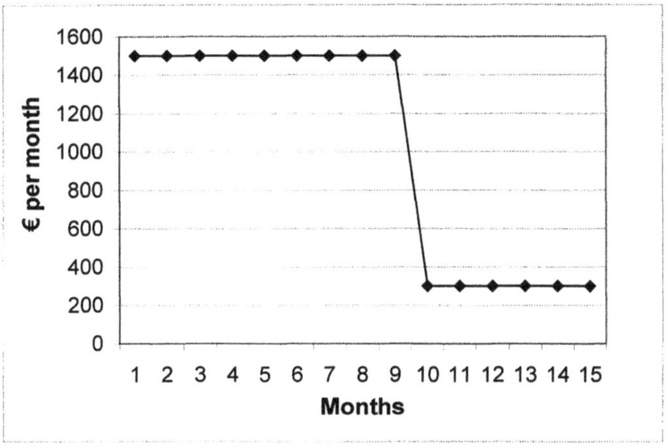

Data: Marco Caliendo/Steffen Kühn/Frank Wießner 2009, S. 11 (own graph). – Recipients are not legally entitled to get a prolongation of the allowance after the first nine months.

Table 1: Interim aid for unemployed persons who want to become self-employed 2000-2006

Year	Bridging allowances	Self-employment grants	Start-up grants (integrated & adapted version)	Readjustment allowance (for long-time unemployed persons)	Sum of newly accepted applicants for interim aid
2000	92,953	---	---	---	*92,953*
2001	96,387	---	---	---	*96,387*
2002	125,721	---	---	---	*125,721*
2003	158,969	97,253	---	---	*256,222*
2004	183,545	171,267	---	---	*354,812*
2005	156,888	91,020	---	17,149	*265,057*
2006	108,266	42,812	33,569	32,571	*217,218*
2007	---	---	121,954	32,177	*154,131*
2008	---	---	119,309	24,794	*144,103*

Data: Bundesagentur für Arbeit 2005: 100-101 / 2007: 96-97 / 2008: 55; Bundesagentur für Arbeit 2009a.

With respect to the German labour market policy these changes mean:

(1) Meanwhile an instrument that temporarily had been in disregard for self-employment grants because of its bureaucratic character, namely: testing the seriousness and the professionalism of the founders, is in use for all attempts to create a firm by formerly unemployed persons.

(2) Step by step the decision to grant or withhold an allowance has been passed over from politics - parliament - to the responsible administration: the employment agency.

(3) As a result, the administrative pressure on the founders is higher than in the early years of the decade.

(4) On the other hand, though the names of the programmes are rather similar, there has been an important change in structure: Whereas the *old allowances had to stop* in case of an *economic success*, the *new interim aid* provides an *incentive for economic success* by a possible prolongation of the financial support.

5. Existing studies and own results

In an evaluation by the research institute (*IAB*) of the Federal Agency of Labour both of the two former programmes received positive comments: In the long run they have been successful, the study states. Not only the bridging allowances, but also the self-employment grants have induced people to become self-employed. Therefore the *IAB* researchers would have preferred a prolongation of the separate programmes rather than their merger into one (Caliendo/Kühn/Wießner 2009: 9-10; similar: Caliendo/Kritikos/Steiner/Wießner 2007).

In detail the *IAB* scientists found:

In the Western parts of Germany 56 months after the establishment of their own firm three fifth of the recipients of self-employment grants and two thirds of those of the bridging allowances were still self-employed. Roughly one fifth had opted out and had taken a job as an employee again, having used the self-employment only as a stepping stone.

Whether the income of the founders could be regarded as "sufficient" or not had to be answered in a differenciated way: On the one hand, the *IAB* research documented an enormous spread in the distribution of incomes, in part depending on the possibility to work full-time that could not be taken for granted. On the other hand, the economic situation of the formerly unemployed founders depended strongly on surrounding factors like family support. If the entrepreneurial activities remained without success, founders accumulated substantial debts: a quarter of the unsuccessful group had to carry a burden of more than 10,000 € afterwards. Some reduced their permanent payments by quitting the old age pension insurance, though this was contrary to the obvious intentions of the red-green government.

The secondary effects of the newly created jobs remained rather limited. At the end of the 56-months-period, there were 80,000 additional employees (calculated as full-time jobs) on every 100,000 self-employed former receivers of bridging allowances but only 16,000 employees for the same number of former receivers of self-employment grants (Caliendo/Kühn/Wießner 2009: 2-6).

Table 2: Characteristics of the interviewees

1st series of interviews		
	Numbers	Percentages
Interviewed persons	78	100%
Gender		
Male	58	74.4%
Female	20	25.6%
Nationality		
Germans	62	79.5%
Non-Germans	16	20.5%
- Turks	13	16.7%
Years of age		
20-29	10	12.8%
30-39	17	21.8%
40-49	31	39.8%
50-60	20	25.6%
Education		
Grammar school ("Gymnasium"): *13 years of school training* ("Abitur"/"Matura")	47	60.3%
Intermediary level of secondary education ("Realschule"): *10 years of school training*	8	10.3%
Upper division of elementary school ("Hauptschule") *9 years of school training*	22	28.2%
No diploma of any school	1	1.2%
Professional training		
University	31	39.7%
University of applied sciences	7	9.0%
Apprenticeship + secondary professional school	31	39.7%
Other/none	9	11.5%

Data: Peniuk 2008: 218-219 (own suvey).

Though the *German Institute for Economic Research* (*DIW* Berlin) also published an all-in-all positive comment on start-up grants as one of only four positively evaluated labour market instruments, the experts of that institute point at deadweight losses, substitution effects and a rather poor income situation of individuals who received support according to the "Me plc." programme (Eichhorst/Zimmermann 2007: 7, 11, 14).

For the PhD-thesis which in part is presented here, a closer look at the living conditions of the founders has been undertaken. The group of interviewees consisted of 78 unemployed persons in the first series and 53 in the second. Of the first group 46 (59.0%) had applied for bridging allowances, only three (3.8%) for self-employment grants. The rest was not eligible for these benefits (Peniuk 2008: 228). The preference for the first alternative is in line with the relatively high qualification of the analysed group, as shown in table 2.

From those data can be infered:

The going-to-be founders among the unemployed members of the labour force showed a much higher percentage of university graduates than the German society in general – in average 7.2% in 2004 (Statistisches Bundesamt (ed.) 2004: 78). Also the share of graduates from "universities of applied sciences" was higher than in general: 4.6%.

That means: According to their formal education, a major part of the interviewed persons was theoretically well-equipped for the labour market.

But: Most of the founders belonged to an age group for which the chances to be employed in a flourishing enterprise after the loss of the previous job were relatively small.

Table 3: Period of unemployment prior to self-employment

	Numbers	Percentages
Less than 3 months	25	32,1
3 to 6 months	31	39,7
6 to 12 months	17	21,8
More than 1 year	5	6,4
Total	78	100,0

Data: Peniuk 2008: 220 (own collection).

With regard to the time-factor, there is a high number of attempts to establish a business of one's own in the early months after the loss of the previous position. But numerous persons hesitated for some months before they gave up their hopes for a new employment on a permanent salaried position. That indicates major problems in adapting for the formerly unemployed founders.

Table 4: Risks anticipated and realized

1st interview (prior to establishment)	Numbers percentages (78)	Numbers percentages (59)	2nd interview (after establishment)
Not willing to found	0 0%	6 10.2%	No founding activity (obstacles)
Major risks expected	7 9%	7 11.9%	Already given up (problems)
Only minor risks envisaged	40 51.3%	30 50.8%	Substantial problems
No doubts in success	22 28.2%	15 25.4%	No problems
No answers	9 11.5%	1 1.7%	No answer

Data: Peniuk 2008: 230-231 (own collection).

The reasons for this finding can be identifyed in the specific situation of the founders: Founders, who are unemployed when they start their business, are predominantly motivated by the chance to get back to work *at all*, not by an original business plan which they might have pursued for a long time. Therefore many of them lack

(a) a concise business concept and
(b) sufficient knowledge of the specific duties of self-employed persons.

The specific personal economic situation for this type of founders is marked by

(a) the loss of their previous job and
(b) their professional expertise in a specific branch which does no longer have a sufficient demand for their working power.

Though 50 out of the 78 tried to optimize their preparation for their self-employed professional activity, 45 felt that the professional counselling which was offered by the employment agency and its partners (among others, especially the chamber of commerce) was of no use for them. Only 9 (or 11.5%) described the counselling as valuable (Peniuk 2008: 224).

With few exceptions the firms which were actually established by the respondents were small, generally consisting only of the founder himself. Less than a quarter of the firms had employees. Therefore nearly two thirds of the founders were registered as self-employed individuals, only a tiny minority had the financial partners needed for a limited partnership or even a company limited by shares.

Dominantly, the newly established enterprises belonged to the services sector. Despite of its growth, the economic success of the individual firm was limited by the services an individual person could offer. In fact, more than two fifth were not working at full capacity in their new jobs.

As a result, the economic success could not be substantial either. Consequently, for 70% of the founders their earnings were lower than in their previous dependant position. 11% achieved the same income and 17% managed to earn more than in the dependent position of an employee (Peniuk 2008: 232).

As the huge majority of those founders never had an original wish to be self-employed, it can be no surprize that the interviewees felt psychologically stressed by their new occupation. Moreover, in one half of the cases, the tensions that resulted from the economic insecurit had negative spill-over effects on the families of the founders (Peniuk 2008: 233).

6. Conclusions

1) The relevant publicly financed institutions show an improvable performance. Besides the financial aspects which already have been modified, an optimization of the programme should include the counselling of the founders.
2) The unemployed founders who were lucky to survive had a comparative cost advantage because they were not obliged to calculate their prices on standard wages fixed by collective bargaining. Instead, if necessary, they could exploit themselves.
3) Nevertheless, more than a third of the respondents could only survive by substantial intra-family transfers. In these cases it seems to be questionable to characterize the newly established firms as economic successes.

This means:

The pictures shown in TV and the images drawn up by politicians, who had envisioned creative new enterprises and secondary effects on the labour market by successful founders, do not describe a likely short-term perspective. Perhaps the *IAB* research gives some hope for surviving founders after several years.

In our own study (Peniuk 2008), the existing problems have been focussed more explicitly than by the *IAB*. In this respect, our results are presented in the more skeptic manner of the *KfW-Gründungsmonitor* (Kohn/Spengler 2008: 3) and the *DIW* (Eichhorst/Zimmermann 2007: 7). Nevertheless, the findings are generally in line with the research pursued by the IAB. But including psychological stress and family situations into the considerations dampens the positive attitudes towards the programmes for unemployed founders. These programmes do not guarantee any success and therefore they are risky for the receivers of the benefits.

Considering the number of created jobs for employees in established firms on the one hand and for self-employed former unemployed founders on the other, it is obvious: The reduction of the number of unemployed persons in recent years from 4.861 million (2005) to 3.268 million (2008, Bundesagentur für Arbeit 2009b) is due to the overall economic development. The contribution of the labour market instruments which have been discussed here, is, however, only marginal.

References

Bundesagentur für Arbeit 2006: Geschäftsbericht 2005, Nürnberg (download: *http://www.arbeitsagentur.de/zentraler-Content/Veroeffentlichungen/Intern/Geschaeftsbericht-2005.pdf*)

Bundesagentur für Arbeit 2007: Beschäftigungsperspektiven sichern. Geschäftsbericht 2006, Nürnberg (download: *http://www.arbeitsagentur.de/zentraler-Content/Veroeffentlichungen/Intern/Geschaeftsbericht-2006.pdf*)

Bundesagentur für Arbeit 2008: Erreichtes sichern - Erfolge ausbauen. Geschäftsbericht 2007, Nürnberg (download: *http://www.arbeitsagentur.de/zentraler-Content/Veroeffentlichungen/Intern/Geschaeftsbericht-2007.pdf*)

Bundesagentur für Arbeit 2008a: Finanzielle Hilfen für Existenzgründer (download: *http://www.arbeitsagentur.de/nn_26400/Navigation/zentral/Buerger/Hilfen/Existenzgruendung/Existenzgruendung-Nav.html*)

Bundesagentur für Arbeit 2009: Chancen des Marktes professionell nutzen. Geschäftsbericht 2008, Nürnberg (download: *http://www.arbeitsagentur.de/zentraler-Content/Veroeffentlichungen/Intern/Geschaeftsbericht-2008.pd)f*

Bundesagentur für Arbeit 2009a: Statistik: Ausgewählte arbeitsmarktpolitische Instrumente - für Personen im Rechtskreis SGB III und SGB II - mit Förderinformationen der zkT (download: *http://www.pub.arbeitsagentur.de/hst/services/statistik/detail/z.html*)

Bundesagentur für Arbeit 2009b: Arbeitslosigkeit im Zeitverlauf, Nürnberg June 2009 (download: *http://www.pub.arbeitsagentur.de/hst/services/statistik/aktuell/iiia4/laender_heftd.xls*)

Caliendo, Marco/Steffen Kühn/Frank Wießner 2009: Ich-AG und Überbrückungsgeld: Erfolgsgeschichte mit zu frühem Ende, in: IAB-Kurzbericht no. 3/2009 of February 2009 (download: *http://doku.iab.de/kurzber/2009/kb0309.pdf*)

CDU 1980: Für Frieden und Freiheit in der Bundesrepublik Deutschland und in der Welt. Wahlprogramm der CDU und CSU für die Bundestagswahl 1980, ed. by CDU-Bundesgeschäftsstelle, Abt. Öffentlichkeitsarbeit, Bonn

CDU 1983: Arbeit, Frieden, Zukunft. Miteinander schaffen wir's. Das Wahlprogramm der CDU/CSU, ed. by CDU-Bundesgeschäftsstelle, Abt. Öffentlichkeitsarbeit, Bonn

CDU 1990: Ja zu Deutschland - Ja zur Zukunft. Wahlprogramm der Christlich Demokratischen Union Deutschlands zur gesamtdeutschen Bundestagswahl am 2.

Dezember 1990, ed. by CDU-Bundesgeschäftsstelle, Abt. Öffentlichkeitsarbeit, Bonn
CDU 1994: Wir sichern Deutschlands Zukunft. Regierungsprogramm von CDU und CSU, ed. by CDU-Bundesgeschäftsstelle, Abt. Öffentlichkeitsarbeit, Bonn
CDU 1998: 1998-2002. Wahlplattform, ed. by CDU-Bundesgeschäftsstelle, HA Öffentlichkeitsarbeit/CSU Landesleitung, Geschäftsbereich Öffentlichkeitsarbeit, Bonn/München
CSU 1976: Das gemeinsame Wahlprogramm der CDU und CSU 1976, edited by CSU-Landesleitung, Ref. Öffentlichkeitsarbeit, München (also published as: Christlich-Demokratische Union Deutschlands: Das Wahlprogramm der CDU und CSU 1976, Bonn 1976)
Eichhorst, Werner/Klaus F. Zimmermann 2007: And Then There Were Four ... How Many and Which Measures of Active Labor Market Policy Do We Still Need?, DIW Berlin (German Institute for Economic Research), Discussion Papers no. 685 (March 2007) (*http://www.diw.de/documents/publikationen/73/56541/dp685.pdf*)
Geißler, Rainer 2002: Die Sozialstruktur Deutschlands, 3rd ed., Bonn: Bundeszentrale für politische Bildung, and Wiesbaden: Westdeutscher Verlag
Herzog, Roman 1997: Das Land erneuern, Hamburg: Hoffmann&Campe
Herzog, Roman 2000: Reden und Interviews, vol. 5/I, Bonn
IHK Limburg 2008: Gründungszuschuss - § 57 SGB III - Starthilfe und Unternehmensförderung, März 2008 (*http://www.ihk-limburg.de/Site%20komplett/2%20Starthilfe/Download/Gr%FCndungszuschuss_0308.pdf*)
Koch, Susanne/Frank Wießner 2003: Ich-AG oder Überbrückungsgeld? Wer die Wahl hat, hat die Qual, in: IAB-Kurzbericht no. 2/2003 of March 3, 2003 (*http://doku.iab.de/kurzber/2003/kb0203.pdf*)
Kohn, Karsten/Hannes Spengler 2008: Gründungen in Deutschland: weniger aber besser - Chancenmotiv rückt in den Vordergrund, KfW-Gründungsmonitor 2008 (*http://www.kfw.de/DE_Home/Service/Download_Center/Allgemeine_Publikationen/Research/PDF-Dokumente_Gruendungsmonitor/Kfw_Grundungsmonitor_2008_32_Internet_Langfassung.pdf*)
Kommission "Moderne Dienstleistungen am Arbeitsmarkt" 2002: Bericht der Kommission, Berlin (download on: *http://www.bmas.de*)
Lampert, Heinz/Jörg Althammer 2004: Lehrbuch der Sozialpolitik, 7th ed., Berlin/Heidelberg/New York
Oschmiansky, Frank/Mareike Ebach 2009: Aktive Arbeitsmarktpolitik im Wandel, Aus Politik und Zeitgeschichte B 27/2009 of June 29, 2009, pp. 15-20
Petzina, Dietmar/Werner Abelshauser/Anselm Faust 1978: Sozialgeschichtliches Arbeitsbuch Band III: Materialien zur Statistik des Deutschen Reiches 1914-1945, München: C. H. Beck
Peniuk, Alexander 2008: Aus der Arbeitslosigkeit in die Selbständigkeit? Individuelle und soziale Faktoren bei Erfolg und Scheitern von Existenzgründern, Diss. phil., Ruhr-Universität Bochum
Plöhn, Jürgen 1996: Mehrheitswechsel in Sachsen-Anhalt. Modellfall oder Sackgasse?, Frankfurt et al.: Peter Lang
Plöhn, Jürgen 2001: Vertrauen und Verantwortung in den politischen Systemen westlicher Demokratien, Habilitationsschrift, Martin-Luther-Universität Halle
Plöhn, Jürgen (ed.) 2008: Roman Herzog: Zukunftsideen. Für die Konrad-Adenauer-Stiftung zusammengestellt von Jürgen Plöhn, St. Augustin: KAS

Redel, Beate 2007: Existenzgründung - Wege in die Selbständigkeit, in: Beruf - Bildung - Zukunft, Ausgabe 2007/2008, ed. by Bundesagentur für Arbeit, Nürnberg (*http://www.arbeitsagentur.de/zentraler-Content/Veroeffentlichungen/BBZ/BBZ-Existenzgruendung.pdf*)

Sahner, Heinz 2005: Die Gesellschaft. Sozialstruktur und Lebenslagen in der Bundesrepublik Deutschland, in: Everhard Holtmann/Oscar W. Gabriel (eds.): Handbuch Politisches System der Bundesrepublik Deutschland, 3rd ed., München: Oldenbourg, pp. 43-88

Schäfers, Bernhard 2002: Sozialstruktur und sozialer Wandel in Deutschland, 7th ed., Stuttgart: Lucius&Lucius

Schumpeter, Joseph Alois 2006: Theorie der wirtschaftlichen Entwicklung, Berlin: Duncker&Humblot (reprint, 1st ed. 1912)

Schumpeter, Joseph Alois 1976: Capitalism, Socialism and Democracy, New York et al.: Harper Torchbooks (originally published 1942)

SPD 1976: Weiterarbeiten am Modell Deutschland. Regierungsprogramm 1976-80. Beschluß des Außerordentlichen Parteitages in Dortmund, 18./19. Juni 1976, Bonn (download: *http://library.fes.de/pdf-files/bibliothek/retro-scans/fc-02947.pdf*)

SPD 1980: Sicherheit für Deutschland. Wahlprogramm 1980. Beschlossen von der Sozialdemokratischen Partei Deutschlands auf dem Wahlparteitag in Essen. 9./10. Juni 1980, ed. by Vorstand der SPD, Abt. Presse und Information, Bonn (download: *http://library.fes.de/pdf-files/bibliothek/retro-scans/a80-03353.pdf*)

SPD 1983: Das Regierungsprogramm der SPD 1983-1987. Beschlossen vom Wahlparteitag der SPD am 21. Januar 1983 in Dortmund, ed. by Vorstand der SPD, Abt. Presse und Information, Bonn (download: *http://library.fes.de/pdf-files/bibliothek/retro-scans/fx01275_1983.pdf*)

SPD 1986: Zukunft für alle - arbeiten für soziale Gerechtigkeit und Frieden. Regierungsprogramm 1987-1990 der Sozialdemokratischen Partei Deutschlands, Bonn (download: *http://library.fes.de/pdf-files/bibliothek/retro-scans/a87-04013.pdf*)

SPD 1990: Regierungsprogramm 1990-1994: Der neue Weg: ökologisch, sozial, wirtschaftlich stark. Beschlossen vom SPD-Parteitag in Berlin am 28. September 1990, Bonn (download: *http://library.fes.de/pdf-files/bibliothek/retro-scans/fa90-05465.pdf*)

SPD 1994: Das Regierungsprogramm der SPD. Reformen für Deutschland, Bonn (download: *http://library.fes.de/pdf-files/bibliothek/retro-scans/fa94-02358.pdf*)

SPD 1998: Arbeit, Innovation und Gerechtigkeit. SPD-Programm für die Bundestagswahl 1998. Beschluß des außerordentlichen Parteitages der SPD am 17. April 1998 in Leipzig, ed. by Vorstand der SPD, Öffentlichkeitsarbeit, Bonn (download: *http://library.fes.de/pdf-files/bibliothek/retro-scans/a98-04467.pdf*)

Statistisches Bundesamt (ed.) 1987: Datenreport 1987. Zahlen und Fakten über die Bundesrepublik Deutschland, Bonn

Statistisches Bundesamt (ed.) 2004: Datenreport 2004. Zahlen und Fakten über die Bundesrepublik Deutschland, Bonn

Statistisches Bundesamt (ed.) 2006: Datenreport 2006. Zahlen und Fakten über die Bundesrepublik Deutschland, Bonn

Statistisches Bundesamt (ed.) 2007: Statistisches Jahrbuch 2007, Wiesbaden (*http://www.bpb.de/files/5Z3DV3.pdf*)

Statistisches Bundesamt (ed.) 2008: Datenreport 2008. Ein Sozialbericht für die Bundesrepublik Deutschland, Bonn

Sternberg, Rolf / Udo Brixy / Christian Hundt 2007: Global Entrepreneurship Monitor (GEM): Länderbericht Deutschland 2006, Hannover / Nürnberg (*http://www.gemconsortium.org/document.aspx?id=581*)

Sternberg, Rolf / Claus Otten / Christine Tamásy 2000: Global Entrepreneurship Monitor (GEM): Länderbericht Deutschland 1999 - Kurzfassung, Köln 2000 (download: *http://www.wigeo.uni-hannover.de/fileadmin/wigeo/GEM/gem1999.pdf*)

Wießner, Frank 1997: Aus der Arbeitslosigkeit in die Selbständigkeit - Teil 1: Existenzgründer bevorzugen Servicebereich, in: IAB-Kurzbericht 10/1997 of Dec. 8, 1997, pp. 1-6 (download: *http://doku.iab.de/kurzber/1997/kb1097.pdf*)

SOCIAL AND HEALTH SERVICES IN THE EU.
AN ANALYTICAL SKETCH WITH PARTICULAR REFERENCE TO THE REPERCUSSIONS OF EUROPEAN LAW ON THE GERMAN DEVELOPMENT OF THE PROVISION OF SOCIAL AND HEALTH SERVICES

FRANK SCHULZ-NIESWANDT / MICHAEL SAUER
(UNIVERSITY OF COLOGNE, GERMANY)

Although Europe, since its emergence after 1945 should be basically regarded as an organisation for peace[1], and although Europe is also eager to define itself culturally, less geographically[2], as a value-driven community space, the EU essentially and primarily represents an economic space that is understood as a free internal market and that has been partly transformed into a currency union (with considerable effects on the monetary and, consequently, on the financial policy of the Member States).

1. The internal market and its dynamics of integration

This internal market has no tariff and non-tariff restrictions to trade. It is characterised by economic freedom of movement (capital, labour, goods and services) increasingly virtually adopted as constitutional law. In essence there is a universal anti-discrimination law.

The process of integration in relation to this common internal market has made great advances and now places further areas of law and regulation of the Member State's societal life under a corresponding pressure towards adaptation and modernisation.

Against this background there is a controversy and discussion as to whether Europe has already acquired its own state character, or at least state-like characteristics, or whether the Member States are still sovereign and in principle have bound themselves only to a horizontal treaty under national law. The Member States are, after all, "Masters of the Treaties", the EU Commission is *only* the "Guardian of the Treaties". Different variants of the interpretation of the EU as a federation of states or a federal state compete with each other. However, the little word "*only*" with regard to the function of the Commission as "Guardian of the Treaties" is central: how are the treaties interpreted? Here the central role of the European Court of Justice (ECJ) takes effect. What consequences must be drawn as a result of such interpretation?

---

[1] This is often no longer questioned.
[2] Both are quite difficult.

2. Social policy as shared competence

However this problem is regarded in jurisprudence and according to the law, the political architecture of Europe as a political system is in any case to be understood as a multilevel system[3] (from the German viewpoint: EU level, federal (national) level, subnational divisions: *Länder* (states), municipalities). The results of this setting do not only matter on issues of division of competences, but also in the vertical interlocking and horizontal intertwining.

2.1 Balances of power and weighting of goods

We assume, against the background of these assessments, that Europe *de facto* already operates shared competences in social policy, including health policy (Hervey 2008). Europe practices these shared competences independently of whether legal regulation will be adjusted on the basis of the Treaty of Lisbon amending the Treaty on the European Union (TEU) and the Treaty establishing the European Community (TEC) – a constitution-compensating treaty, which might even fail again. These shared competences, i.e., the practice of a common exercise of power, do not contradict the idea of subsidiarity under Art. 5 b TEC. Art. 137 and Art. 152 TEC do not necessarily run counter to this power-sharing arrangement in the European multilevel system since the sovereign legislation and policies of the Member States nonetheless still have to test and respect the correspondence of their own national action with EU law.

The EU Member States are therefore sovereign and responsible themselves for the social and health policy, but only conditionally: they must, in fact, customise the development of their law and policies according to EU law (and to GATS: Lipson 2002). The necessity of accordance leaves room for manœuvre as both must be defined and given a specific form. To that extent this legal problem is by no means free of questions concerning power and the balance of power in the multilevel system, nor is it free of political weighting of goods between the internal market dimension on the one hand and other esteemed historic, cultural and social characteristics of Europe and its Member States on the other. However, here again it must be stressed how precisely the internal market has become the core of the process and the motor of the (intensifying but also expanded) European integration. In this context "Brussels" is often accused of an antipathy towards federalism, a deep-seated cultural and political incomprehension of historically

[3] For further discussion about the multilevel-governance approach please refer to Knodt and Hüttmann (2005) or classically Hoghe and Marks (2001).

developed institutions and, in general, for the diversity of cultures of Europe - accused although the primary law of Europe explicitly takes account of these attributes and values the cultural diversity.

2.2 The European Court of Justice (ECJ)

This adaptation and correspondence that has started with regard to gaps forming between the dynamics of the internal market on the one hand and the national legal situations and institutional arrangements on the other is now the reason why and how the ECJ dispenses justice only in the form of (contentious in the theory of democracy) the creation of law: it must provide general answers as to how the gaps are to be filled. To that extent the ECJ has become the motor of development in many areas of law and, consequently, of life. That is contentious in jurisprudence and politics, but results from the development gap between the degree of the economic integration and other stages of integration in Europe in social, political and cultural respects and, in fact, with an only limited existing supranational political system of the EU. Since the national governments are naturally not willing or inclined to close the gaps, the closing is initiated at the supranational level.

2.3 Europeanisation of social policy[4]

Certain areas of a Europeanised social policy have therefore already come into being in the sense of a shared competence. Though not all sub-areas can be mentioned or included here, the strategy concerns:

- coordinating labour and social law,
- aspects of the European Structural Fund (especially the European Social Fund [ESF] and the European Regional Development Fund [ERDF]),
- the Open Method of Coordination (OMC) policy (Umbach 2009)[5],
- the redefinition of the manner of functioning (of the markets) of services of general (economic[6]) interest (GIS or SG[E]I), and
- the basic social rights of the Unions' citizens (in the framework of their general as well as their economic and political) basic rights

[4] For a retrospective overview of developments as well as for the political and technical procedure adopted for progressing social policy in the European Union, refer to Threlfall (2007).

[5] E.g. Borrás and Jacobsson (2004) deliver an analytical framework for studying the impact of the OMC, while Büchs (2007) presents a more detailed analysis regarding the design and evaluation process of the OMC.

[6] Or even non-economic interest, which however remains controversial, since all offers are basically a market reference, that is, a situation of competition.

(European Union Charter of Fundamental Rights, proclaimed at the European Council meeting in Nice, 2000 [7]).[8]

These dimensions are interdependent. Examples: the citizen's freedom of movement as an insured person in the role of a patient requires coordination of social law; or: the basic rights of persons with handicaps to participate in the world of employment requires supporting activities, e.g., by the ESF. The redefinition of the provision of social services is closely linked to the question of the basic freedoms in the internal market that are practically already "adopted as constitutional law". Just like the objectives of the OMC, these new arrangements assume the increasingly market-driven and economically guided forms of provisions of social services:

- the citizen's basic social right to free access to the social protection systems and to facilities and services,
- the quality should be guaranteed at a high level,
- however, the services should also be offered at the lowest possible prices and efficiently (which accounts for the opening up of the market and economic guidance),
- and, finally, the social protection systems must be sustainable, that means financial viability and long term stability.[9]

In the following, we only discuss the problem of the GIS or SG(E)I, but we relate this interdependence to other dimensions of an increasingly Europeanised social and health policy (as shared competence in a multilevel system) in the examinations.

3. The dynamics of the SG(E)I

Person-specific services targeted at physical and mental aspects of the individual cannot simply be organized through markets:

- an asymmetric distribution of information between providers and clients is the rule, not the exception,
- the quality of the products/services is not easily to be judged beforehand or afterwards,

---

[7] Probably the most modern catalogue of human and basic rights in the world.

[8] Refer e.g. to Menéndez (2002).

[9] The dependence of social protection systems on demography has become a theme of EU policy. A Green Paper has been presented on that issue. This is generally in line with the EU Lisbon Strategy. Regarding the relations between the labour market and social protection systems reference is made to the employability strategy and to the Flexicurity Strategy ("Workfare" instead of "Welfare").

- not all services can be judged comparably in repeat purchases, correspondingly, trust and confidence play a constitutive role,
- corresponding contracts cannot be made completely specific.

As a rule, however, there are situations concerning provisions estimated as having high social value, so that the goods are assured or guaranteed in their production, provision and access (so-called merit goods).

However, complete failure of the market does not happen, especially since non-market controls are likewise incomplete (state or policy failure, failure of administration, failure of the third sector).

In the context of this finding of the basically only incomplete allocation solutions it may be said that, therefore, the EU policy envisages the creation of regulated quasi-markets. Where it *does* concern, it concerns the opening up to competition "in" markets and the opening up to competition "around" markets if - in cases of "natural monopolies" - there can be only one (regional) provider. It further concerns approaches to competition solutions in the form of surrogates for competition.

The EU policy tends analogously to transfer the new forms of regulated markets in the core areas of economic welfare (transport, energy, postal services and telecommunications, waste and sewage management, and increasingly water in any case) to the sectors of provision on social and health services. In-house solutions (where the governments - for instance: the local authorities[10] - provide the production themselves, i.e., in the form of public enterprises) are marginalized as possibilities with a strict subordination to market solutions and economically steered assignments to private carriers and pushed to the edge or the background. The science of the public economy occasionally articulated clear criticism on this topic (GÖW 2007a).[11]

In general an obligatory best-bidder competition is emphasised for the selection of private providers/suppliers of services. The corresponding rules and procedures for the provision of social services are accordingly affected via the transparent, discrimination-free route of opening of the market and the competitive selection of providers/suppliers. To that extent the national practice of service provisions must comply with this European system of competition, (the prohibition of) subsidies and the award of contracts. Where contracting out is dispensed with the deed of assignment, it must not only be transparent in accordance with European law, it must also incorporate benchmark instruments. Other further

[10] Reference is made here to the possibility of the local authority self-administration economy, anchored in constitutional law in Germany.

[11] Also printed in English: GÖW (2007b)

instruments (such as a market-oriented direct award of contract) are not further discussed here.

In everyday life social and health services are thus increasingly treated in much the same way as services in the economic-technical goods area. The EU Commission has clearly promoted this analogy through the relevant Green Papers and White Papers as well as through announcements and consultation processes. The results of this regulation policy, the form of sector-specific or framework directives remain open. This counts especially for the compatibility with other relevant decrees and directives and the question how the whole theme will finally be anchored in the EU's primary law in which the SG(E)I is also evaluated with reference to constitutional law (cf. Art. 16 ECT in conjunction with 86, Section 2 ECT). Therefore the questions of (limited and certainly rather restrictively applicable) exemption and leeway rules likewise remain unresolved.

The reason for this policy of market opening and control through competition can be seen in the existence of competitive tendering. Besides the social enterprises of the free welfare care, private, commercially oriented enterprises are also active in these sectors.[12] Since such a market reference exists in the production and operation of these social services the functional concept of enterprise becomes effective.

From the functional point of view of the EU Commission and the ECJ, this is *neither* a matter of the particularities of the carrier or legal form *nor* of the presence of cooperative forms of production. The dominance of the business-management objective in the context of a complex cooperative stakeholder philosophy and action and the analogous creation of laws by the ECJ does not play any fundamental role for the EU Commission. The whole debate around the social production function of the social economy ("added values" thesis[13]) and its insertion in a "Third Sector" between state, market and primary networks (family and relations as well as friendship: see also Bettio 2004 in relation to gender aspects; also Schulz-Nieswandt et al. 2006) is barely adequately

---

[12] This is strongly pronounced in the care sector according to the German Social Law Code XI. However, also in the hospital sector there is competition between public, free (free-cooperative) and private carriers.

[13] Reference is generally made to the production of "social capital" by free welfare care. Local effects of intensified social integration and social cohesion that also increase the individual's quality of life and contentment with life are connected with this. Economic theory speaks in a related sense of positive external effects. But even this perspective of a welfare-economic consideration does not lead in simplified manner to the replacement of market through State production but, possibly, only to forms of regulation of markets.

assimilated by the EU Commission, despite the consultations held and the discourses on the subject and despite the received expert scientific opinions (Huber, Maucher and Sak 2008).

In this connection the own development in the national implementation of a "new control" or the New Public Management does not, however, make it possible to speak only of a purely exogenous modernization in the rules and procedures of the production of (social) services of general (economic) interest. The problem is also "home-made".

4. The guarantor State

Looking at this interplay of European (i.e. *supranational*) and *national* modernization impulses, we must speak in general terms of a trend towards a "*welfare state contract management*". Even in the light of the (social) trends towards adoption in EU constitutional law, the sovereign Member State remains free in this respect concerning the setting of general-interest service objectives to guarantee the provision of access opportunities to social infrastructures of high societal significance: the guarantor State. However, the rules and procedures for the creation of services by the guarantor State should be left up to market-driven providers within the limits of a delegation principle (Cox 2008 and Obermann 2007). Here the said forms of a quasi market-opening or control of competition - even if they are nothing more than approaches to market solutions, given the above-mentioned imperfections of market and non-market allocations - serve as comparison.[14]

The German model of service provision in the framework of the social law codes closely approximates this European system through the prioritization of free (free-cooperative) and private (for-profit) carriers, but the extent of the formation of regulated quasi-markets has not yet been elaborated to the last detail in compliance with the (law of the) internal market. And this is where conflicts arise around narrowness or width in view of interpretation and incorporation of the necessary internal market harmonisations of national practices regarding the control of service provision markets on the social and health sector. This will be the theme for the years ahead. The EU Commission closely focuses on the aspect of "welfare-optimum" prices and interprets this (theoretical) concept to a large extent in the sense of lowest-possible prices, thus running the risk, however, of fading out or marginalising more complex, integrated price-quality parameters in the orientation towards competition.

---

[14] The corresponding principle is: seek the least-incomplete solution compared to other incomplete solutions of the problems of awarding a contract.

In the socio-political perspective this constriction is grave because relevant aspects and dimensions of the problem are neglected. Market solutions seem to be difficult, particularly in complex need situations, "bad risk" situations, of individual persons. We should perhaps think of a mix of chronic illnesses, assistance and care requirements and handicaps in the light of simultaneous network deficits, more particularly in the case of older and elderly persons. The situation may be different for simple risks. A more extensive socio-political discourse could be given here regarding the problems of the development and protection of suitable (e.g., transsectorally and multi-professionally integrated) care landscapes. The Commission, more familiar with the economic-technical core areas of general-interest services, seems to have little understanding for the social-spatial, social environment and district-specific issues of guaranteeing complex services in the sense of accessibility, reachability, availability and acceptance. It largely assumes only political market power interests of the social economy established by the State.

The special tax law status of non-profit-making enterprises is broadly held to distort competition. This crystallizes in the issues of zero-tax-discrimination recognition of the non-profit character of the EU foreign enterprises in connection with transborder activities – and also questions of zero-discrimination calls for tenders, awards and the contract and allocation law. The discussion is not yet closed in this respect.[15]

In general, the development of European law and policy largely blanks out the question of the transaction costs of the induced regulation system (for the creation and opening up of modes of provision close to the market). These welfare gains of an increasingly efficiency-driven market opening and steering through competition are offset by the costs of the necessary regulatory authorities and their regulatory practice. Here it might help to take a look at the telecommunications or energy markets. After all, even in the case of an extensively competition-based ordering of health care, for instance in the form of purchase models from suppliers and supply networks by single social insurance funds in competition[16], the idea of leaving the supervision of the quality (and of the spatial provision situation[17]) to the regional regulatory authorities is being entertained.

---

[15] Which actually makes welfare services increasingly problematic, considering the need for strategic management in connection with the formation of reinvestment funds.

[16] Individual instead of collective contracts.

[17] This is a fundamental argument in Germany on account of the imposition under constitutional law of an "equivalence of life relations" in space. To that extent it was always a political affair to structure medical care in an integrated manner,

5. Problems of adaptation of the German national health service

The transborder mobility of patients alone has required adaptations of the German health service, including hospitals and nursing. With a greater degree of patient mobility, problems could also arise in the current practice of capacity planning in the outpatient and ward admissions areas. Extra fiscal charges could also be imposed for health insurances. This is connected with the details of the practice of compensation in Germany. Transborder formations of contracts, on the other hand, should proceed discrimination-free as per European law.

Basically, the German traditions of professional licensing of panel doctors and the nature of investment promotion remain a controversial theme in the context of the federal *Länder* demand planning, in terms of both, constitutional and European law. There are still unresolved (competition and contract award law-related) questions[18] regarding the licensing and franchise models that are effective here. Legal and political conflicts loom in respect to the weighting of goods, between basic liberties, rights of freedom of movement, national laws securing financial sustainability and the freedom of the State as the guarantor with regard to goods of general interest. But, even independently from dynamics of the retroactive European law, that was already a topic in Germany of the (not isolated) administration of justice by the Federal Social Court and the Federal Constitutional Court.

The pressure for adaptation of the German social and health service with regard to the European regulations in the areas of competition, subsidy and the law on contract awards will, however, only increase. Particularly in view of health services a trend (promoted especially [but not only] in the integration arrangements under § 140a-d SGB V) can be recognized towards transition to an individual contract system, that is to say, to a selective "purchase" of providers and care structures through individual funds that are in competition with each other. The traditions of a professional licensing system and a corresponding planning for the setting up of practices on the outpatient side consequently break up. If it ever will come to a (long-considered but still controversial) abolition of the dual hospital financing in favour of a monistic system (financing of the operating and investment costs of hospitals "from the one hand" of the insurances), then the capacity planning would also (have to) be transferred to the individual funds. In the framework of such a "purchase model" the relevant internal market-centred European law

aligned with available health care, with general town planning (settlement structures) etc.

18 These are of a terminological and also a legal strategy nature.

would acquire greater significance for the German health and social services.

Hitherto the practice of solidarity financing has been assessed by the ECJ based on the view that the funds are no economic enterprises. So they may, e.g., jointly establish fixed amounts for drugs and medicines, which under other circumstances would constitute an abuse of a position of dominance in the market and would have to be forbidden on the grounds of anti-trust law.

Nor is there any change to the current legal assessment of the non-commercial enterprise character of social insurances in the most recent reform[19], which provides for the creation of a health fund (initially) with uniform contribution rates and a change of the risk structure balance (RSB) between the funds. However, the German health service, in the wake of the national reform legislation, is moving more and more to the model of a "solidarist competition order", that will seriously increase the relevance of European competition, subsidy and contract award law. That does not concern the fact that the German system of public missions delegation to public-law corporations through State self-administration and the priority under social law of non-public providers (including the equal ranking of free [cooperative] and private carriers) in principle, but not in concretisation, was always oriented towards a public-private-partnership model in the sense of the guarantor State.

6. A European social model?

It is again apparent not only which far-reaching adaptation requirements result from the dynamics of the internal market, but also how fraught the evident abbreviation of the idea of European integration is for questions of economic space alone. Against this background questions arise regarding the diversity of social protection systems in Europe (Pestieau 2006; Bambra, 2008) and their competition (Arts and Gelissen 2002; Cerami 2006 with relation the Central and Eastern Europe; Korpi 2003). Here the OMC plays a fundamental part, regarding the criteria of access opportunities, quality and sustainability. The search for better solutions, the process of "invited dutifulness", a mixture of bottom-up discursive elements and socialising top-down effects (Büchs 2007: 26) places the Member States under the pressure of the learning and benchmarking process and, insofar as they are slowly harmonising, triggers at least changed[20] processes. In this framework, the restructuring of the SG(E)Is,

[19] I.e., the GKV-Wettbewerbsstärkungs-Gesetz (GKV-WSG).

[20] That may architectonically question the institutional identity (self-image) as known now.

certainly on the basis of the recognition of a fundamentally socially-minded guarantor State, belongs to the core elements of the discussion of a "European Social Model".[21]

References

Alber, J. 2006: The European Social Model and the United States, in: European Union Politics, vol. 7 (3), pp. 393-419

Annesley, C. 2007: Lisbon and social Europe: towards a European 'adult worker model' welfare system, in: Journal of European Social Policy, vol. 17 (3), pp. 195-205

Arts, W. / J. Gelissen 2002: Three worlds of welfare capitalism or more?, in: Journal of European Social Policy, vol. 12 (2), pp. 137-158

Bambra, C. 2008: Cash Versus Services: „Worlds of Welfare" and the Decommodification of Cash Benefits and Health Care Services, in: Journal of Social Policy, vol. 34 (2), pp. 195-213

Bettio, F. 2004: Comparing care regimes in Europe, in: Feminist Economics, vol 10 (1), pp. 85-115

Borrás, S. / K. Jacobsson 2004: The open method of co-ordination and new governance patterns in the EU, in: Journal of European Public Policy, vol. 11 (2). pp. 185-208

Büchs, M. 2007: New Governance in European Social Policy. The Open Method of Coordination, Houndmills/New York: Palgrave Macmillan

Cerami, A. 2006: Social Policy in Central and Eastern Europe. The Emergence of a New European Welfare Regime, Münster: LIT

Cox, H. 2008: Public enterprises and service providers in institutional competition and undergoing structural change, in: Annals of Public and Cooperative Economics, vol. 79 (3+4), pp. 527-547

GÖW 2007a: Ausschreibung oder Direktvergabe öffentlicher Dienstleistungen - Plädoyer für ein Wahlrecht der Gebietskörperschaften. Stellungnahme des Wissenschaftlichen Beirates der Gesellschaft für öffentliche Wirtschaft, Berlin: GÖW. Also printed in: Zeitschrift für öffentliche und gemeinwirtschaftliche Unternehmen, vol. 30, 2007, pp. 207-227

GÖW 2007b: Tendering or Direct Awarding of Public Services - Plea for the Right to Choose for Territorial Authorities. On the Need for Legal Provisions on the In-house Concept in the European Union. Statement of the Scientific Council of the Gesellschaft für Öffentliche Wirtschaft, Berlin: GÖW

Hervey, T. K. 2008: The European Union's governance of health care and the welfare modernization agenda, in: Regulation & Governance, vol. 2 (1), pp. 103-120

Huber, M. / M. Maucher / B. Sak 2008: Study on Social and Health Services of General Interest in the European Union. Final Synthesis report. Prepared for DG Employment, Social Affairs and Equal Opportunities. DG EMPL/E/4. VC/2006/0131

[21] For the discussion about the European Social Model refer e.g. to Scharpf (2002) and Alber (2006); for a special view - that of an *adult worker model* - more precisely Annesley (2007); see also Maydell et al. 2005.

Korpi, W. 2003: Welfare-State Regress in western Europe: Politics, Institutions, Globalization, and Europeanization, in: Annual Review of Sociology, vol. 63 (5), pp. 589-609

Lipson, D. 2002: GATs and health services. Implications for EU candidate countries, in: Eurohealth, vol. 8 (4), pp. 39-41

Maydell, B. v. et al. (eds.) 2005: Enabling Social Europe, Berlin: Springer

Menéndez, A. J. 2002: Chartering Europe: Legal Status and Policy Implications of the Charter of Fundamental Rights of the European Union, in: Journal of Common Market Studies, vol. 40 (3), pp. 471-490

Obermann, G. 2007: The role of the State as guarantor of public services: transactions costs issues and empirical evidence, in: Annals of Public and Cooperative Economics, vol: 78 (3), pp. 475-500

Pestieau, P. (2006). The Welfare State in the European Union. Oxford: Oxford University Press

Scharpf. F. W. 2002: The European Social Model: Coping with the Challenges of Diversity, in: Journal of Common Market Studies, vol. 40 (4).,pp. 645-670

Schulz-Nieswandt, F. et al. 2006: Care Regimes for the Elderly in South Eastern Europe in a European Comparative Perspective, in: U. Laaser / R. Radermacher (eds.): Financing Health Care. A Dialogue between South Eastern Europe and Germany, Lage: Jacobs Verlag, pp. 257-277

Threlfall, M. 2007: The Social Dimension of the European Union. Innovative Methods for Advancing Integration, in: Global Social Policy, vol. 7 (3). pp. 271-293

Umbach, G. 2009: Intent and Reality of the European Employment Strategy. Europeanisation of National Employment Policies and Policy-Making?, Baden-Baden: Nomos

Attachments:

ABSTRACTS (IN ALPHABETICAL ORDER)
EDITORS AND CONTRIBUTERS

ABSTRACTS

Chobanov, George: ***Walras Law and Flow of Funds Analysis in an Open Economic System***

The Walras law was originally stated for a closed economic system without money and public goods on the level of the usual microeconomic markets. Later on, Walras's law was proven for a closed economic system without public goods, but aggregated macroeconomic markets and involving money as a macroeconomic phenomenon. Further developments in economic theory came to overcome the separation of the micro and macro approach, giving the Walrasian model a central role, like a "Charta magna" for the economic theory.

Here, Walras's law is formally proven for aggregated markets in an open economic system (with public goods), closing it by taking into account the exchange with the rest of the world. Thus, a complete version of the Walras law in an open economy system is derived, concerning the excess demands of the aggregated macroeconomic markets of private goods, money, public goods, labor, capital and foreign exchange.

The Walras law of a dynamic equilibrium in an open economic system is considered as a proper theoretical base for economic policy mechanisms, like a flow-of-fund analysis, financial programming and especially for a balance of payment equilibrium.

Key words: Walras law, open economy, aggregated macroeconomic markets, private goods, public goods, money, labor, capital, foreign exchange, economic policy mechanism, flow-of-funds analysis, social accounting matrix, financial programming.

JEL classification: D5, E44, E52, F32.

Dardac, Nicolae / Iustina Alina Boitan: ***Assessment of the Romanian Banking System Performance. A Non-Parametric Approach***

The study assesses the performance, expressed in terms of efficiency and productivity, of a number of 16 Romanian credit institutions, for a time period between 2004 and 2006, a period characterized by an expansion of the retail credit activity. In order to evaluate the relative efficiency of their financial intermediation activity, we have applied a non-parametric technique, named Data Envelopment Analysis (DEA). Subsequently, the individual efficiency scores obtained by means of DEA have been included in the computation of the Malmquist productivity index. A particularity of this index is that it allows both, the identification of the productivity change and its decomposition on influence factors. The results obtained indicated that small and medium size credit institutions, with foreign and private capital, registered the most significant increase of their activity, which was reflected in the level of the performance indicators analyzed.

Key words: banking system, efficiency, productivity, Data Envelopment Analysis, Malmquist indexes.

JEL classification: C14, C67, G21.

Dimitrova, Kalina: ***Monetary and Fiscal Policies in Bulgaria:Lessons from the Historical Record***

The paper starts with a brief review of the literature arguing that inflation could be classified as a "fiscal phenomenon". Then the historical background of the study is introduced, the legislation defining the relations between the central bank and the

government institutions, and the research studies of that time providing evidence for the presence of a strong influence of fiscal policy on the money creation. In the following section an empirical analysis is conducted and econometric estimations are derived in order to draw some conclusions and policy implications on the interaction between the monetary and the fiscal policy under different monetary regimes. The time span of the study is the monetary history of Bulgaria from the establishment of the Bulgarian National Bank in 1879 until 1947.
Key words: Central bank, banking system, gold standard, credit, budget, government, money, monetary history, monetary policy, fiscal policy.
JEL classification: E52, E58, N13, N14.

Dolgopyatova, Tatiana G.: ***Corporate Control and the Role of Business Integration in Russian Companies***

In this paper I examine the role of business integration in the development of a form of intra-corporate control, based on the separation of executive management from ownership in Russian companies. After an empirical investigation of a set of determinants of owners' choices of hired management vs. manager-shareholders against the background of high ownership concentration, I found the following main results: a) business integration promotes a gradual separation of management from ownership in the rank-and-file membership of company groups; b) a company's affiliation or non-affiliation with a company group predefines different roles of various factors in this choice. The study is based on the data of a survey of 822 top-managers of large and medium-sized joint stock companies in industry and communications.
Key words: stock ownership, corporate governance, separation of ownership and management, corporate integration, Russia.
JEL classifications: D23, G34, P26 .

Egbert, Henrik / Maria Ivanova / Georgi Chobanov: ***New Data on the Bulgarian Transaction Sector: 1997 to 2006***

Chobanov and Egbert (2007) measured the transaction sector between 1997 and 2003 for the Bulgarian economy. They report an increase in the transaction sector from below 40% to more than 50% of GDP. This indicates a fundamental institutional change within a short period of time. Here, we repeat this study because more precise data have become available since January 2008. The National Statistical Institute recalculated the GDP and it is the basic reference point in our study. Furthermore, we are able to include the years 2004 to 2006, thus providing data for a full decade. We also improved the methodology of Chobanov and Egbert, coming closer to the original concept of the transaction sector.
Key words: Transaction Sector, Bulgaria.
JEL classifications: L 14, N74.

Gern, Jean-Pierre: ***Sustainable Development: a Challenge for the Decisional Process***

The paper deals with the problem of sustainable development. By this term we understand an evolution of techno-economic and social structures, which tend towards an equilibrium between human activities and the natural environment, as well as a social equilibrium.

To minimize the impact of human activities on the environment and to avoid building up social tensions, objectives for production and a new approach to "needs" are required. The determinant factors of the constant increase in the production of goods and services have to be analysed, as well as their dynamics. The attention is concentrated on one issue: How far are today's societies able to take efficiently the decisions needed to achieve sustainable development?

Two levels of action and decision making are considered: (a) within a relatively homogeneous social system in areas like Europe, which are called "regions" (b) the relations between such "regions".

Key words: Sustainability, environment , regions, decision making process.

JEL classifications: Q01, Q58.

Ivanov, Ivan / Julia Dobreva: ***Social Effects of Government Subsidies to Local Public Goods***

This paper examines the problem of the social effect caused by government subsidies to local public goods. The analysis is based on the optimization model and it provides a comparison between centrally subsidized public and private goods and government transfers for the financing of local public goods. Our model provides evidence that the subsidies allocated to the local self-governments are more effective and have a greater positive impact on the social effect of the financed public goods than the centrally supported public goods. We argue that the effect of these subsidies is highly localised – the provided public goods are consumed directly by a closed community, comprising of narrow income groups where there is no leakage of subsidies. Further evidence to the support of our analysis is that the locally subsidized public goods may be also supported by private contributions of local residents in the form of donations. Our conclusions are in favor of an economy with a decentralised state budget management and support the notion that the subsidy to local public goods has a significant and direct social effect and should be preferred to the central government financing schemes.

Key words: optimization model, duality, the Slutsky equation, central public goods, local public goods.

JEL classification: C61, D61, H24, H25.

Lenk, Thomas / Oliver Rottmann / Tatsiana Makarevich: ***Challenging Budgetary Situations – Municipal Management***

On the municipal level services of general interest (SGIs) cover, for example, water, energy supply and waste disposal, healthcare and social services, pre school education and postal deliveries. Originally maintained by local or governmental authorities and financed by subsidies, since the late 1970s new forms of ownership, maintenance and financing of SGIs occured: public procurement, private ownership and financing, public-private-partnerships, subsidies of European or other funds. Since the late 1980s, the European Commission has pursued a policy of market-opening to create competition in the so far public sectors.

The article examines the consequences of these facts and developments on the municipal policy within the European Union. Firstly, we will consider the framework conditions of public or municipal management. In doing so, we will put particular emphasis on services of general interest and their framework conditions changed by the implementation of EU-legislation. Secondly, demographic and regional political planning implications of services of general interest are discussed and the possibilities for the use of the EU-support policy are outlined. Finally, the option of privatisation of public services and, especially, the role of public-private-partnerships (PPP) are to be discussed.

Key words: EU, municipal policy, general interest, public services, regional political planning, privatisation, public-private-partnership.

JEL classifications: G28, H41, L33.

Oros, Cornel/Camelia Romocea-Turcu: ***Monetary Shocks in Central and Eastern Europe: Evidence from a VAR Analysis***

The paper analyzes the monetary policy transmission channels of six CEECs (Hungary, Poland, Czech Republic, Romania, Slovakia and Slovenia) over recent periods, corresponding to stable monetary regimes. Three channels have been taken into account - the interest rate, the exchange rate and the domestic credit - whose relative importance was accounted for using a structural VAR model. The results show that all the countries share a weak domestic credit channel while they are highly heterogeneous with regards to the relative effectiveness of the interest rate and exchange rate channels. Thus, Hungary and Poland's distinctive feature is the presence of a price puzzle effect combined with a high influence of the exchange rate which acts both as a mechanism of monetary policy transmission and as a supply and demand shock absorber. On the contrary, just like in the case of the Euro zone countries, it is the interest rate channel that has the major influence in the cases of the Czech Republic, Slovakia, Slovenia and partially Romania. Therefore, this latter group appears to be more apt to join the EMU in the near future, which can be confirmed by the Slovenian case.

Key words: VAR models, monetary policy transmission, CEECs.

JEL Classifications: C32, E52, E58, P24.

Plöhn, Jürgen/Alexander Peniuk: ***From Unemployment to Self-Employment. Political concepts, economic realities, and social effects in Germany***

Since 1975 German governments try to cope with a rate of unemployment that was unknown in the two previous decades. Various attempts to accelerate economic growth did not generate satisfying results. When the immediate positive effects of the German reunification on the demand of goods and services withered away, the shut down of inefficient East German production sites produced extremely high degrees of unemployment in the New Länder of Germany.

German politicians tried to overcome the crisis on the labour market by enlarging the number of self-employed persons. For decades, the percentage of the self-employed part of the working force had been shrinking. But in the phase of the "New Economy" some politicians expected major positive effects on the economic growth by switches from unemployment to self-employment.

The paper examines several aspects of that problem: (1) the development of economic data on the German labour market; (2) contradictory political concepts of the two major political parties in response to the economic challenges; (3) economic effects of the realized measures; (4) social effects of the measures on the respective parts of the labour force as shown by a survey in the Ruhr area.
Key words: unemployment, self-employment, labour market, service sector, Germany, New Länder, Ruhr area, party platforms.
JEL Classifications: J28, J44, J48, J64, O14, O52.

Schulz-Nieswandt, Frank/Michael Sauer: ***Social and health services in the EU. An analytical sketch with particular reference to the repercussions of European Law on the German development of the provision of social and health services***

Although Europe, since its emergence after 1945 should in essence be regarded as an organisation for peace, and although Europe is also eager to define itself culturally, less geographically, as a values-driven community space, the European Union primarily represents an economic space that is understood as a free internal market and is in part already transformed into a currency union - with considerable effects on the monetary and, consequently, in the financial policy of the Member States.

The architecture of Europe as a political system is to be understood as a multilevel system. Different variants of the interpretation of the EU as a federation of states or a federal state compete with each other. How are the treaties on the EU to be interpreted? Here the central role of the European Court of Justice (ECJ) takes effect. Which consequences must be drawn as a result of such interpretation?

We assume that Europe de facto already operates shared competences in social policy, including health policy. Certain areas of a Europeanised social policy have therefore already come into being in the sense of a shared competence. Looking at this interplay of supranational and national modernization impulses, we recognize a trend towards a "welfare state contract management". In the end we consider the question whether there is a European social model.
Key words: EU, European Court of Justice, health services, social services, welfare state contract management, guarantor state.
JEL Classifications: H 11, H41, I18.

EDITORS and CONTRIBUTORS

Boitan, Iustina Alina, Academy of Economic Studies, Faculty of Finance, Insurance, Banking and Stock Exchange Bucharest (RO), *iustinaboitan@yahoo.com*

Chobanov, George, Prof. Dr., Sofia University "St. Kliment Ohridski", Dean of the Faculty of Economics and Business Administration and head of the Department of Industrial Economics and Management, Sofia (BG), *georgech@feb.uni-sofia.bg*

Dardac, Nicolae, Prof. Dr., Academy of Economic Studies, Faculty of Finance, Insurance, Banking and Stock Exchange Bucharest (RO) *iustinaboitan@yahoo.com*

Dimitrova, Kalina, Sofia University "St. Kliment Ohridski", Department of Economics and Business Administration, Sofia (BG), *dimitrova.ka@gmail.com*

Dobreva, Julia, PhD student, Sofia University "St. Kliment Ohridski", Department of Economics, Faculty of Economics and Business Administration, (BG), *dobreva_julia@abv.bg*

Dolgopyatova, Tatiana G., Prof., Dr., State University Higher School of Economics (SU HSE), Moscow, (RUS), *longheel@hse.ru*

Egbert, Henrik, PD Dr., Justus-Liebig-University Giessen, Behavioral and Institutional Economics, Giessen (D), *Henrik.Egbert@wirtschaft. uni-giessen.de*

Gern, Jean-Pierre, Prof. (em.) Dr., Université de Neuchâtel (CH), *jean-pierre.gern@unine.ch*

Ivanov, Ivan, Prof. Dr., Sofia University "St. Kliment Ohridski", Faculty of Economics and Business Administration, Department of Statistics and Econometrics, Sofia (BG), *i_ivanov@feb.uni-sofia.bg*

Ivanova, Maria, Sofia University "St. Kliment Ohridski", Faculty of Economics and Business Administration (BG), *mariaiv@feb.uni-sofia.bg*

Lenk, Thomas, Prof. Dr., Leipzig University, Institute for Public Finance and Public Management, Leipzig (D),
iff_fiwi@wifa.uni-leipzig.de

Makarevich, Tatsiana, Dipl.-WiMa, Leipzig University, Centre for International Economics, Leipzig (D),
makarevich@wifa.uni-leipzig.de

Oros, Cornel, Université de Poitiers, CRIEF Laboratory, Faculty of Economics, Poitiers Cedex (F),
cornel.oros@univ-poitiers.fr

Peniuk, Alexander, Dr., Essen (D),
apeniuk@gmx.de

Plöhn, Jürgen, PD Dr., Martin-Luther-University Halle-Wittenberg, Institute for Political Science and Japanese Studies, Halle (D),
ploehn@hotmail.com

Romocea-Turcu, Camelia, Université de Poitiers, CRIEF Laboratory, Faculty of Economics Poitiers, Cedex (F),
camelia.turcu@univ-poitiers.fr

Rottmann, Oliver, Dipl.-Vw., Leipzig University, Institute for Public Finance and Public Management, Leipzig (D),
rottmann@wifa.uni-leipzig.de

Sauer, Michael, Dipl.-Pol.-Wiss., University of Cologne, Department of social policies, Cologne (D),
michael.sauer@uni-koeln.de

Schulz-Nieswandt, Frank, Prof. Dr., University of Cologne, Department of social policies, Cologne (D),
schulz-nieswandt@wiso.uni-koeln.de

Sofia Conferences on Social and Economic Development in Europe

Editors: Prof. Dr. George Chobanov, PD Dr. Jürgen Plöhn,
Prof. Dr. Horst Schellhaass

Band 1 George Chobanov / Jürgen Plöhn / Horst Schellhaass (eds.): Towards a Knowledge-Based Society in Europe. 10th International Conference on Policies of Economic and Social Development, Sofia, October 5 to 7, 2007. 2009.

Band 2 George Chobanov / Jürgen Plöhn / Horst Schellhaass (eds.): Policies of Economic an Social Development in Europe. 11th Annual Conference of the Faculty of Economics and Business Administration. Dedicated to the 120th Anniversary of St. Kliment Ohridski University of Sofia, Sofia, October 10 to 11, 2008. 2010.

www.peterlang.de